PEERING BEHIND THE CURTAIN

Studies in Modern Drama
Kimball King, *Series Editor*

PEERING BEHIND THE CURTAIN

DISABILITY, ILLNESS, AND THE EXTRAORDINARY BODY IN CONTEMPORARY THEATER

EDITED BY THOMAS FAHY AND KIMBALL KING

ROUTLEDGE
NEW YORK AND LONDON

Published in 2002 by
Routledge
29 West 35th Street
New York, NY 10001

Published in Great Britain by
Routledge
11 New Fetter Lane
London EC4P 4EE

Routledge is an imprint of the Taylor & Francis Group.
Copyright © 2002 by Routledge

10   9   8   7   6   5   4   3   2   1

Library of Congress Cataloging-in-Publication Data

Peering behind the curtain: disability, illness, and the extraordinary body in contemporary theater / edited by Thomas Fahy and Kimball King.
    p. cm. — (Studies in modern drama ; v. 18)
    ISBN 0-415-92997-0
    1. American drama—20th century—History and criticism. 2. Handicapped in literature. 3. English drama—20th century—History and criticism. 4. Physically handicapped in literature. 5. Abnormalities, Human, in literature. 6. Body, Human, in literature. 7. Diseases in literature. 8. Medicine in literature. 9. Sick in literature. I. Fahy, Thomas Richard. II. King, Kimball. III. Series.

PS338.P4 P44 2001
812'.50935208—dc21   2001048571

Printed on acid-free, 250-year-life paper.
Manufactured in the United States of America.

Contents

PART II

General Editor's Note

Linking together the essays in this volume is the underlying conviction that what is generally regarded as a "disability" is in large part a social construct. The "able"-bodied make the world's rulers, and an individual's sense of self-worth too often depends upon the way he or she is evaluated by those "in charge." A great deal has been written about "marginalized" people—those who have been relegated by the "mainstream" culture to a shadowy borderline beyond its official parameters. Women, racial and religious minorities, homosexuals, the poor, the elderly, and countless others often exist on the fringes of a patriarchal society based on power, wealth, and hereditary entitlement. If the marginalized agree to accept the limits society presently imposes upon them, they may be tolerated by the mainstream, especially when they assume a posture favored by the establishment. Nevertheless, people whose physical faculties have been severely impaired or destroyed are often unable to coexist peacefully with the majority. They remain apart from the mainstream; their admittance is steadfastly denied. Any study of currently perceived incapacities reveals what concepts society believes it must value and preserve. And it cruelly selects for survival those best able to maintain its present equilibrium.

The bourgeoisie appropriated modern theater, and the novelty of seeing ordinary doctors, lawyers, professors, and clergymen, in plays like Ibsen's or Shaw's, grappling with emergent social conditions, almost masked the hegemony of contemporary culture. The theater has been much slower to acknowledge the painful dilemmas of physically "different" people than have other literary genres, such as the novel.

Even more than stage plays, contemporary movies have mirrored the ideals society aspires to—a specific kind of physical beauty, bodily strength, and engaging personality being the traits that define the "star" of modern cinema. Thus, two of the most accessible cultural forms, theater and film, reinforce stereotypes of physically perfect people who possess the qualities essential for success.

Curiously, one of the founders of the modern theater, Ibsen, was one of the first to note the presence of the disabled, yet he focused on issues believed to be more relevant to the bourgeois establishment, such as gender inequalities, a disregard for the environment, and ethical versus unethical leadership. But the specter of disability always darkened his mise-en-scènes: Dr. Rank's mysterious terminal illness, Oswald's syphilis, Lovborg's alcoholism, Hedwig's blindness, to name a few examples. Still, Nora becomes an icon of the women's movement in *A Doll's House* as we bristle at her being treated as an inferior, unable to borrow money without a man's permission and beholden to the whims of an autocratic, moralizing husband. It's easy to forget that the play is also about her husband, Helmer, whose illness, probably tuberculosis, necessitated Nora's risky and disastrous forgery in the first place. To be physically unable to care for his family made any Scandinavian male feel emasculated and worthless. Weakness of body was equated with weakness of spirit. Therefore, Helmer's response to his illness and recuperation is predictably one of utter denial. Nora waits in vain for Helmer to acknowledge her sacrifices on his behalf. To thank her for taking on his role as family provider and authority figure would have betrayed his own warped sense of masculinity. Yet Ibsen never probes the issue of disability in a contemporary society newly dominated by the middle class.

As the dominant modes of drama moved from realism to naturalism, expressionism, and eventually absurdism, philosophical issues of social injustice took precedence over individual suffering. When personal tragedies were emphasized, the individual characters were more frequently handicapped by emotional rather than physical infirmities.

Critical interest in multiculturalism, a recognition that the "outsider" in the modern world is nearly anyone who is not male, white, able-bodied, and of European descent has given expression in the theater to explorations of "otherness": African-American and Asian culture, women's issues, and all aspects of society unfamiliar to the world's dominant forces. Plays that concentrate on people who differ so dramatically in appearance and behavior from the world's accepted power brokers have begun to appear on stage and will command an increasing share of audience attention. Already a dozen major universities offer curricula in disability studies, and the University of Chicago awards a Ph.D. in that subject. Thomas Fahy and I hope that this present contribution to the Studies in Modern Drama series will foster a new awareness of a large segment of humanity frequently neglected on stage, as well as in life.

Kimball King
General Editor

Peering behind the Curtain: An Introduction

THOMAS FAHY

At the end of Alfred Hitchcock's *Rear Window* (1954), L. B. Jeffries (James Stewart), who has been watching his neighbors through binoculars and a telephoto lens for days, is finally caught in the act of looking. Lars Thorwald (Raymond Burr), the man Jeffries suspects of killing his wife, sees him spying from across the courtyard. Like Stewart's character, the audience has participated in the transgressive and voyeuristic pleasures of this mystery, but the safety of Stewart's dimly lit apartment, and by extension the darkened theater, is shattered when Thorwald looks back. He catches both Jeffries and us peering into his "secret, private world," and the dramatic tension of the film's final moments comes, in part, from our own sense of guilt.

If, as Jeffries's nurse Stella (Thelma Ritter) laments earlier in the film, "we've become a race of Peeping Toms," what does this desire say about us? About our need to observe and then create narratives to explain the strange and unusual? The film repeatedly moralizes on the dangers of such surveillance ("What people ought to do is get outside their own house and look in for a change"), but the problem of rear-window ethics is never resolved, particularly in regards to disability. At the opening of the film, we stare at Jeffries's disabled body, and Hitchcock immediately answers our unspoken questions about his condition: How did this happen? Is it permanent? Photographs of car crashes and explosions hang from the apartment walls like trophies to Jeffries's mobility and masculinity, and the magazine editor who mistakenly calls him with a new assignment one week before his cast comes off chastises Jeffries for breaking his leg while taking risky photographs at an auto race. Hitchcock is clearly not interested in a narrative of disability—relegating Jeffries to a wheelchair only temporarily and presenting Thorwald's invalid wife as mobile. Instead, the wheelchair, like the walled-in courtyard, becomes a metaphor for his reluctance to get married and serves as a plot device to justify his voyeurism: "You've got to get me out of here. Six weeks sitting in a two-room apartment with nothing to do but look out the window at the neighbors." His captivity mitigates his (as well as our own) ethical reservations about gazing into the private lives of others. How else would one spend long, hot summer afternoons?

Disability not only demands its own narrative—an explanation of the deviant body—but its inherent difference calls attention to all of the bodies on screen and on stage. It informs our perceptions and interpretations of the drama, in part because images of physical difference are so unexpected. Like the sequestered Jeffries in *Rear Window,* disability is so often hidden from view in contemporary society that most able-bodied viewers have no frame of reference for responding to it. As Rosemarie Garland Thomson explains when discussing disability performance art, the body is "an object to be viewed and to be explained. The disabled body is not only the medium but the content of the performance. The disabled body on view *is* the performance. [And] in the social context of an ablist society, the disabled body summons the stare, and the stare mandates the story."[1] The same is true in films and plays that represent disability. Jeffries's convalescence not only becomes the excuse for staring at and objectifying the able-bodied (an ironic inversion of the gaze[2]), but it also invites us to compare the long, beautiful legs of Lisa Fremont (Grace Kelly) and Miss Torso the ballet dancer with his cast-bound body. Just like Mrs. Thorwald's illness, disability makes Jeffries vulnerable; it is presented as a sign of social dependency and physical inadequacy. In this way, physical disability reveals social anxieties about power, control, and self-worth; like the figure of the "cripple," "freak," and "invalid" in most literature, *Rear Window* tries to relegate disability to the metaphoric, ultimately contributing to the pervasive misrepresentation and marginalization of disabled people.

Unlike this film, a widely available text to most readers and therefore indicative of familiar cultural constructions about disability, theater makes it much more difficult for audiences to escape into comfortable inaction, to accept these messages about the disabled body passively. This volume examines some of the ways that disability theater challenges the culturally constructed images and meanings ascribed to disability by nondisabled people. By disability theater, I mean drama written and performed by disabled artists, and/or staged works about disability and the social constructions of physical difference. The stage confronts viewers with a physical reality, asking them both to stare at the bodies on display and to see them as individuals, not objects. Through the proximity of the actors and the spontaneity of performance, audiences feel a sense of intimacy and community with those on stage. This moment—energized and made possible by live performance—can be a powerful tool for undermining stereotypes and misconceptions. When the disabled, suffering, or freakish body appears on stage, it raises certain questions (How did this happen? Is this condition permanent? Can this happen to me? Is the actor really disabled?) that challenge the audience's assumptions about and interpretations of this body. By not defining characters by their bodies, disability theater hopes to transcend these questions, fashioning narratives that individualize experience and move beyond the metaphoric. It ultimately challenges audiences to reevaluate preconceived notions about disability, and the stage becomes a space where social and political changes are possible.

Overview

Part I of this collection is a scholarly exploration of twentieth-century disability theater in America and Britain. In the first essay, "Between Two Worlds: The Emerging Aesthetic of the National Theater of the Deaf," Kanta Kochhar-Lindgren examines the "double language of sign and speech" that has been used by the National Theater of the Deaf (NTD) since the late 1960s. The NTD makes "deafness visible" in its productions through an aesthetic that both challenges traditional assumptions about performance and asks audiences to reconsider the relationship among space, sound, silence, and the body on stage. With a specific emphasis on their 1988 production of *In a Grove,* Kochhar-Lindgren discusses the ways that the NTD uses performance to raise questions about the cultural and social constructions of hearing. The nonlinguistic meaning established between audience and performer in these shows "creates new possibilities for understanding, as well as, potentially, for political change."

Robert C. Spirko also explores the cultural constructions of deafness, but as they relate to Deaf education. In "'Better Me Than You': *Children of a Lesser God,* Deaf Education, and Paternalism," Spirko argues that popular and critical attempts to defuse the political dimensions of Mark Medoff's play and film come from a "flawed empathy"—one "grounded solely in abled experience . . . that proceeds without recognizing genuine otherness." He also criticizes readings of the play that use disability as a metaphor for gender relations. This reading, Spirko argues, minimizes the "Deaf politics" of Medoff's work and prevents readers from both seeing "disability and gender as a joint articulation" and recognizing the audist paternalism limiting the deaf characters in the play.

Moving from discussions about cultural constructions of deafness to those dealing with the body, Pamela Cooper examines the spectacle of pain in Margaret Edson's *Wit* and the paintings of Francis Bacon. Both present violence through the lens of medical science, making the body a site for torture, decay, pain, and pleasure. For Edson, "this sensationalizing of pain within a framing problematic of knowledge (its limits, methods, and effects) gives *Wit* its vertiginous dramatic energy and intellectual shape." It also enables the play's powerful critique of medicine and academia. Cooper goes on to argue that protagonist Vivian Bearning's deterioration makes her "the perfect Baconian subject," comparing Bacon's aesthetic presentation of pain to that of Edson.

Tess Chakkalakal continues this discussion by examining images of suffering in Bill T. Jones's *Last Supper at Uncle Tom's Cabin/The Promised Land.* "Making an Art out of Suffering: Bill T. Jones's *Uncle Tom*" specifically analyzes the way Jones uses dance to explore the history of positive and negative images associated with Harriet Beecher Stowe's character Uncle Tom. His production plays with the tensions between hero and victim "to formulate the terms of victim art as a form of creative expression in the later twentieth century." Chakkalakal goes on to explain that "by using his own body, Jones shows how the intersections of race, sexuality, and disease alter the constitutive features of victims and heroes to elide the differences between them." The various representations of Tom on stage both challenge and enhance stereotypical images of the black figure in American culture, raising important questions about the construction of black male bodies. These images not only validate suffering and disabled bodies in the production of art, but they also give audiences a new way to evaluate victims on and off the stage.

Ruby Cohn surveys suffering and disability throughout Beckett's oeuvre in "'It Hurts?': Afflicted Bodies in Beckett's Drama." "Beckett exploits corporeal affliction

Peering behind the Curtain: An Introduction

to dramatic ends, and he does so in two main modes: (1) familiar bodies that resemble our own and (2) fragmented bodies that are nevertheless sentient." Focusing on blindness, mutism, and injured legs in his works, she argues that Beckett never places disabled and fragmented bodies into a meaningful social context. Ultimately, "through both kinds of affliction Beckett implies the inadequacy of our corporeal equipment for human life on this planet."

The suffering body in Marsha Norman's *'night Mother* is not visible, but, as Sarah Reuning argues in "Depression—the Undiagnosed Disability in Marsha Norman's *'night Mother,*" her unseen illness refutes traditional interpretations of this play that validate suicide as a victory and triumph for the main character. These readings assume "that Jessie (the protagonist) has complete control of her mental faculties and that her suicide is a rational act. However, this assumption of rationality ignores the presence of mental disability." In fact, Jessie suffers from major depressive disorder, and her suicide cannot be understood apart from this disability. Reuning, therefore, sees Jessie as not in control of her final act, and presents depression both as a tool for interpreting *'night Mother* and as a means for reevaluating the criticism that has, in a sense, misdiagnosed Jessie.

The suffering body on display is often perceived and constructed as a type of freakish spectacle, and the next two essays present "freakishness" as a powerful tool for social critique and personal awareness. In "Some Unheard-of Thing": Freaks, Families, and Coming of Age in *The Member of the Wedding,*" I examine the use of freak shows in Carson McCullers's dramatic adaptation of *The Member of the Wedding*. As social and political tensions regarding homosexuality intensified during the 1930s and after World War II, sexually ambiguous freaks, such as bearded ladies and hermaphrodites, were increasingly seen as visible threats to compulsory heterosexuality and the nuclear family. In adapting this novel for the theater, McCullers made significant changes "to capitalize on the ways a staged production could enact the dynamics of a freak show," and to criticize heterosexual imperatives. By featuring the struggles of Frankie Addams, a young adult poised to make her own choices about sexuality, McCullers juxtaposes freakishness with same-sex desire to capture the debilitating impact of these imperatives, suggesting that sexuality had become another tool for preserving white, middle-class hierarchies.

The "freakish" becomes a site for finding compassion in Johanna Shapiro's "Young Doctors Come to See the Elephant Man." As part of a class on the doctor-patient relationship, Shapiro asks several of her second-year medical students to read and respond to Bernard Pomerance's *Elephant Man*. In their exploration of the complex, multifaceted, and flawed figures of Joseph Merrick and Frederick Treves, they grapple with a relationship that is defined by exploitation as well as caring and compassion. This class came to view *The Elephant Man* as a play about the need to view others with love. As Shapiro concludes, Merrick's closing remarks imply "that unless the physician's clinical gaze, so routinely directed toward the vulnerable, suffering patient, is suffused with love, it becomes unbearable. Perhaps in the ultimate summing up of the Elephant Man, Treves has seen the importance of gazing on patients with love as well as scientific detachment."

Part II of this volume features interviews, essays, and a play by artists currently working in the theater. In "Acting without Limits: Profiles of Three Physically Disabled Performers," Lilah F. Morris talks with three performers who have worked in disability theater throughout the United States and share their experiences and opinions on the direction of disability theater in the twenty-first century. Nancy Bezant's "Two-Act Play" describes her own struggles and accomplishments as a blind actress with a theater group in North Carolina, and playwright James MacDonald discusses his writing and the role of disability in contemporary British theater and society. The volume concludes with his play *Balance Is Stillness*.

In part, this collection hopes to lift the profile of disability theater. As disability theater challenges people to reexamine the cultural assumptions imposed on disability, it teaches us to look without embarrassment, without resistance, at bodily difference. The narratives created by this drama enable an interactive exchange—one that asks audiences to identify with the *experiences* of those on stage, to recognize disability as a social construct, and to acknowledge our own role in this phenomenon.

NOTES

1. See Rosemarie Garland Thomson, "Staring Back: Self Representations of Disabled Performance Artists," *American Quarterly* 52.2 (2000): 334–35.
2. In Laura Mulvey's terms, this inversion occurs in the sense that Lisa is free to assume the active role usually reserved for the male hero. His disability inverts the power dynamic—as illustrated by her "aggressive" sexuality and Jeffries's unresponsiveness. See Mulvey's "Visual Pleasure and Narrative Cinema," *Screen* 16.3 (1975): 8–18.

PART I

Between Two Worlds:
The Emerging Aesthetic of the
National Theater of the Deaf

KANTA KOCHHAR-LINDGREN

In 1967, the National Theater of the Deaf (NTD) began creating performance works that bridge the deaf and hearing worlds through their combination of American Sign Language (ASL) and speech. In this new theatrical form, both signing and speaking performers are on stage at the same time, and the double language of sign and speech merges image and sound to explore the potential of language as action-in-space. As a result the hearing audiences must learn to listen with their eyes as well as their ears, and because deaf individuals speak visually and kinesthetically in ways unfamiliar to the hearing population, these works challenge the traditional limits of language, poetry, and the use of voice.

Broadly speaking, NTD's work makes deafness visible, and, because the group focuses on classical theater pieces, it achieves this visibility by inserting the deaf into the cultural and theatrical mainstream. NTD's work presents a moment in the discussion of the theory of deafness that "severs the 'natural' connection between voice and language" (Bauman, 1996). W. J. T. Mitchell, for example, has noted the potential of sign language poetry to extend the contemporary discussion about the distinctions between textuality and performativity. Mitchell remarks that

> The poetry of the deaf stages for us in the most vivid possible form the basic shift in literary understanding that has been occurring before our eyes in the last decade; the movement from a "textual" model (based on a narrowly defined circuit of writing and speech) to a "performance" model, exemplified in the recent work in the semiotics of drama, film, television and performance art and in the interplay of language with the visual or pictorial field. (1989, 14)

Deaf studies theorists Lennard Davis and Dirksen Bauman have also suggested ways—for example, through Davis's notion of the "deafened moment" and Bauman's critique of the relationship between signing and painting—that the examination of deafness can lead to the development of new models for the construction of meaning. NTD's work, in particular, rearticulates the presence of the body, its silences, and the ways in which visuality can speak to us.

This article examines how the sensory modalities involved in the staging practices can facilitate a multisensory, synaesthesiac engagement with performance. Because a language of shape and space is emphasized rather than a language of speech, understanding unfolds through a type of body-to-body listening. In particular, *In a Grove*, a 1988 NTD production, provides a striking example of how deafness informs NTD's aesthetic, and it articulates ways in which voice, as it crosses between signing and speaking, also refracts the ambiguities involved in listening to another.

In order to hear these multiple voices, the interpretive concept of the third ear[1] enables us to track the ambiguous articulations of sound, silence, and image. Through the third ear, we shift our attention from the overt content of the performance to its forms of expression, listening "less to the plot, the narrative, the development of the story . . . and more to the mode of telling" (Miller 1997, 11). We become more involved in the felt sense of the performance as it unfolds: the silences, the gaps between image and sound, the incongruities between movement and text, dissonant intercessions of noise and gesture, and the positions of the performing bodies that speak to us.

Part of the success of NTD's work lies in its ability to invoke a nonlinguistic, visceral meaning that emerges between performers and audience members, and, through the third ear, we "hear" meaning as it emerges in the performativity of the moment. By disrupting traditional and expected linkages between the normatively audial and visual, the numerous combinations of the performance of sound create new possibilities for understanding, as well as, potentially, for political change.

Homi Bhabha, for example, has written of the power of the performative to insert new realities into social space. This performative dimension occurs in what he calls the space "in-between." He remarks:

> It is in the emergence of the interstices—the overlap and displacement of the domains of difference—that the intersubjective and collective experiences of nationness, community interest, or cultural value are negotiated. How are subjects formed "in-between," or in excess of the sum of the "parts" of difference (usually intoned as race/class/gender)? (1994, 2)

Bhabha articulates the *interval* between identity and difference, a central index by which to chart the shifting terrain of contemporary identity politics. The interval, rather than emphasizing an original source for cultural identity, schematizes the way in which identities and cultures are actively *produced*. Cultural identity, always the result of multiple intersections of meaning, manifests itself through the power of the performative, "emergent" subjectivities.

As new possibilities for multiple voices are created, the very process of hearing requires further examination. Even in its most basic terms "hearing," as it is embedded within traditional cultural paradigms, is not a perceptual experience of simply registering the presence or absence of sound and concomitant meaning. It also indicates the process of engaging in a cultural and political selectivity. Consequently, a crucial component of hearing the other entails the question of *how* we hear. Hearing cannot be fully examined without also unpacking the trope of deafness.

This analysis of the intersection of the world of hearing and deafness will be contextualized within the theoretical and historical framework of the National Theater of the Deaf, which is performing an eloquent, newly emerging aesthetic. This aesthetic calls for a sophisticated critical response to how such performance extends deaf culture, examines the trope of deafness, raises the issue of perceptual difference, and suggests ways of reconfiguring what we mean by performance in general.

Overview of NTD's Background

The concept for a professional theater of the deaf began in the late 1950s with Dr. Edna Simon Levine, a psychologist who worked in the area of deafness. She envisioned a professional theatrical venue for the deaf that showcased the use of American Sign Language, mitigating the stigma that was then attached to the use of sign language. Originally, Dr. Levine approached Arthur Penn, who at the time was directing *Miracle Worker*, and Anne Bancroft, the lead actress, about heading the project to form a company. David Hays, a successful set designer for Broadway productions as well as George Balanchine's ballets, was working with Penn at the time, and he was invited to go along with Penn and Bancroft to Gaulladet College to see the current performance of *Our Town*. When Penn and Bancroft had to back out of the endeavor because of other commitments, Hays was encouraged to take on the project. In 1967, backed by a $310,000 grant from the Department of Education and a home base in New London, Connecticut, at the Eugene O'Neill Theater, David Hays produced NTD's first performance season.

An initial grant, in 1965, from the U.S. Department of Health, Education, and Welfare allowed for the planning stages of the project. Additional funds from the U.S. Office of Education allowed for the development of a summer school program that provided professional training. Hays remarks that

> Those were the dark ages. The deaf population desperately needed role models; they had no heroes. Some states would not even license them to teach, because their English wasn't too good. So the government was very practical—it wanted to take people off the dole and turn them into taxpayers. (Quoted in Grandjean 1993, 38)

Despite the fact that the time of the inception of the company was one fraught with social and political problems for the deaf, Hays remained focused on the use of sign language and the creation of the theater as a new form. He has always focused on the "stageworthiness" of ASL:

> When you see the words at the same time that you hear them, it gives them an additional meaning. Your eye is caught everywhere by the movement of

the language onstage; it's like sculpture in the air. (Quoted in Grandjean 1993, 38)

Because Hays approached the challenge of addressing both social and artistic concerns while professionalizing his actors, the company has been highly successful in inserting deaf performers into the cultural mainstream.

Nannette Fabray, a prominent television actress who was hard-of-hearing, helped spearhead publicity during the early stages of the company. In particular, she hosted *The Theater of the Deaf*, an NBC experiment in TV that was produced in 1967. In describing the challenge of creating a particular scene, she says that "We want to evolve a theater so compressed, so charged that to speak is unnecessary." She added that "We think we can touch the edges of such total involvement that the body becomes a silent singing instrument of infinite range" (NTD 1967). This vision for NTD argues for the transformative potential of merging sign and speech into a single "charged" form that transfigures the prescribed pathways of communication. Fabray's oxymoron of the "silent singing" of the body illustrates the vision that was driving NTD.

In addition to experimentation with the combined form of sign and speech, Hays also initiated work on new forms of music. NTD is known in particular for their work with the Baschet sculptures, sound structures that create a visual and sonic background for the performances. These new instruments had been created over a fifteen-year period by François Baschet and his brother Bernard and were used in the premiere of NTD in 1967.

The instrument sculptures were as tall as twelve feet, and included a twelve-foot gong. The xylophone-like instrument was covered by luminous glass rods and gleaming metals. The musicians played these sculptures with moistened fingers and rubber mallets or bows, and they plucked them like a harp or played them like a piano. The various sounds possible included those reminiscent of African drums, bells, strings, and brass instruments. These instruments provided the means for a sonic and visual staging of music. This approach helped orient the hearing audience, provided vibrations as cues for the deaf performers, extended the possibilities for scene design since the metals could reflect colored lights, and also acted as visual cues for the performers.

Because there were no prior models for the development of theater that used both ASL and English, Hays turned to whatever he sensed would work. One such direction was Japanese theater. In their first season, Yoshio Aoyama directed *The Tale of Kasane*. While the available description is scant, it is particularly interesting to note that in the Kabuki form the narrators stand to one side while the performers "move" out the action. Rather than being an issue of translation or compensation, the aesthetic form itself—through the separation of sound and image—creates a third, or new, space for the unfolding of the drama.

In addition to Aoyama's *Tale of Kasane*, the 1967 season also opened with three other works: Gene Lasko directed William Saroyan's *Man with the Heart in the High-lands*, John Hirsch, *Tyger! Tyger! And Other Burnings*, and Joe Layton, *Gianni*

Schicci. Although only six people attended the first performance, word spread quickly. Hays attributed the low initial turnout to social misconceptions of deaf people as "freaks."

The Third Eye, put together and toured in 1972–73, is one of the few works in NTD's repertoire that deals directly with the deaf experience. There were four sections in the work, each one attempting to address deaf/hearing issues from the deaf perspective. One of the sections, "Side Show," was directed by Open Theatre's Joe Chaikin and NTD's Dorothy Miles. In order to depict normality from the point of view of the deaf, the company portrays the everyday activities of the hearing as freakish. Two hearing creatures, captured for the circus because they hear, are displayed in a cage. The other performers, astonished, gawk and gesticulate at their habits of using a variety of sound-based instruments, such as the telephone, record player, and alarm clock. Further commentary is offered on how the hearing communicate using their mouths rather than their hands. In another section, the performers do a "theater of the ridiculous" version of a familiar children's song. In this section they do a sign-along of "Three Blind Mice" that is reminiscent of a Mitch Miller sing-along.

The Third Eye comments on the difference between perception in a hearing and deaf world without a specific editorializing of the situation. This approach allows the audience to take in the images and absurdities and to make their own connections. At the very least, *The Third Eye* points out the way in which the hearing population tends to take hearing for granted and all that it implies. Davis notes, for example, that "Disability is a specular moment" (1995, 13), and here we have an inversion of this looking as the deaf—through the *third eye*—look back at the hearing and position the hearing as the freakish ones.

Shortly after this season, NTD, in 1973, was invited to do a workshop with Peter Brook, who is noted for his experimentation with pushing the boundaries of classical theater. His highly physical approach explored sonic and kinesthetic possibilities, and Brook was particularly interested in developing a universal language for the theater that he pursued in his two most recent works, Ted Hughes's *Orghast* and Peter Handke's *Kasper*. *Orghast*, for example, relied on "a whole new language for its dialogue—also called Orghast" (Croyden 1973, 7). Orghast was a "language of pure, concrete sounds," "an imageless, concretely operative language of direct connotation that was supposed to operate in the affective manner of music or gesture" (Zinder 1980, 129). Brook was extremely interested in creating "a universal language of theatre that [could] be understood by human beings anywhere in the world, regardless of cultural, social, or geographical differences" (Zinder 1980, 129).

For his upcoming piece, *The Conference of the Birds*, which he planned to tour in Africa, Brook wanted his company to develop a system of signs, syllables, and silence, as well as bird sounds. "Brook [was] striving for the meaning of *sound* rather than the meaning of *words* and for a theatrical language that is more theatrically expressive than English, and more universal, able to be grasped emotionally anywhere in the world" (Croyden 1973, 7). To this end the company worked on Greek, sonic essences,[2] and Japanese and African songs.

NTD was invited for three weeks to further the discussion on what sign language could contribute to theatrical communication. One exercise involved the use of sticks to communicate as they became extensions of the body, the voice, and the psyche. In another activity the actors were asked to work with boxes—creating playlets out of yet another extension of personal space. This exchange with Brook not only provided a testing ground for his theatrical techniques but NTD also absorbed and extended his ideas.

> For the National Theater of the Deaf, the experience with Brook "opened up new avenues," said Hays. "For example, we are working toward extending communications without using sign language. In our new piece, *Gilgamesh*, the Deaf use a good deal of abstract sound. They are trying to use their voices on a purely emotional level since they have no way of monitoring sound. (Croyden 1973, 7)

The experimentation in staging expressivity through the use of tonality enlarged the parameters for NTD. This example, along with the previously mentioned one of the Baschet sculptures, suggests new ways to think about sound and how it can be used with deaf actors.

That there were no preexisting models for the development of a theater of the deaf that combined sign and speech from which NTD could draw, founding director David Hays explains, facilitated the development of NTD's aesthetic through a process of trial and error.[3] Nevertheless, NTD has a long history of interaction with a variety of performance modes that include Kabuki, Bharata Natyam, opera, modern dance, Peter Brook's theatrical experiments, Pilobolus's choreography, and more recently, Ping Chong's performance compositions.[4] Through these contacts, NTD has sought to develop language theater that is grounded in a viable form and that activates the sensory registers in new ways, all aimed at making space speak. In other words, in the space of the performance, the use of signing as a visual and kinesthetic language has its own organizing principles that differ from the speech as a sound-based model of language. NTD, while basing their aesthetic on a viable coupling of sign and speech, continues to develop an acting style that emerges from the pictorial baseline that governs ASL.

In a Grove

In a Grove, the National Theater of the Deaf's work based on a Japanese short story by Ryunosuke Akutagawa and directed by Arvin Brown, was first produced in 1986 and revived for the Tokyo International Theater Festival in 1988. Using the *rashomon* technique,[5] the story revolves around the mystery of a presumed murder, and it involves the testimonies of seven different people—a woodcutter, a priest, a policeman, the mother, the bandit, the wife, and the husband as they are delivered in a court. The audience does not see or hear the judge, and except for several remarks by the testifiers, the judge is an unvoiced presence.

The work unfolds through a set of shifting, harrowing images in which the gaps between stories reinforce not only the partiality of each one's perspective, but also the impossibility of acquiring a complete picture. *In a Grove* shows how each individual is trapped within his or her own story, answering, finally, not to an objectively deferred symbolic law of the courtroom, but to his or her own fantasies of personalized forms of law. The voice highlights the ways in which the individuals are trapped between two worlds, that of their own stories and that of the symbolic order. The unvoiced, unspeaking presence of the judge, to whom each speaker addresses his story, does not even reply at the end when the husband, speaking through a medium, sinks back down "into the space between two worlds." Embedded with this testimonial insularity is the issue of aborted attempts at hearing one another.

At a literal level, the various testimonies enable the audience to reconstruct the likely, but always fragmented, events surrounding the husband's death. Briefly, the story revolves around a chance encounter between a couple and a bandit while they are traveling. Because the young woman is so beautiful, the bandit plots to have her at any cost, and he concocts a story to get the couple to detour into the woods with him. There, after tricking the husband into a helpless position, he binds his arms and his legs so that he cannot escape. The wife becomes enraged with him, and tries to knife him, and the bandit not only restrains her, but also forces himself on her. Shortly after that, in an unclear sequence of events, the husband dies and the wife apparently disappears.

Although the actual time of the testimonies is that in which the courtroom scene unfolds, and despite the fact that that experience of that level of time remains steady, there is no closure or response at the end of any of the individual testimonies, even after the final one. As a result, the stories are suspended in a time frame of their own without reference to the ones that have gone before. Within that context, we hear the voices one after another, but we cannot determine the truth of the presumed "facts." Left to our own silences, we also do not answer back.

Each testimony surfaces as a result of a simple comment from the court announcer: "The testimony of——." There is no particular order to the testimonies themselves except that the last three involve the three people most directly related to the murder: the bandit, the wife, and the husband. The woodcutter, for example, talks about finding the body; the priest goes further back in time to the belief that he passed the husband on the road walking alongside his wife, who was on horseback. Then the plot jumps forward to the policeman, who finds the bandit at some unknown length of time after the crucial sequence of events. As we hear/see each story, the disorienting, irregular time frame disrupts the compulsion to accumulate the facts about what happened. It reminds us that speaking is partial and related to one's own viewpoint.

By the time that we hear the husband's testimony, his expression of anger subsumes and overrides the laying out of facts. Significant truth emerges in the play of passions much more so than in the "actual" details of the event surrounding the man's death. Despite the way in which the testimonies accumulate toward this intensity of passion, the disparities in each individual's testimony, particularly between the wife, bandit, and husband, undermine the possibilities of creating a unitary and coherent sense of the "time" of the murder. What we hear are narrative fragments and occlusions.

The use of space also evokes an amorphous flux, creating a sense of how testimony, or any sort of narrative, is an attempt to escape from the unyielding presence and flux of space. In particular, the staged images are poetic, suggesting the atmosphere of a place rather than a specific location itself. The stage setting is sparse except for the use of long poles that mark the places of the grove and the Baschet sculptures that stand off to one side and provide the musical accompaniment. Lighting is manipulated to play with, and offset, the long lines of the poles and the shadows they make next to the performers who hold them up.

The actual use of the stage space itself also works to create scenes that change shape in a mysteriously driven fashion. The sections of the grove appear and disappear, riding on the waves of motion, as the performers form and reform themselves with their long poles in the space of the stage. At one point the poles, in order to create the impression of a wall, are positioned together tightly and in a straight row. In other sections the trees of the grove encircle the performers, in order to hide them (as in the case of the rape scene).

The grove is everywhere; it moves as though driven by a power and pulse of its own. The grove also forms the backdrop of the court space, and the space of the grove permeates the courtroom. It is from this blurred space of the in-between that the testifiers emerge and to which they return after they have spoken. Many of the performers, when they are not giving testimony, wear black masks across their faces to create a uniform, choruslike identity between them. Each of the characters steps out of the wall of trees to claim his or her individual part when it comes time to speak, and then steps back into the communal anonymity that the figure of the grove provides.

When, for example, the chorus-member steps forward to give the testimony of the woodcutter, he must, as do each of the subsequent witnesses, transform into the one who speaks. He does so by draping a piece of clothing in a ritual-like fashion over the original attire. Additionally, the speaker raises the mask, which hides his eyes, from his head so that his entire face is visible. This maneuver further distinguishes the character from what he has been, a member of the grove, to what he is, and it is signified through a change in the visual image of the body.

The pattern of changing one's physical position and look in the narrative in order to testify echoes the dynamics of testimonial itself in *In a Grove*, and it traces the transformation from the nonvoicing presence of the grove to the voice of the character who must speak. Rather than as in a production predicated on hearing, moving from silence to sound, the metaphor moves from one physical image to another—that is, from one body to another—in order to illuminate the shift in perspective from the wall of "silence" to speaking the testimony through the hands. The chorus is established not by what they *say*, but by what they *do*, how they are positioned and move through the space. Despite the testimonies that we see/hear from each of the individuals, what happens "in the grove" remains a question. Since the play is titled *In a Grove*, we are reminded that we are not sure what has happened in the play either.

The use of tonality further reinforces the sense of fluctuating time and space. When the woodcutter, as he tells his version, steps back into the grove, which has split and fallen to either side, he advances toward the dead body that he had not recognized. As he moves into the space of death, the use of tonality—moans, whistles, screeches, and sighs—distorts the space, giving it a distant and ghostly air. After he has finished his testimonial, the woodcutter leaves the space, and again we hear these tones. They come out of nowhere and recede back to nowhere, further multiplying the spheres of voice.

After the testimonies of the woodcutter, the priest, the policeman, and the mother, who says she does not know where her daughter is, we hear from the three main individuals involved. The bandit confesses his lust for the wife, and he claims that she told him, after the rape, that one of the men would have to die. The bandit decides to duel the husband, and he claims that he killed him with his sword. In the next testimony, the wife mysteriously appears to give her account. She insists that the bandit violated her, and that as a result of her disgrace, she wanted to die. But the woman is tormented and in the process of her despair, she can feel her husband's eyes piercing through her. The wife finally kills her husband because, as she says, she feels his eyes telling her to do so. But after she kills him, she does not have the strength to kill herself, and so she runs away.

The final testimony that we hear is that of the dead husband, and this testimony is delivered through a medium. As the transition unfolds from the grove to the character, the performer we are to discover as the medium pounds the pole into the ground. We feel, hear, and see the trembling of this part of the grove as both a commentary on the story and the eruption of a greater moment than those that have been revealed. What is happening in this shift? Does the grove summon the dead man? Or has the dead man, as a part of the vortex of nonvoicing, forced an outbreak from the world of the dead into the courtroom of the still living?

Because there are three levels of speaking for another, the last scene, in particular, heightens the issue of multiplication of voices. We simultaneously see and hear voices in several registers. This scene explores the way in which the medium speaks for the dead man, but also the way in which the voicing actor speaks for the medium, as her speaking voice. At the beginning of this section, there is the sign language of the medium, the voice of the speaking actress, and the minimal movement of the dead husband as he passes his voice to the medium. Eventually the scene shifts and we see/hear the dead man himself speaking. It is a shift that we accept; we are now close enough to the sphere of the dead that we can hear him across the divide without the help of the medium.

In this version, we discover what is probably the most likely version of the story. This version, in fact, contradicts the accounts of the bandit, who claims that he killed the husband, and of the wife, who claims that even though she killed her husband, she was too powerless to go ahead and kill herself. The husband, we learn, overheard his wife tell the bandit to "take me, whoever you are," and from this moment the husband was trapped in his own anger and resentment, unable to find any other way out of his predicament than to kill himself. *In a Grove* closes with this revelation, and as the husband lies there dead, with medium hovering over him, the last words we hear are "I sank down in the space between two worlds."

The semiology of NTD's double form of sign and speech provides a dimension to *In a Grove* that makes it especially powerful. In this production, the voicing actors are also a part of the grove, and because the grove is often shrouded in half-shadows, it is not always clear where the sounding voice is coming from. This structure seems particularly suited to the thematic frame of the story. As the various images unfold, the performers move in and out of their positions in the grove, or the testifiers sign their testimony, the story takes shape primarily in pictorial terms. The use of the speaking actors underscores, but does not explain or substitute for, the visuality of the production. This double form creates a heightened experience of the words—a sonic and kinesthetic echo chamber.

Furthermore the deaf performers, through the use of sign language, both embody and speak their story. Viewed through the use of *deixis*, the story that they tell involves the coordinates of the here and now of the speaker and the body of the person. According to Brenda Farnell, "Time/space is measured from the here and now of the embodied person as mover and speaker in a space that is simultaneously physical and social" (1995, 94). As a result of this complex layering of body, memory, and the social realm, the audience's involvement with the pictorial motion of the signing body, even if partial, also creates a different sense of time and space.

Additionally, sign language has cinematic properties, as noted by deaf performers Bernard Bragg and Gil Eastman:

> In a signed language . . . narrative is no longer linear and prosaic. Instead, the essence of sign language is to cut from a normal view to a close-up to a distant shot to a close-up again, and so on, even including flashback and flash-forward scenes, exactly as a movie editor works. (Cited in Sacks 1989, 90)

This aspect of sign language helps to explain the rhythm of the scenic changes and the logic of the spatial organization of each retelling as cinematic cuts. In other words, the "filmic" logic of sign extends into the larger choices about spatial organization and change.

While we do not know for sure whether the last version of the events is most true, it is certainly the most important one. The spaces of two worlds could refer to many possibilities, but they obviously refer to the worlds of life and death, speaking and nonspeaking, and the enclosed stories of the bandit, wife, and husband and their inability to perform within the symbolic order. These individuals have come before the judge, but they do not receive any answers. We are reminded, once again, that here are no stable places and no stable narratives—and of the inevitabilities of an only partial hearing.

NTD's work is striking in how signing, the spoken, and the use of sound effects are combined to create the visual multispatial analogy of what is communicated in the speech. These scenes are examples of ways in which the combined use of sign and speech has led to extensive exploration of the pictorial possibilities of language through the hearing eye. According to William Stokoe,

> Speech has only one dimension—its extension in time; writing has two dimensions; models have three; but only signed languages have at their disposal four dimensions—the three spatial dimensions accessible to the signer's body, as well as the dimension of time. And Sign fully exploits the syntactic possibilities in its four-dimensional channel of expression. (Cited in Sacks 1989, 90)

This difference in the spatial experience of language and its expression in the ASL that NTD uses, a heightened and poeticized version, promotes a radical shift in perception and the understanding that can pass from performer to audience. The audience views and hears through the double sensory mode of sign and speech as well as the musical instruments that are used, which are also highly visual and sculptural.

By providing the context for exploring the threshold between speech and sign, or words and visual-spatial images, the type of ASL that NTD uses further explores not only the physicalization of the word, but also a type of writing in space.[6] Bauman remarks that "A line of ASL poetry may bear more resemblance to a line in a painting or drawing than to a line in a written poem." The mix of speech and sign leads to a hybrid theatrical form, a sign language poetry, which "adds a new perspective in the historical tradition of relating poetry to blindness and painting to silence or muteness" (1997, 176).

The original style for NTD that founding director David Hays fostered through collaboration with various experimental directors is seeing a resurgence and a new phase in the work of the current artistic NTD directors, Will Rhys and Camille Jeter. For example, in August 1998, Ping Chong was invited to lead a workshop at NTD for two weeks on a topic of his choice. Rhys explained that his interest in Chong centered on his work in movement and text as well as his collaborative approach to directing, a style that NTD promotes and also wants to extend. In 2000, NTD began to collaborate with Geiji Ito, an experimental music composer, on their millennium touring production, *The Unwritten Song*. While each of the groups that NTD works with reflects differing aesthetics and methods of theatrical production, they all share a focus on the use of sound, silence, and image, and they all work collaboratively. Rather than setting productions according to a preexisting vision, these works evolve as the participants—hearing and deaf—bring their various sensibilities to bear on the projects. Out of these intersections new forms are forged.

Through an active listening through the third ear that involves both hearing and seeing, we can better grasp the double nature of the performances of the National Theater of the Deaf. These performances, as well as NTD's professional training programs and their outreach work, have led to radical revisionings of the possibilities for theater as well as shaking up and transforming "entrenched ideologies based on the 'normal hearing body' " (Bauman 1997, 171). Disrupted, resisting the normative, we learn to hear differently, and we are oriented in new ways toward a perceptual and conceptual openness that shifts not only our understanding of difference but also the transformative power of performance.

NOTES

1. For more on the third ear, see Reik 1948. Elsewhere I am also developing a new model of the third ear and its application to performance studies.
2. Brooks's study involved finding the range of tonality that could communicate across language groups.
3. Personal interview, April 1998.
4. Personal interview, April 1998.
5. *Rashomon* refers to a technique that presents several viewpoints on an event in such a way that the truth is seen to be relative. This term derives from a 1950 film with that title by Japanese filmmaker Akira Kurosawa. In this film a "single" story is depicted through the eyes of four different characters.
6. It is important to reiterate that the type of signing that NTD uses is a version for the stage, in which the dramatic potential of the language is paramount. Deaf audience members have at times expressed confusion over the ASL that NTD uses.

References

Bauman, H. Dirksen L. "Beyond Speech and Writing: Recognizing American Sign Language Literature in the MLA." *Profession 1997*. New York: MLA, 1997.
———."Derrida and Deafness: Phonocentrism, Audism, and Sign." MLA Conference paper, 1996.
Bhabha, Homi. *The Location of Culture*. New York: Routledge, 1994.
Croyden, Margaret. "Peter Brook's 'Birds' Fly to Africa. *New York Times*, January 21, 1973, 1, 7.
Davis, Lennard J. *Enforcing Normalcy: Disability, Deafness, and the Body*. New York: Verso, 1995.
Farnell, Brenda. "Where Mind Is a Verb: Spatial Orientation and Deixis in Plains Indian and Sign Talk and Assiniboine (Nakota) Culture." In *Human Action Signs in Cultural Context: The Visible and Invisible in Movement and Dance*. Lanham, MD: Scarecrow Press, 1995, 82–111.
Grandjean, Pat. "David Hays," *Connecticut* (February 1993): 32–39.
Miller, David. "Myth and Folktale," *Mythosphere* 1.1 (1997): 9–22.
Mitchell, W. J. T. "Gesture, Sign, and Play: ASL Poetry and The Deaf Community." *MLA Newsletter* 21.2: 13–14, 1989.
National Theater of the Deaf. *Peer Gynt*. Videocassette. NTD Archives. Chester, CT, 1996.
———.*Ophelia*. Videocassette. NTD Archives. Chester, CT, 1992.
———.*Farewell My Lovely*. Videocassette. NTD Archives. Chester, CT, 1990.
———.*In a Grove*. Videocassette. NTD Archives. Chester, CT, 1988.

————.*Woyzek*. Videocassette. NTD Archives. Chester, CT, 1971.

————.*Tales of Kasane*. Videocassette. NTD Archives. Chester, CT, 1967.

Reik, Theodor. *Listening with the Third Ear: The Inner Experience of a Psychoanalyst*. New York: Farrar, Straus, 1948.

Sacks, Oliver. *Seeing Voices: A Journey into the World of the Deaf*. Berkeley: University of California Press, 1989.

Zinder, David G. *The Surrealist Connection: An Approach to a Surrealist Aesthetic of Theatre*. Ann Arbor, MI: UMI Research Press, 1980.

"Better Me Than You":
Children of a Lesser God, Deaf Education, and Paternalism

ROBERT C. SPIRKO

> Sarah: *So your mother told you you were God.*
> James: *So my mother told me I was God. Yes, that's correct.*
> Sarah: *And that's why you want to make me over in your image.*
> —CHILDREN OF A LESSER GOD, ACT I

> James: *. . . Right. And we'll have deaf children.*
> Sarah: *Right!*
> James: *Who's going to educate them? You?*
> Sarah: *Better me than you.*
> —CHILDREN OF A LESSER GOD, ACT II

It is one of the givens of Deaf[1] education that the Deaf are, more often than not, educated by the hearing.[2] As Deaf studies and disability studies have shown, the political and cultural implications of this for the Deaf community (and, it might be noted, for the hearing community) are profound.[3] In fact, the education of deaf children is one of the primary sites of intervention that the hearing majority makes on the Deaf minority. Since the Milan congress in 1880, the general tide in education of the Deaf has been toward oralism and speech training, and away from sign language–based instruction of the deaf, carried out by hearing people for/on deaf people, "for their own good." There has been a long-standing Deaf resistance to this trend, whose most notable victory was in the Gallaudet Revolution in 1988[4]: the student protests succeeded in both winning the first Deaf president for the college and raising the profile of the Deaf community in the national consciousness.

Eight years before the Gallaudet Revolution, however, deafness had come to the public consciousness in the form of Mark Medoff's *Children of a Lesser God*, which virtually swept the Tony awards in 1980 and ran for over eight hundred performances on Broadway. The issue returned on an even wider scale when the film version was released in 1987 (perhaps not coincidentally the year before the protests at Gallaudet), and Marlee Matlin won the Oscar for best actress as Sarah Norman, the Deaf protagonist.

16

Given the explicitly political nature of the issues that the play deals with, it is interesting to observe how in both the contemporary reviews and the film version, issues of deafness and power are glossed over in the face of the love story between a hearing man and a deaf woman. In this reading, the fact that the story is about a romance between a hearing speech teacher and a deaf student, and that the play is centered on a residential school for the deaf, fade into the background.

It is not surprising, given that the majority of audiences for the play and the film are hearing, that this fade has taken place. As Harlan Lane points out, the "mainstream" construction of deafness as a disability requiring medical intervention and support services is long-standing, well entrenched, and supported by a medical establishment with vested interests in maintaining itself (1997, 166). In terms of the average audience member, "hearing people led to reflect on deafness generally begin by imagining themselves without hearing—which is, of course, to have a disability but not to be Deaf" (166). That is, they have no experience with the Deaf community and the fact that in this community, Deaf people are not disabled.

This response of the hearing audience to the play is influenced not only by this flawed empathy—only partially putting themselves in the place of the other—but also by other cultural constructions of normality and difference and of the nature of literature. These constructions can be seen in contemporary reviews of the play. Robert Brustein, in *The New Republic*, categorizes *Children* as a "disability play" in which a crusading "normal" tries to save/cure a disabled protagonist but encounters resistance. Through a process of conflict and emotional connection, the "normal" hero comes to the realization that we "share a common humanity, regardless of our defects" (1980, 23). Presumably, through identification, the audience maps the hero's experience onto their own. The problem here is that "common humanity" is a bit vague as a category. In fact, the identification as "common humanity" proceeds on abled terms: common, normal, normative. In this formulation, it seems that only by disregarding defects can we recognize the other as human. Such an approach denies the possibility that one might actually identify with their "defect" and take it as the ground of their humanity, rather than what must be pared away before an underlying humanity can be revealed. As I noted above, at issue is not empathy as a way of understanding, but an empathy grounded solely in abled experience, one that proceeds without recognizing genuine otherness.

There is a paradigm other than that of the abled by which the play might be read: that of gender relations. The love story was given central focus in the movie, presumably because it was more commercial. Even in the play, however, critics found the romance compelling; Edwin Wilson, in *The Wall Street Journal*, found deafness to be a "powerful" symbol of "the difficulties a man and a woman have in communicating with each other" (22). This reading reduces a complex interaction of culture and power to a "men are from Mars, women are from Venus" dynamic. Reducing disability to a metaphor for a "real" interaction renders disability as secondary to gender in this case. Medoff's play, which actually does an admirable job in depicting some of the very real issues that the Deaf community faced in the late 1970s and still faces today, becomes a simple matter of (mis)communication. If deafness becomes a metaphor, we are not encouraged to read the "Deaf politics" of the play for themselves, and we leave the play with little more appreciation for the real issues facing the Deaf than when we came. Furthermore, there are particularly disturbing issues surrounding the use of disability as a metaphor, as critics have pointed out: "not only do such figures of speech further objectify and alienate people with disabilities, they perpetuate stereotypes" (Linton et al., 6). In a literary field marked by metaphoric reading and the search for deep meanings, however, such a reduction may be unavoidable. Rudolf Erben, in his study of Medoff's work, persists in reading disability as a metaphor:

> *Children of a Lesser God* is the second of three dramas in which Medoff uses the disability metaphor. The heroine's mental retardation in *Firekeeper* serves the same purpose as the protagonist's deafness in *Children of a Lesser God* and *The Hands of Its Enemy*. Their handicaps demonstrate women's victimization in a patriarchal society. . . . In the end, both James and Sarah abandon gender stereotypes and respect each other as equals. (1995, 39–40)

The problem with Erben's reading is that, like Wilson's, it subsumes disability under the cover of gender relations as a metaphor.

Pace Erben, at the end of the play, what happens is emphatically *not* that "they both abandon gender stereotypes and respect each other as equals" (39), but that a hearing person and a deaf person agree to try to meet in a different space, one "not in silence or in sound but somewhere else" (Medoff 1982, 91). There are gender issues at work, to be sure, but the growth of the characters is not about the abandonment of "gender stereotypes"—such language is found nowhere in the play, and the issue of gender relations as such is hardly foregrounded. It is only present in a metaphorical reading of deafness that, as I pointed out above, eviscerates a great deal of the politics that the play grapples with.

The question we are then faced with is: How do we approach the play? Given that, as majority readers, we[5] have to be cautious about the way our empathy and identification work with the characters, and given that few majority readers have much direct experience with the Deaf community, close attention to what the play actually says may be helpful. We also need to be able to realize our own situatedness, both in terms of this essay and the play itself, that we understand ourselves as not "speaking in place of Deaf people . . . but rather, as hearing people engage[d] in self-reflective conversation about the audist oppression of the Deaf community" (Bauman and Drake 1997, 309). Below, I want to offer a reading of some of the elements of *Children* in the hopes of resisting a normative, audist interpretation of the play.

The challenge here is not to see disability as a metaphor for woman's state in the patriarchy (although it can be read as such), but of disability and gender as a joint articulation: "Join. Unjoin," in the language of the play. As the feminist and disability critic Rosemarie Garland Thomson points out, "both the female and the disabled body are cast within cultural discourse as deviant and inferior" (1997, 279). The problem is not so much that Sarah is subject to a generic "patriarchy," but that she, along with the other deaf characters, is subject to a specific audist "paternalism" that infantilizes the deaf and takes from them power over their own lives.

Harlan Lane, in *The Mask of Benevolence*, makes a strong case for reading the relation between hearing and Deaf culture as a colonial one, one marked by paternalism: "like the paternalism of the colonizers, hearing paternalism . . . sees its task as 'civilizing' its charges: restoring deaf people to society. And hearing paternalism fails to understand the structure and values of deaf society" (1992, 37). This colonial paternalism "deals in stereotypes" (37) and "places its beneficiaries in a dependent relation and keeps them depending for its own psychological and economic interest" (39). Looking at the teachers in *Children*, we can see this dynamic at work.

Mr. Franklin, the supervising teacher at the school, is perhaps the most direct representative of the "audist establishment." Toward the end of Act II, in the context of the students' legal challenge to the lack of Deaf teachers, Franklin says he will fight their challenge to the end, appealing as many times through the legal system as necessary. He justifies these actions because "despicable as it may seem, I won't continue in this field if the subjects of my efforts are going to tell me how to minister to them" (Medoff 1982, 82). Franklin absolutely rejects any claims that the Deaf students may have to self-determination, or to being taught by native speakers of their language. In fact, Franklin is resolutely dismissive of the idea of Deaf educators: "Would you hire your wife [Sarah] to teach? What—sign? That'd be like a football team hiring a guy to do nothing but hold for extra points" (82). This spoken by the man who is responsible for the atmosphere and teachers at a residential school for the Deaf. In this character, Medoff has condensed the most egregious forms of audism and speech-centeredness. Franklin also demonstrates the audist establishment's desire to maintain its own power in the face of challenges from the Deaf.

Franklin is an obvious target for criticism: he is not a likeable character, and is overt about his need for control and his disdain for Deaf culture. James, however, is also a paternalistic figure, though in more subtle ways. Throughout the play, he clings to his conviction that a speech-centered approach is best, from his first interactions with Orin and Sarah, to the emotional climax of the play, where he and Sarah confront their differences.

From their first meeting, James and Sarah clash over speech. She refuses to learn to lip read or to mimic speech from him; the challenge intrigues James. He invites her to dinner off-campus, and they begin to fall in love. Read in a purely cynical way, when James cannot win Sarah's compliance in the classroom, he pursues her in the bedroom. The actual emotional dynamic in the play is more complex than this, certainly, but from a distance it seems to resemble very closely the behavior of the colonizer toward the colonized. There are certainly gender dynamics at work, but the gender roles are seen through a decidedly colonial lens. James, somewhat paternalistically, is trying to teach Sarah the language of the dominant culture. For him, Sarah is the exotic Other, who needs to be domesticated—and she is quite literally domesticated in the course of their romance, taking on the role of a contemporary housewife after their marriage. Her impulse toward literal domesticity is seen in the wish list she and James discuss toward the end of the first act: it includes a house, car, garden, microwave, food processor, and children (37–38). Tellingly, Sarah emphasizes that she wants *Deaf* children, a stipulation with which James is uncomfortable. In a colonial paradigm, if children are too much like the colonized parent, they will be unable to pass.

Passing as a theme is raised explicitly in the play. Sarah's mother tells James in no uncertain terms: "you're still trying to force her to speak and lip read so she can pass for hearing" (7). The idea of passing has received a great deal of attention in African-American studies, as it marks a moment of cultural instability, when someone from one race slips into the codes of another. In a Deaf context, passing as hearing requires an adherence to the norms of the dominant society, particularly in the form of communication: this adherence requires a great deal of work and practice. As in racial passing, ability passing is not available to all: only light-skinned African Americans might pass, just as only Deaf people with some residual hearing might. In both cases, the bodies of the oppressed class become a contested site that must conform at least partially to the norms of the dominant culture. For those whose bodies do not conform, passing is not an option.

After their marriage, James's insistence on Sarah's conformity to the hearing world begins to lessen, but resurges in their emotional confrontation near the end of the play. He pins her arms, silencing her, and speaks to her without sign language:

> Shut up! You want to talk to me, then *you* learn *my* language! Did you get that? Of course you did. You've probably been reading lips perfectly for years; but it's a great control game, isn't it? You can cook, but you can't speak. You can drive and shop and play bridge but you can't speak. You can even make a speech but you still can't do it alone. You always have to be dependent on someone, and you always will for the rest of your life until you learn to speak. Now come on! I want you to speak to me. Let me hear it. Speak! Speak! Speak! (86)

Sarah's response to this tirade is to speak, but as Medoff specifies in the stage direction, it is "*not a positive demonstration of speech—only of passion. Only a few words are even barely understandable*" (87). James is confronted with the absolute physical limitation on Sarah's speech. What he is not directly confronted with, however, are the assumptions he makes in his orders to her. He assumes that she has been "reading lips perfectly for years," although nothing actually bears this out in the play. He also treats Sarah's limited bid for control over her own life and communication as a "control game": not a valid response to a society bent on erasing her, rendering her invisible as long as she might "pass as hearing." James also seems unable to dissociate normal functioning from speech. He enumerates the daily activities she can do, and is incredulous that she can do all these things—cook, drive, shop, play bridge—but cannot speak. In this moment, the depth of his failure to understand her disability is clear.

Similarly, his inability to understand Deaf cultural values (one of the hallmarks of paternalism) comes to the fore. He accuses her of always being dependent, and hinges independence on learning to speak. Independence is a mainstream U.S. cultural value, but one that certain subcultures do not share (not only the Deaf—one thinks of ethnic immigrant communities as well).

It is evident from this exchange that Sarah's joke earlier in the play, about James being a God who wants to remake Sarah in his own image, rings true. James, despite his liberal good intentions and his deep emotional commitment to Sarah, cannot get past his hearing assumptions.

We can see the effects of Franklin's and James's paternalism on the deaf characters in the play. Orin represents a rejection of the overt paternalism of the hearing establishment, but he unfortunately reinscribes paternal gender relations. In him, we see the tendency of unreflective radicalism to carry over gender power imbalances: male dominance operates within the Deaf community as well as around it. Orin wants to lead the revolution—he wants Sarah to work with him, to be "pure deaf" but also to be under his control—to be his weapon against the audist establishment. Being "pure deaf," she is the silver bullet that can strike at the monster's heart. There is also a subtext of jealousy between Orin and James, as if Orin considers Sarah to be (because of their deafness) "his" woman.

In a sense, Orin and Lydia represent two different relations to James's father-figure: Orin rejects him, ultimately, in anger. Lydia wants to seduce him, to be the good student and the good lover. She tries the hardest of any deaf character to pass: in a stage direction, James brushes back her hair, *"revealing two large hearing aids running from her ears into her shirt pockets; obviously, she uses her hair to try to camouflage the amplifiers"* (12). Her crush on James is almost painful to watch: constantly in need of attention from him, reading every book he gives her, seeking him out whenever she can, Lydia is the "good colonial subject" who follows the colonizer's rules in the hopes of gaining power and self-worth. There is no indication that Lydia is conscious of what she is doing, but Sarah recognizes the process and accuses James of fostering Lydia's dependency. James responds initially with "would that be so terrible if she became dependent on me?" (25). Again, we see the unreflective paternalism James harbors—while later in the play he castigates Sarah's own dependence, he also secretly wants Deaf dependence on him generally, as it bolsters his power and importance. When Sarah presses the accusation, James becomes defensive: "Jesus Christ, that's quite a little leap you made there; from helping someone to learn something to dependency because of it, to falling in love as a result of the dependency. That's very nice, but it happens to be bullshit" (25).

Far from being bullshit, it indicates that Sarah is aware of the colonial relations between hearing and Deaf. Sarah charts a third course—neither complete rejection nor complete submission. In a telling moment during their first meeting, Sarah asks if James was a radical in the 1960s. When he fails to understand her sign, she writes "RADICAL" on the chalkboard, coincidentally opposite her name. From the audience's introduction to her, then, the association Sarah—RADICAL is made. Her Deaf radicalism is in some ways more pure than Orin's—she refuses to learn speech, while he is willing to learn it. But her attraction to James, and to the consumer world that her relationship with him enables, means that disengagement is not an option. It is ultimately this connection between them that enables James to grow in his understanding of deafness, to realize that his audist insistence on speech is problematic.

The danger, of course, is that the audience will believe James in his bad moments. Despite Medoff's assertion that Sarah is the true protagonist of the play (xv), James remains the filtering consciousness through which the play is told. A great deal of interpretation would here depend on the staging, on whether James was obviously defensive in the exchange about dependency, obviously aggressive and enraged in his argument with Sarah at the end. Still, a hearing audience will be more likely to find in a hearing character their identification point with the play. They may see Sarah as James sometimes sees her: a needy, controlling, defensive deaf person, rather than an organic intellectual, bent on resisting the hearing world but not given the intellectual material to do so. Still, Sarah insists, toward the end, on her own point of view. Rather than giving in to a colonizer-colonized model that inevitably dichotomizes and splits, Sarah, in her speech to the commission investigating the school, calls for a joining:

> Well, I want to be joined to other people, but for all my life people have spoken for me: *She* says, *she* means, *she* wants. As if there were no *I*. As if there were no one in here who *could* understand. Until you let me be an individual, an *I*, just as you are, you will never truly be able to come inside my silence and know me. And until you can do that, I will never let myself know you. Until that time, we cannot be joined. We cannot share a relationship. (84)

On the surface, this may seem like an appeal to a "common humanity," as Brustein reads it (1980). However, once one considers the real implications of treating a deaf person as "an *I*, just as you are," it becomes apparent that more is at stake. What Sarah demands is to be met on her own terms, in her own language, by a culture that is always used to operating on its own terms, in its own language. James, thoroughly steeped in that culture, is initially unable to do so. It is an open question whether the audience is able to meet her on that ground.

This ground is unstable territory: it tears her relationship with James apart, for a time. It is a utopian space that cannot yet be envisioned, only hinted at, between the radical Deaf rejection of speech and the audist establishment's insistence on speech as the only real method of communication. The final words of the play, "I'll help you if you'll help me," are simultaneously spoken and signed—but Sarah has the last word with the sign *join*.

NOTES

1. *Deaf* will be used throughout to refer to members of the Deaf community, while *deaf* will be used to indicate absence of hearing.
2. The history and political implications of this fact are well documented by Harlan Lane (1992).

3. Lane's studies *The Mask of Benevolence* (1992) and *When the Mind Hears: A History of the Deaf* (1984) are among the most forcefully argued studies of this phenomenon. Other examinations of the political/cultural issues involved with Deaf culture are Bauman and Drake 1997 and the essays in Wilcox 1989.

4. The Gallaudet Revolution started on March 6, 1988, when the Gallaudet University board of trustees announced their selection of Elisabeth Ann Zinser, a hearing woman, over two Deaf candidates as the new president of the university. Students responded with a week of demonstrations and marches, effectively shutting down the college, until their demands were met. For more information, consult Gannon 1989 and Christiansen 1995.

5. I include myself with the majority readers in this "we," even though I could be considered disabled—as a mild to moderately severe hearing-impaired individual, I identify with both communities. However, as I was mainstreamed as a child and am not fluent in ASL, I cannot count myself as Deaf.

References

Bauman, H. Dirksen L., and Jennifer Drake. "Silence Is not without Voice: Including Deaf Culture within Multicultural Curricula." In *The Disability Studies Reader*, ed. Lennard J. Davis. New York: Routledge, 1997.

Brustein, Robert. "Robert Brustein on Theater," *The New Republic*, June 7, 1980, 23–24.

Christiansen, John. *Deaf President Now! The 1988 Revolution at Gallaudet University*. Washington, D.C.: Gallaudet University Press, 1995.

Erben, Rudolf. *Mark Medoff*. Boise, ID: Boise State University Press, 1995.

Gannon, Jack. *The Week the World Heard Gallaudet*. Washington, D.C.: Gallaudet University Press, 1989.

Lane, Harlan. "Construction of Deafness." *The Disability Studies Reader*. Ed. Lennard J. Davis. New York: Routledge, 1997. 153–71.

———. *The Mask of Benevolence: Disabling the Deaf Community*. New York: Knopf, 1992.

———. *When the Mind Hears: A History of the Deaf*. New York: Random House, 1984.

Linton, Simi, Susan Mello, and John O'Neill. "Disability Studies: Expanding the Parameters of Diversity," *Radical Teacher* (Fall 1995): 4–10.

Medoff, Mark. *Children of a Lesser God*. Oxford: Amber Lane Press, 1982.

Thomson, Rosemarie Garland. "Feminist Theory, the Body, and the Disabled Figure." In *The Disability Studies Reader*, ed. Lennard J. Davis. New York: Routledge, 1997.

Wilcox, Sherman, ed. *American Deaf Culture: An Anthology*. Burtonsville, MD: Linstock Press, 1989.

Wilson, Edwin. "Broadway: Two Openings and One Closing," *Wall Street Journal*, April 1, 1980, 22.

Violence, Pain, Pleasure: *Wit*

PAMELA COOPER

God created man in health, but health continued but a few hours, and sicknesse hath had the Dominion 6,000 years.

—JOHN DONNE, SERMON 2

[T]he image must be twisted if it is to make a renewed assault on the nervous system.

—FRANCIS BACON

At the core of *Wit* is a suffering body. Vivian Bearing, distinguished professor of seventeenth-century poetry, succumbs to ovarian cancer, and her physical ordeal gives the play its dramatic and imaginative center. Indeed, the title is almost a misnomer. The word *wit* refers broadly to mental agility and knowledge. More specifically, it describes the brilliant verbal tactics favored by the Metaphysical poets—most notably John Donne, whose Holy Sonnets Bearing has spent a lifetime studying. While all these modalities of the word apply, the topic of the play is less intellect than flesh. Margaret Edson names her protagonist for endurance, and embodies in her the corruption to which all flesh is heir. *Wit* details the torment and embattled resilience of a body caught up not only in the abyssal drama of illness, but in the ghastly apparatus of modern healing. As fiercely compressed as one of the sonnets on which Bearing is an expert, the play chronicles the betrayal of the intellect by a body turned rebel in the grip of disease.[1]

Committed to the life of the mind, Bearing finds her scholarly enterprise mocked by an invasion of the mindlessly material. Her peritoneal cavity, she tells us, is "crawling with cancer" cells eager only to reproduce, unresponsive to the researcher's skill, unreachable by knowledge (Edson 1993, 53). Epistemology and the strategies of both scientific and humanist knowing are powerful themes in *Wit*. The play's fascination with knowledge and its shrewd grasp of medical procedure as spectacle effectively theatricalize pain and offer it as entertainment. The result is a disturbing, sometimes baffling exposure of the body as an object of discipline, obscure punishment, and perverse sensuality. Bearing's flesh becomes abject—a warning, a sacrifice—and also irresistible: an atrocity exhibition, a crucifixion, a show. This

24

sensationalizing of pain within a framing problematic of knowledge (its limits, methods, and effects) gives *Wit* its vertiginous dramatic energy and intellectual shape. The properties of that energy and the details of that shape are the subject of this chapter.

Delineating the sick body as eerie and threatening, *Wit* explores flesh as an epistemological border for the inquiring mind. Bearing tries to grasp decay and death within an inflexible taxonomy of logic derived from her academic study of Metaphysical poetry. As she struggles to master her experience with the tools of literary analysis, the spectacle of the diseased scholar deepens into a kind of revenge play; Bearing is destroyed by the flesh she has neglected. Gender bursts upon the scene of bodily torment. Married to texts, Bearing finds that her supine reproductive system revolts by hatching in itself a tumor the size of a grapefruit (47). The body avenges itself on the mind. The lessons taught by this furiously didactic play are visceral, its meanings summarized in the brutal wisdom of the putrefying organ.

Wit is a violent work. Like the British painter Francis Bacon's studies of mutilated figures in austere, featureless settings, *Wit* strips the human being to an essence, a flayed scarecrow bound uncomprehendingly to the scene of its torment. Like Bacon, who drew on X rays and diagnostic photographs for his images of screaming faces and contorted limbs (Peppiatt 1996, 71, 224), Edson dramatizes a medical presence at the scene of suffering, and brings her own precise clinical eye to the depiction of the anguished body. Coercion is endemic to the expression of these contemporary artistic visions; for both Bacon and Edson, violence brings, along with its horror, voyeuristic excitement and a strong shiver of arousal. But whereas in Bacon's work violence assumes a kind of amoral, free-floating exuberance, Edson shows it as an instrument of ideological conformity.

In *Wit*, violence is the agent of orthodoxies that the play seems at once to despise and to endorse. The presence of a norm—of health, of scholarship, of femininity, of beauty—haunts the action. Bearing's treatment for cancer is an effort to "normalize" her delinquent body; her own pedagogy is based on the expounding of correct textual interpretation. The radiant woman into whom Bearing transmogrifies in the play's last moment manifests an aestheticized "ideal feminine" from which her scourged body has departed. In its engagement with gender and femininity, *Wit* applies sexuality as a hermeneutic lens to the spectacle of pain. Thus mediated, the play's indignant critique of knowledge refocuses as an invitation to sadistic enjoyment. Normative violence and the excitement of cruelty define Edson's didacticism. Hierarchy, authority, and rigor—with humiliation and pain as their by-products—characterize the pursuit of both medical and academic/literary knowledge in *Wit*. Femininity is the phantasmatic bridge between these two epistemological systems: "woman" as the institutional Imaginary. Subject to rebuke and coercion, the female body becomes their vehicle and scapegoat.

The play's revenge mechanism, and the stern morality that accompanies it, relies on force as both a motif and a strategy. Bearing's presumptive authority as a professor is dismantled by disciplinary practices as coercive as those she herself has inflicted on

her students. Economical in method, the play sets up a parallel between the disciplinary apparatus of the hospital and that of the university; the techniques of investiga-
tive medicine echo those of an excoriating pedagogy. The classroom, like the
circumscribed space of the hospital room, becomes the site of surveillance—examination—in *Wit*. Invasion and the sadistic manipulation of the multisensorial gaze
inform the power dynamic of each location, while female vulnerability articulates the
oblique, apprehensive pleasure such sadism draws.[2] The important scene in which
Bearing undergoes a pelvic exam at the hands of a former student, now the intern
assigned to her case, mixes vengeance and voyeurism into a crude kind of poetic justice. Bearing has used her authority and her analytical skill not only to torment students but even, the play hysterically implies, to torture poems into bloody submission.
In this scene—her feet in the stirrups and her monstrous mass "frankly palpable" (37)
to the sophomoric curiosity she so despises—Bearing is hoist with her own petard.
She becomes the freakish text, the twisted cell under the microscope. Her former cruelty is reduced to a happy memory: "If they were here, if I were lecturing: How I
would *perplex* them! I could work my students into a frenzy. Every ambiguity, every
shifting awareness. I could draw so much from the poems. I could be so powerful"
(48; emphasis in original).

This episode of humiliating examination is almost a mise-en-abyme for the play as
a whole. Dramatically, it convenes the spaces both of pedagogy and medical treatment
as theaters of revelation, pain, and ambiguous delight. In a metatheatrical sense, the
classroom and the exam room also become scenes of entertainment. Structurally, the
play arranges this "theater of coercion" around the woman's body as object of investigation. Recalling Alfred Hitchcock's fail-safe dictum "Torture the women,"[3] the pelvic
exam configures Bearing's suffering as a kind of medicalized or gynecological pornography. Here the female body is made to confess its hidden truths in the interest of a scientific practice able to disavow its own prurience in the name of knowledge.[4]
Discussing Francis Bacon's human subjects, John Berger remarks on the oddly titillat-
ing quality of their alienation—its combining of loneliness with hyper-visibility: "Their
isolation does not preclude their being watched. . . . His figures are alone but they are
utterly without privacy" (1980, 114). Bereft, solitary, but transfixed by the gaze, the
body in this kind of porno-clinical scenario is more than examined: it is penetrated, dis-
emboweled. Bearing's pelvic exam suggests itself as a rape: an ostensibly functional but
effectively harsh claiming of (sexualized) knowledge; an assertion of power.

Deploying its own grammar of pain, humiliation, discipline, and what comes to
look a lot like punishment within the overarching specular frame of drama itself, *Wit*
invites pornography and sadomasochism into the scenes of healing and teaching. This
strategy is by no means new. Like courtroom drama, hospital drama is a literary sta-
ple, and school stories, at once harrowing and sentimental, continue to move readers
from *Jane Eyre* through to *Harry Potter*. *Wit* shrewdly articulates the contemporary
referent of such dramas by combining the ruefulness of the school story with the high
tension of the TV hospital series. Shows like *ER* and *Chicago Hope*, which exploit the
hospital as a prime site of excitement, suspense, and overwrought emotion, stalk the

play's more serious dramatic gestures. One reason for *Wit*'s popularity is Edson's sharp attunement both to popular culture, with its strong basis in traditional narrative forms, and to the current political climate in America. *Wit* is scathingly (if ambivalently) critical of two of the culture's most mistrusted institutions: medicine and the professoriate.[5] The medical establishment and the academy—broadly representing knowledge in both its scientific and humanist avatars—are the internal tumors that vitiate the body politic in *Wit*. On the one hand, the play invites an audience to assuage its sense of helplessness before the entrenchment of such institutions by endorsing the triumph of the individual spirit. On the other, the humiliation and inevitable death of the (uppity, presumptuous) individual allows the audience to chastise the authority she represents. Taking revenge to a feel-good extreme, *Wit* offers us the double thrill of watching a plucky protagonist battle corrupt institutional authority only to be felled by the very power she has both vilified and wielded. We are given the emotional release of critique with the indirect assurance that in the end, nothing much has changed. For Edson, the dark magic of violence brings itself, finally, within the fold of a political orthodoxy only slightly reconfigured.

Despite its suspicion of the intellect, *Wit*'s own intellectual matrix recalls Foucault's politically based analyses of the suffering flesh—the imbrication of the body in mutually reinforcing systems of power and knowledge. By focusing upon a woman whose reproductive system has been overdetermined by disease, *Wit* evokes what Foucault calls the *scientia sexualis*: the scientific taxonomy whereby Western culture arranges its comprehension of sexuality in ratiocinative terms, accommodating desire between the lines, as it were (Foucault, 1978, 58). The high drama and righteous tone of Bearing's agony suggest what Foucault, in *Discipline and Punish*, describes as both premodern and modern modes of spectacular and/or corrective punishment. *Wit* combines the severe exhibition of the public execution—wherein the power of the sovereign was inscribed literally on the flesh of the condemned—with the objectifying of the body through the corrective regimes of the prison and the hospital: disciplinary modes that engage individuality in order more precisely to draw it within the normative classifications of knowledge (7–13). The play's attack on institutional power, and on knowledge itself, is usefully illuminated by the Foucauldian paradigm; *Wit*'s further audacity lies partly in the meeting it engineers, over the probed and mutilated body of a woman, between Foucault and John Donne.

In *Wit*, as I have suggested, medicine and teaching are dehumanizing disciplinary systems. The university and the hospital are claustrophobic, narcissistic places where the will-to-knowledge/power entrenches itself—through agents like Bearing and her doctors, Kelekian and Posner—and the "docile body" of the fully inscribed social subject is violently produced (Foucault, *Discipline* 138). The punitive impulse that animates *Wit* underlines the austere circularity of Bearing's fate: having lived by the sword of knowledge, she also dies by it. Despite the currency of its referential frames—a bewildering medical culture, a cutthroat academy—the play's justice is not only poetic in the proverbial sense, but witheringly biblical.

The linguistic and technical armature of this justice is literally poetic. *Wit*'s violence, while thoroughly modern in most of its preoccupations, is tactically embedded in the workings of Metaphysical poetry. The play's critique of American medicine as bureaucratic and callous involves the portrayal of healing as the systematic inflicting of pain. The conceit that organizes the play is the simple but devastating one of the deadly cure; the chemotherapy that Bearing receives is at least as effective a means of destruction as her cancer itself. In this paradox lies the play's ironic impact and its considerable poignancy. At the end, Bearing dies a martyr to knowledge, claimed alike by the esoteric imperatives of literary inquiry and cancer research. The peculiar completeness of such violence again recalls Metaphysical poetry's tense economies of poetic compression. The very procedures of wit as a literary device rely on violence, for the conceits they generate require the forceful yoking together of opposites.

A good example of the savage paradoxes coerced by wit occurs at the end of Donne's Holy Sonnet 14.[6] In the famous couplet, the desperate speaker importunes God: "Take me to You, imprison me, for I / Except You enthrall me, never shall be free: / Nor ever chaste, except You ravish me." Donne's poetry revels in stark, almost surreal juxtapositions: the shock of contraries registered as a jar on the nerves, a shimmering fault line in the usual order of perception. In particular, his frank application of sexual terms to religious experience disrupts the traditional boundary between the erotic and the spiritual, the body and soul. Compelled together, sexual desire and yearning for God intertwine as both metaphors and metonyms; the relations among different aspects of the human being are reinterpreted by the rhetorical alchemy of wit. Through a kind of technical force majeure, sexuality provides Donne with a vocabulary for spiritual anguish—a vocabulary that inevitably mobilizes the erotics of violence and the inseparability of pleasure and pain. For Donne, wit often articulates the fierce, irresistible romance between torture and joy.

Wit appropriates this kind of paradoxical violence in interesting and disturbing ways. Its basic conceit of the deadly cure liberates the verbal energy, the exhilarating perceptual rearrangements of wit into the dramatic action. But this energy remains oddly homeless, unfocused, and superfluous in the play. Loosening the violence of seventeenth-century wit from its theological moorings in Christianity, and from its affective base in spiritual apprehension, the play deploys sexualized violence in the purely secular context of physical trauma and its treatment by a scientific medical establishment.[7] There is no real struggle with God, no sickness of the soul, in *Wit*. Bearing's brief postmortem appearance in the final scene suggests resurrection shaped crudely, and in a spiritual vacuum, by the imagery of Norman Rockwell, or by cliché depictions of the afterlife in Hollywood movies like *All That Jazz*. There is none of the probing, with the cunning tool of wit, the interplay of body, soul, and mind that informs so strongly the impassioned violence of Donne.

In Holy Sonnet 5, for example, which Bearing analyzes, this interplay gathers as a sudden, painful shift of direction and tone. The speaker cries out: "O God, Oh! Of thine onely worthy blood, / And my teares, make a heavenly Lethean flood, / And drowne in it my sinnes black memorie" (Edson 1993, 49). Bearing dismisses this moment of anguish as "an unconvincing eruption of piety" (50), but it may be read more descriptively, as the mind's encounter with the limits of its own comprehension. Resonant with longing, the lines suggest a prayer for the surrender of human intellect, and our baffling physicality, to an enigmatic spiritual forgetting: the merciful grace of God.[8] By interpreting the struggle depicted in the sonnet as mere theatrics, Bearing simplifies the "poetic encounter" (50) of man and God into a spat between a braggart and a gruff but kindly curmudgeon. Uncoupling in this way intellectual energy and bodily suffering from spiritual searching, *Wit* (misnamed again?) effectively strips wit of its complexity—its metaphysical obsessions, its craving for transcendence, its lust for God.

Instead, the play adopts a reading of wit that suits its mistrust of intellect and apparent smoothing-over of spiritual conflict. As mediated through Bearing, wit becomes mere mental agility—an arid verbal exhibitionism that reifies complex thought out of fear for the "simple truth" of the heart. In Edson's play, wit is not about engagement with life—the mind's battle with both its epic capacities and limitations, the tension between human reach and grasp. Rather, wit in *Wit* is about fleeing life: a flight conceived in pop-psychological terms as fear of emotion and a consequent retreat into intellect. As one of Bearing's students, arguing for simplicity, observes, "I think it's like [Donne's] hiding, I think he's really confused, I don't know, maybe he's scared, so he hides behind all this complicated stuff, hides behind this *wit*" (60; emphasis in original). Here truth emerges from the mouths of babes, not doctors, or poets. As limpid as a child's story and as easy to consume as a popsicle, truth in *Wit* is witless. It is summed up in Bearing's motherly nurse, Susie Monahan, who speaks for the play's diluted Romantic ideal of truth as the holiness of the heart's affections—a secularized holiness, however, and one effectively severed from what Keats called the truth of poetry.

Narrative, though, seems to be one linguistic source of such veracity. Toward the end of the play, Bearing's former teacher, E. M. Ashford, reads her *The Runaway Bunny* as she dies. This moment is significant, for it represents the recasting of two authoritative scholars in the domesticated, familial roles of mother and child. Ashford, in town to see her great-grandson, visits Bearing under the sign of a matriarch rather than that of a mentor or colleague.[9] Bearing, stripped at last of her powerful eloquence—the armor of words—moans incoherently, falls asleep, and peacefully dies. "It's time to go," says Ashford, "And flights of angels sing thee to thy rest" (80). No longer Hamlet, the narcissistic intellectual, Bearing becomes as a little child and is permitted finally to enter the play's version of heaven.[10]

The reading of *The Runaway Bunny* is the necessary, subliterary prelude to the transformation, at the moment of death, of the frigid professor into the sweet woman she never allowed herself to become. In the brief image of the rejuvenated Bearing that ends the play, violence is sanitized; the revenge play and the get-well card, Webster and Walt Disney, come together in a sentimental parody of Metaphysical wit. Sliding from judgment to redemption, from Jehovah to Mother Mary, *Wit* proffers a vision of mercy as a bromide for its own cruelty. Entertained by a sadistic spectacle, the audience is absolved from such dubious enjoyment by a brief image of the body restored. The cinematic glimpse of the angelic Bearing that ends the play not only releases the agonized body from the scene of its torment; it effectively erases the marked body of the sufferer and substitutes for it a form healed through regression. The child/seraph replaces the woman/monster. If, as Ashford says, *The Runaway Bunny* offers "a little allegory of the soul" (80), *Wit* performs its own little allegory—of gender, intellect, and the corrective disciplining of both. The child's story, with its gentle description of the fortitude of maternal love, is symbolically set against the textual body of the Holy Sonnets in order to declare at the end of the play the triumph of heart over mind—of transparent, soothing simplicity over "Itchy outbreaks of far-fetched wit" (20).[11]

Such a deployment does wit a disservice. As I have argued, Metaphysical wit, far from excluding the body, bridges the flesh, the intellect, and the soul. It constitutes verbally the medium of their struggle. The energy of wit is relational, not "only" intellectual in any reductive or elitist way. It is sparked by the mind in ferocious play with both body and spirit. When the soul is discounted and spiritual hunger is replaced (as it is in *Wit*) by a generalized endorsement of human kindness, the connectedness of body, mind, and spirit—the fervid intermingling compelled and consummated by wit—fades. The pain-wracked, diseased body becomes a hunk of meat. The intellect, its energies divorced from spiritual purpose, becomes a weapon: the gratuitous instrument both of pain and sadistic pleasure. In this formulation—separated from its theological/affective roots and so radically dehistoricized—Metaphysical wit is severed from the matrix of its passion. It leaves behind only the crude fact of its violence and a residual coldness that lends itself to sensational uses.

Strikingly, *Wit* translates this factual violence and coldness into aesthetic terms. Bearing's passage into death is portrayed, as I have said, as a regression to childhood. In a grotesque echo of *The Picture of Dorian Gray*, her postmortem appearance suggests a sublime moment of youthful purity restored: "she is naked, and beautiful, reaching for the light" in her play's last scene (85). As in Wilde's fable, problems of knowledge, power, gender, and morality are registered in visual terms. Recalcitrant and complex, such issues are schematized—rendered diagrammatic—through the awesome return of an unsullied form: the mystical restoration to the visible world of an original ideal of physical beauty and innocence. In *Wit*, the radiance of this recuperated form bleaches out the darkness of the text, meeting its interrogations not with resolution but with glamour; beauty here is a deferral, a seductive blinding. For Edson (as for Wilde), the brilliant charisma of beauty reprojects intellectual and ethical questions visually, as the preternaturally cleansed body. Such bewitchment becomes a kind of solvent for the unanswerable horrors the text has unfolded.

Recalling Wilde's fascination with the language of the aestheticized body, Edson comes to articulate physical pain as a matter of beauty. Given the virulence of chemotherapy and its attack on the body, Bearing—under the scrutiny of the medicopornographic eye and on the brink of death—represents a physically degraded spectacle. As the stage directions imply, she is ugly; "completely bald," she "wears two hospital gowns—one tied in the front and one tied in the back—a baseball cap, and a hospital ID bracelet" (5).[12] In her last appearance, though, Bearing is explicitly described as beautiful, and this restored loveliness, the play suggests, triumphs over the muddle and flurry of the code team's misplaced efforts to revive her. Edson's aesthetic vocabulary here recalls that of the modernists—Joyce, Eliot, and before them, Wilde—for she freezes the sublimely visible object in the familiar syntax of wholeness, harmony, and radiance: "naked, and beautiful, reaching for the light."

But *Wit* does not simply reiterate an outdated aesthetics: the play's modernism is agonized, its postmodernism emergent. Like the paintings of Francis Bacon, *Wit* illustrates what Milan Kundera calls "the modernism that closes the way again": intellectually and historically, a threshold modernity where traditions are both celebrated and abused (Borel 1996, 15). The play's ardently hostile nostalgia for that modernist fetish of literary mastery, Metaphysical poetry, confirms its involvement with representational traditions etiolated or dying, but available for experiment nonetheless.

The echoes of Wilde, Joyce, and Eliot reinforce what I am presenting as an imaginative interplay between Bacon and Edson. Haunted by the specter of Dorian Gray, Bacon—like Edson—is drawn to revisit that aesthetic tension between coherent and disintegrating forms that so fascinated his modernist forbears. "[U]nlovely, unloved, and unloving" (Harmsworth 2000, 257), Bearing's degradation, her immolation by catheters and syringes, render her effectively as the perfect Baconian subject. At the end of the play, as the code team pummels her, she could be one of the artist's hairless hysterics, caught in a rictus of futile movement. In the earlier scenes, with her outraged authority, she might be one of his infamous screaming popes.

In the name of physiological honesty, both Bacon and Edson push the aesthetic envelope, breaking down the perceptual barrier between traditional notions of beauty and ugliness. For Bacon, pain is a gorgeous spectacle; but he never evinces nostalgia for the restored and uncorrupted body. Refusing to categorize the artist as a modernist in any narrow sense of the word, Kundera claims: "for Bacon the issue always and above all is beauty, the explosion of beauty, because even if the word seems nowadays to be hackneyed, out of date, it is what links him to Shakespeare."[13] France Borel's summary of Bacon's technique as a portraitist could be applied, I think, to Edson's depiction of Vivian Bearing: "A vibrant individual, ripped apart, whom the painter experiences from the inside with which he merges, whom he penetrates . . . and lashes with the brush. He even uses his hands. . . . Blurred faces, nausea, migraines, misplaced eye, distorted mouth, mucous membranes turned inside out like a glove, tunic of Nessus" (189). Such an effort both to demolish and reconstruct or reinscribe the body in a nakedly visceral way, from the inside out as it were, is an aesthetic and rhetorical endeavor. It seeks a distortion that captures the visible shape of suffering: its forms, languages, and sensual textures. This quest leads Bacon to express in his oeuvre an ever more precise aesthetics of extremity—repeatedly to explore suffering as another modality of the beautiful.

Bacon was quite frank about his aesthetic responses to pain, the combination he sought of emotional distance, voluptuousness, and a rapacious intensity of perception: "I wanted to paint the scream more than the horror. . . . I like, you may say, the glitter and colour that comes from the mouth, and I've always hoped in a sense to be able to paint the mouth like Monet painted a sunset."[14] These comments describe some of the aesthetic ground that *Wit* also traverses—and the link Kundera sees between the Baconian aesthetic of agony and Shakespearean richness resonates interestingly with the play's immersion in early modern literature, the work of Shakespeare as well as Donne. Bearing appears on stage as "unaccommodated" woman, the kind of "bare, fork'd animal" that Shakespeare depicts in *King Lear*—the same one that reappears, in various stages of violation, in Bacon's scenarios of suffering.

In the work of these artists, both liminally modernist and postmodernist, a sense of organic richness—what Bacon called an "obsession with life"—combines with the peculiar aloofness, the moral objectivity, of the aesthetician. As Bacon remarked, "[I] would love to be able in a portrait to make a Sahara of the appearance—to make it so like, yet seeming to have the distances of the Sahara."[15] The artists' deepest fascination is with the flesh: what it looks and feels like, what might be done to it. Yet their projects diverge—implicitly, over the Sahara as a metonym for an ultimate aesthetic of desolation and dismemberment. The difference between Bacon and Edson as connoisseurs of pain is summed up in the final moment of *Wit*. When Bearing, restored as fully as Dorian Gray's portrait, steps into the light, the aesthetics of extremity—the strange pulchritude of mutilated forms—give way to a traditional ideal of wholeness and the expression of an idealized, pure, feminine beauty.

What moves us at the end of *Wit* is only partly the victory (compromised, as we have seen) of the human spirit, of heart over head. To a great degree, we are moved by the recovery of beauty—the reinstatement of a familiar aesthetics of the unmarked (female) body. Having entertained the Baconian edge, *Wit* drops the troubled logic of evisceration, with its buried echo of the Unheimlich, and returns the audience to a representational comfort zone. Like the runaway bunny, we are claimed finally by the recognizable—the equivalent, in artistic terms, of mother and home. The erasure of Bearing's suffering and the literal spotlighting of beauty at the end of the play offer the audience the aesthetic counterpart of the play's political/ethical/sexual quietism: the reassuring and well-known spectacle of a beautiful naked woman.

Favoring glamour, and obliquely converting the difficulties of connection into an image of accessible beauty, *Wit* blots out suffering with sentiment. By the end of the play, the tonal register has shifted from sulphurous to sweet—from the bite of cancer to a soothing popsicle, from chemotherapy to the sleep of morphine. Like Bearing's agon, the vitiating otherness of death is met with an image of the afterlife as pleasant and facile as the baby oil that Susie Monahan rubs on her dying patient's hands (78). In its turn from corrosion to viscosity, from acid to balm, *Wit* tries for the sublime. The play seeks the moving vision of bodily renewal that John Donne saw as the endpoint of mortal pain: "a consumption hath attenuated me to a feeble macilency and leanness, and God raises me a body such as it should have been if these infirmities had not intervened and deformed it."[16] But Vivian Bearing's restoration is rooted in a struggle without deep spiritual resonance; the pugnacious, chastened scholar remains aloof from the witty conviction that consoled the poet: "My flesh shall no more be none of mine than Christ shall not be man as well as God."[17]

NOTES

I should like to thank Jonathan Howle, Thomas Fahy, and Jennifer Lockard for help and inspiration with this essay.

1. *Wit* has been well received by most critics. For a sampling of critical opinion, see Bregman, Brodesser, Franklin, Harmsworth, Kanfer, Renner, Shewey, Simon, and Zinman.

2. In chapter 7 of *The Birth of the Clinic*, "Seeing and Knowing," Foucault reads clinical perception in terms of touching as well as sight: "The clinical eye discovers a kinship with a new sense that prescribes its norm and epistemological structure; this is no longer the ear straining to catch a language, but the index finger palpating the depths. Hence the metaphor of 'touch' (*le tact*) by which doctors will ceaselessly define their glance" (1973, 122).

3. Quoted in Williams, 1989, 206.

4. See Williams's first chapter, "Speaking Sex," for a reading of pornography as the body's physiological confession of the "truth" of its pleasure, and the scopic drive as the instrument of such disclosure. The trope of confession works well with Foucault's thinking on the probing glance—"clinical experience sees a new space opening up before it: the tangible space of the body, which at the same time is that opaque mass in which secrets, invisible lesions and the very mystery of origins lie hidden" (1973, 122)—which also offers an interesting perspective on Bacon's spectacles of evisceration.

5. Both Bregman and Kanfer consider the parallels drawn in *Wit* between medicine and the academy.

6. Not quoted in the play.

7. For a discussion of Donne's roots in the theological assumptions of his day—particularly his understanding of illness in the context of original sin and Christian redemption—see Goldberg.

8. My sense of a lack of spiritual urgency in *Wit* is contrary to Edson's own sense of the play. In an interview, she described the work as "about redemption, and I'm surprised no one mentions it. . . . Grace is the opportunity to experience God in spite of yourself, which is what Dr. Bearing ultimately achieves" (Martini 1999, 22). Edson's expression of surprise suggests that the theme of grace does not emerge very emphatically in *Wit*; I argue for the play's involvement with issues of redemption as schematic and nominal.

9. The transposing of the collegial and the familial in *Wit* is indirectly reinforced in a 1999 comment by Judith Light, who replaced Kathleen Chalfant in the lead role at Union Square Theater. Remarking on the friendliness that has characterized productions of the play, Light declared that she was "honored to join the *Wit* family" (Martini 1999, 22).

10. My thanks to Jennifer Lockard for pointing out this implied Christian reference.

11. The words are Donne's, quoted in the play. For a critique of *Wit* based on its narrow treatment of Donne's art—and its stereotyping of the woman academic—see Iannone.

12. There may be a reference, in this latter detail, to Donne's poem "The Relic," with its macabrely sensual—and witty—image of a "bracelet of bright hair about the bone" (Smith 1971, 75).

13. Quoted in Borel 1996, 14.

14. Quoted in Berger 1980, 115.

15. Quoted in Borel 1996, 191.

16. John Donne, Sermon 1, quoted in Witherspoon and Warnke 1963, 106.

17. John Donne, Sermon 14, quoted in Witherspoon and Warnke 1963, 106.

References

Berger, John. *About Looking*. New York: Pantheon, 1980.

Borel, France. *Bacon: Portraits and Self-Portraits*. Trans. Ruth Taylor and Linda Asher. New York: Thames and Hudson, 1996.

Bregman, Bertie. "Blame the Scholar Not the Discipline," *The Lancet*, March 6, 1999, 851.

Brodesser, Claude. "Edson's *Wit* Wins Pulitzer for Drama," *Variety*, April 19, 1999, 53.

Edson, Margaret. *Wit*. New York: Faber and Faber, 1993.

Foucault, Michel. *The Birth of the Clinic: An Archaeology of Medical Perception*. Trans. A. M. Sheridan Smith. New York: Vintage, 1973.

———. *Discipline and Punish: The Birth of the Prison*. Trans. Alan Sheridan. New York: Vintage, 1977.

———. *The History of Sexuality, Vol. I: An Introduction*. Trans. Robert Hurley. New York: Pantheon, 1978.

Franklin, Nancy. "*Wit* and Wisdom: High Humor and Holy Sonnets in the Hospital," *The New Yorker*, January 18, 1999, 86–88.

Goldberg, Jonathan. "The Understanding of Sickness in Donne's *Devotions*," *Renaissance Quarterly* #24 (1971): 507–17.

Harmsworth, Madeleine. "*Wit*," *British Medical Journal* (January 22, 2000): 257.

Iannone, Carol. "Donne Undone," *First Things: A Monthly Journal of Religion and Public Life* (February 2000): 12.

Kanfer, Stefan. "*Wit*," *The New Leader*, October 5, 1998, 22–24.

Martini, Adrienne. "The Playwright in Spite of Herself," *American Theatre*, October 1999, 22.

Peppiatt, Michael. *Francis Bacon: Anatomy of an Enigma*. New York: Farrar, Straus, and Giroux, 1996.

Renner, Pamela. "Science and Sensibility," *American Theatre*, April 1999, 34–37.

Shewey, Don. "When Death Comes Knocking," *The Advocate*, December 8, 1998, 79.

Simon, John. "*Wit*," *New York*, September 28, 1998, 78–80.

Smith, A. J., ed. *John Donne: The Complete English Poems*. New York: Penguin, 1971.

Williams, Linda. *Hard Core: Power, Pleasure, and the "Frenzy of the Visible."* Berkeley: University of California Press, 1989.

Witherspoon, Alexander M., and Frank J. Warnke, eds. *Seventeenth-Century Prose and Poetry*, 2nd ed. New York: Harcourt, Brace, 1963.

Zinman, Toby. "Illness as Metaphor," *American Theatre*, October 1999, 25.

Making an Art out of Suffering: Bill T. Jones's *Uncle Tom*

TESS CHAKKALAKAL

> 1989: I read *Uncle Tom's Cabin*. I find it to be hokum, misinformation.
> I find it moving, infuriating, beautiful, embarrassing and important.
> —BILL T. JONES, *LAST NIGHT ON EARTH*

Since the publication of Harriet Beecher Stowe's novel *Uncle Tom's Cabin; or, Life Among the Lowly* in 1852, the name "Uncle Tom" has evoked a plethora of positive and negative associations. Despite the various ways in which this name is used in contemporary, everyday life, Uncle Tom also continues to refer to a fictional character created in the nineteenth century by a white woman to provide a model of black male virtue and heroism. As Stowe asserts in the opening pages of her novel, "Tom is an uncommon fellow . . . good, steady, sensible, pious" (4). His docility, unflagging faith in Christian doctrine, and a passive acceptance of injustices committed against him also establish the terms for the opposite of Stowe's fictional hero: Uncle Tom's heroic beginnings confer on him the preeminent status of the victim. Furthermore, Uncle Tom's widespread dissemination in American culture has raised this figure from his "lowly" beginnings as a fictional hero to a national stereotype of the black American male. In 1990, dancer and choreographer Bill T. Jones examined the dialectical shift between the positive and negative formulations of Uncle Tom through dance in *Last Supper at Uncle Tom's Cabin/The Promised Land*. In doing so, Jones effectively elides the distinction between the categories of heroes and victims. It is this elision that helps to formulate the terms of victim art as a form of creative expression in the late twentieth century.

Jones's performance develops a narrative for Uncle Tom's circulation among African Americans. Whatever the virtues attributed to this character in Stowe's novel, it has become clear that through repeated stagings and citations of Uncle Tom in the twentieth century, the figure now represents some of the ways in which social inequality operates in the United States; that is to say, Uncle Tom's docility and Christian faith are transferred onto African-American males whose social and economic success are viewed as the result of complying with the terms of an implicitly racist sociopolitical infrastructure. The ephemeral nature of the Uncle Tom figure in

American culture makes it somewhat difficult to delineate its specific terms; nonetheless, the widespread circulation of the Uncle Tom figure in American literary, social, and political discourses warrants attention. By considering a recent example of Uncle Tom's appearance on the American stage this essay traces the process by which this literary hero has become a source of shame and contempt for African Americans in the twentieth century.

Drawing upon Uncle Tom's beginnings from the realm of literary fiction to his various appearances on stage, Jones develops the conflicted status of this great American hero to produce a version of Uncle Tom that establishes the value of victimized and otherwise disabled bodies in the production of art. In his performance of *Uncle Tom*, Jones traces the movement of this figure from the pages of literature to the stage, screen, and finally onto the streets of America. While moving fluidly between these various forums of performance, Uncle Tom upsets the terms of his conception only slightly. Rather than naming the hero of Stowe's nineteenth-century novel, Uncle Tom names "spineless, obsequious blacks who appease white culture through their victimized Uncle Tom behavior."[1] "Uncle Tom behavior," in this sense, refers specifically to black men who use the effects of white racism to their social, political, or economic advantage. Clarence Thomas, for instance, is exemplary of someone who warrants the epithet of an Uncle Tom in the late twentieth century, as he effectively cast himself as a victim of white aggression against black men to protect himself against accusations of sexual harassment.[2] It is the personification of Uncle Tom into real black bodies that occurs in its twentieth-century renderings that Jones stages in his dance production. What distinguishes Jones's adaptation of *Uncle Tom's Cabin* from previous versions of the novel is its attempt to reproduce the movement of Uncle Tom in the twentieth century. That is, rather than produce a twentieth-century version of Uncle Tom that simply brings this nineteenth-century literary hero up-to-date, so to speak, Jones's production incorporates these very "other" stagings of Uncle Tom to call into question and undermine the strict binary between Uncle Tom's heroic and victimized positionings.

As a gay, African-American, HIV-positive artist, Jones is no stranger to epithets that call into question identity assertions as celebrations of vicitimization. For instance, Arlene Croce, dance critic for *The New Yorker* magazine, refused to attend Jones's widely acclaimed performance *Still/Here* (1994) because, in her view, the only effect of including video clips that present people who are terminally ill talking about their particular experiences in the production is that "Jones is putting himself beyond the reach of criticism" (1994, 54–60). In other words, Croce views Jones's representation of so-called victims on stage as an attempt to circumvent critique, rather than challenge the viewer's capacity to judge and recognize "good art." Judging from his repertoire—and the critical responses to it—Jones's name has, in many respects, become synonymous with the term *victim art*. The term suggests that those who operate within the medium of victim art lack the creative talent and originality to produce work that does more than simply invoke the sympathies of its viewer. Croce's repudiation of the form thus rejects the notion that the parameters of art can be so loosely drawn so that almost *anyone* can be an artist. Through his representation of one of the most popular and controversial victims in American culture, Jones examines what constitutes the terms of victim art as it has become a convention of performance in the United States.

Stowe's novel, then, introduces readers to the character of Uncle Tom as constituting the terms of "black purity." Unlike the other central black characters of the novel, namely George and Eliza Harris, who are light enough to pass and escape slavery, Uncle Tom is "a large, broad-chested, powerfully-made man, of a full glossy black, and [has] a face [representing] truly African features" (26). The emphasis on Uncle Tom's blackness in Stowe's account conflates his physical features with a certain attitude of "kindliness and benevolence" (26) that attributes the character's power not to his physical strength but rather to his moral strength. Uncle Tom's strength in this sense makes it possible for him to suffer the cruelties of white masters who subject him to various forms of abuse and, by finally dying at the hands of his white masters, the character effectively achieves his heroic status.

Jones's reproduction of the novel draws upon the terms of Uncle Tom's heroic status to produce a conception of black heroism that operates outside the strictures of Christian moral doctrine. Jones's production opens with a view of Tom's Cabin: it is set behind a gingham drape around the entire proscenium of the theater, surrounded by stylized magnolias and hanging moss. The audience hears rasping saxophones as two figures appear on stage; the first functions as the story's narrator and the other represents Stowe's authorial voice. While these figures recite an abbreviated form of the novel, dancers appear on stage to act out the characteristics of the story's primary players: "the fidelity of Uncle Tom, the purity of Little Eva, the tragic reluctance of the liberal master Mr. St. Clare and the twisted values of the evil slave trader Simon Legree" (Jones 1995, 209). With the exception of those playing the role of Uncle Tom, all performers remain masked throughout this opening scene.

Although this opening scene situates the audience in the novel's plot, Jones importantly alters Stowe's story. Skipping over some of the novel's fine details, he makes no mention, for instance, of Little Eva's death, nor does he mention Eliza's reunion with her husband and their eventual departure for a more prosperous life on the shores of Africa. Jones uses these departures from Stowe's story to manifest the changes that occur in the development of the character of Uncle Tom when he moves from the pages of Stowe's novel to the American stage. The appearance of Uncle Tom in the theater marks both a departure and an intensification of stereotypical formulations of black characters in American culture. As Eric Lott points out in his analysis of nineteenth-century stage adaptations of the novel, the play *Uncle Tom's Cabin* incorporated minstrel tunes and blackface makeup not only to entertain its largely white audiences but also to dramatize political conflict between the North and South over the issue of slavery. In doing so, theatrical performances of *Uncle Tom's Cabin* were deployed to achieve specific political ends.

The masks worn by the dancers in the opening scene of the production signify upon the politics of Uncle Tom on stage. Jones introduces his audience to the figure of

Uncle Tom by drawing upon minstrel conventions as they were practiced on the nine-teenth-century American stage. Both the mask worn by the dancers and the tune of atonal musical rhythms played throughout the opening sequence alludes to blackface and minstrel performances of the nineteenth century. The conjunction between black-face performance and the Uncle Tom character give rise to a convention of racial stereotypes in the public sphere that are effectively coopted in the twentieth century to serve, once again, strategic political purposes. Jones's Uncle Tom, as the only figure on stage without a mask, indicates that wearing one would only be redundant to the representation of his character. Uncle Tom embodies the mask worn by black men to defend themselves against acts of white racial violence.

Because Jones draws upon the Uncle Tom convention of the minstrel stage, rather than the Uncle Tom of Stowe's novel, Jones *performs* the characteristics endemic to this hero/victim. Part 1 concludes then with a coup de théâtre—an avant-garde conven-tion of the late-twentieth-century theater wherein the scene of Tom's whipping is played in reverse so that the audience is returned to the moment just before Legree is about to unfurl the first lash of his whip against Tom's back. In Jones's words, "I then take the liberty of inserting a 'correct' ending—the one we would like to have seen, in which Tom, instead of dying at the hands of his aggressors, stands up with all the other slaves and resists Simon Legree" (247). Jones's "correct" ending takes the viewer out of time and into the world of the artist's imagination, in which anything—even a slave revolt led by the passive hero of Stowe's novel—is possible.

Part 2 of Jones's *Uncle Tom* moves from Tom's story to a revisioning of Stowe's other black character, Eliza. Unlike Uncle Tom, Eliza does not accept the conditions of white oppression and slavery. Eliza's heroic status in the novel stems from the amazing dangers her character overcomes not only to protect herself from being sold, but, more important, to maintain the physical bond between herself and her son. What is significant, then, about Stowe's portrayal of Eliza's character is her ability to draw readers into the narrative so that they feel for Eliza's plight not as a black character as such, but rather as manifesting more "universal" characteristics—that is, her role in the relationship between mother and child. Eliza's role in *Uncle Tom's Cabin* pro-vides the reader/viewer with a point of identification whereby any mother, white or black, rich or poor, could understand and, more to the point, sympathize with her actions and feelings. Like his rendering of Uncle Tom, Jones is primarily interested in the image of Eliza as a figure of blackface performance; however, rather than the Eliza produced *for* the stage, Jones reproduces Stowe's Eliza on stage as a production of, in Angela Davis's words, "white motherhood incarnate, but in blackface" (Davis 1981, 27).

Part 2 of Jones's performance, "Eliza on the Ice" offers to the viewer the signifi-cance of "race" to Eliza's character, an aspect not present in Stowe's novel. Here, Jones introduces four silhouetted women "crisscrossing the stage performing signature movements" (211). These four women provide more personal narratives of their con-temporary experiences of "living on the margins" of mainstream American culture. Rather than adapting Stowe's story to suit the demands of these diverse experiences, the narrator/Stowe figure begins to recite Sojourner Truth's "Ain't I a Woman?" speech,[3] to which each of the Elizas performs her particular versions of femininity, black or otherwise. As the scene concludes, the narrator/Stowe figure crawls slowly off stage reciting Truth's address in reverse, reminding the audience of the previous scene, in which the company reversed the sequence of Tom's death in order to affect a scene of liberation and revolution. Stowe's undignified exit from the stage reveals, finally, a male dancer in drag; throwing into disarray the terms by which femininity and masculinity are conventionally understood. By indicating the importance of Eliza's "race" to Stowe's fictional representation, Eliza becomes a black woman who operates on several social registers, rather than one who is bound strictly to her maternal capacities.

Following the exit of the Elizas, Jones appears on stage himself with his own mother; now, the choreographer-director remains silent while his mother sings a version of "I Shall Not Be Removed." The appearance of the author's real mother at this point in the production undercuts the terms of an authoritative narrative voice that is permitted to dictate the terms of, in Stowe's word, the "right" moral feeling and judgment. While Jones submits and receives his mother's (Christian) blessing in this scene, it is clear from his silence that he does not accept the terms of a religious doctrine that considers homosexuality a sin. Following the departure of Jones and his mother from the stage, a male rap artist appears to assert the claims of black identity more broadly, a claim that is premised upon specific exclusions. This performance concludes with a tableau of Leonardo da Vinci's *Last Supper* table. At this point in the performance, the audience is given a moment to pause and to reflect upon the terms by which black male identity is constituted: Uncle Tom, Christian doctrine, and homophobic rhetoric. Taken together, the black male body is effectively contained within the terms of a particularly oppressive infrastructure. Following this momentary pause in the narrative, Jones appears on stage alone to pose a number of questions to the audience: "What is faith? Is Christianity a slave religion? What is evil? Does God punish us? Does hell exist? Is homosexuality a sin? Is AIDS punishment from God?" The audience does not have the opportunity to respond. Instead, upon uttering the final question, the stage becomes flooded with an organized group of about sixty people—none of whom is a professional dancer per se. Interspersed between these bodies are members of the Jones/Zane Dance Company performing a series of stereotypical black moves, moves that Jones calls "Warming up Dixie"—moves culled from the first successful minstrel troupe, the Virginia Minstrels, the group that included Dan Emmett, the composer of the pre–Civil War hit song "Dixie." These rather random acts of black minstrelsy are rounded up with an enactment of Amiri Baraka's *Dutchman* (1964).

Dutchman's principal character, Clay, provides the audience with an example of a modern-day black minstrel, or Uncle Tom; that is, a black man who embodies the characteristics of black acquiescence in his interactions with white society at large. The performers focus on the scene in *Dutchman* where Clay becomes the object of the abuse and derision of a white woman, Lula. The dramatic exchange between Clay and Lula reaches a climax when Lula concludes what Werner Sollors calls "her Uncle

Tom invective" (1978, 125) against Clay with the words "Uncle Tom-Big-Lip," an utterance that provokes Clay to slap her, as thirty dancers strike the floor with their open palms. The final scene reveals all performers without clothes and moving in long lines across the stage performing thirteen gestures "culled from religious iconography as varied as [the] Tiepolo fresco in Venice, a bit of kitsch pottery from Little Italy, or an ancient painting from a church in remotest New Mexico" (Jones 1995, 223). The performance ends to the sound of a lulling saxophone, to which, in Jones's words, "a stage covered with the fat, skinny, rich, poor, old, young, male, female, Asian, Spanish, gay, straight, black, Native American, and European, naked, [are] singing together" (223).

What provides the cohesion to this display of extravagant multiplicity and diversity is the figure of Uncle Tom. In taking up this figure in his dance production, Jones exhibits the various ways in which his own black male body diverges from and contradicts the terms of this stereotype. By using his own body on stage, Jones shows how the intersections of race, sexuality, and disease alter the constitutive features of victims and heroes to elide the differences between them. Jones thus uses the figure of Uncle Tom to provide the necessary common ground to join these otherwise separate and highly invidious identity categories. The elision of difference in this regard produces some rather startling consequences. In deploying the Uncle Tom stereotype as a means of self-representation, Jones's performance of Uncle Tom, alongside his other "victim art" productions, poses a latent threat to the singular terms by which the black male body is constituted as a national subject.

Jones's subsequent production, *Still/Here*, moves from the realm of the sexual body to the ill or diseased body. *Still/Here* displays human suffering in all its gory detail and, much to the chagrin of various critics, confirms Jones's propensity to make an art out of suffering. Jones's tendency to foreground suffering and the personal in his performative projects has raised specific questions concerning the place of unhealthy bodies on stage. More broadly, Jones's art form calls into question the terms of legitimacy. While previous critics of Jones's work have raised the problem of legitimacy in relation to Jones's work, this analysis continues to be preoccupied with Jones's identity and work as constituting art as such. In other words, the terms with which Jones's work is discussed (or undiscussed as in Croce's analysis) disregard the political content of his work to debate only its artistic merits. My analysis of Jones's Uncle Tom departs from the terms of dance/dramatic criticism in order to consider how he uses this figure to alter the terms by which we understand the requirements of citizenship.

By telling the story of his life through the figure of Uncle Tom, Jones works to dismantle the terms of this national stereotype that enforce a doctrine of Christian piety and submissive tolerance wholly devoid of all sexual content as emblematic of the African-American male body. In doing so, Jones produces, or, more accurately, performs an identity category that exists *within* the constraints of national boundaries but one that is visibly marked by these very constraints. Jones formulates this category for visibly marked bodies through his depiction of the Uncle Tom stereotype in retrograde.

Jones's twentieth-century Uncle Tom relies heavily on the terms of Uncle Tom produced for nineteenth-century audiences as its necessary point of departure. The production's trajectory operates on several levels. First, Jones begins his production by taking his audience back to the origins of his (and our) present condition; hence the Cabin becomes the so-called birthplace of the African American male body. Second, Jones reverses the sequence of the Uncle Tom narrative in order to insert a new, "correct" ending that takes his audience out of both its past and present conditions into a yet-to-be-realized future. Third, the back-and-forth movement of the naked and undisciplined bodies in the production's final scene seems to suggest a decline or deterioration in the narrative's progressive movement forward. That is, what establishes these bodies apart from the audience is not only their nudity, but also the fact that they are not going anywhere: these bodies do not ever exit the stage/theater, they simply remain locked together, behind the curtain. The bodies become entangled with one another, forming a unity as a result of the limited space on stage. Retrograde movement, finally, uses the image of the degenerate body to produce a cessation to the constraints maintained by the movement of the Uncle Tom stereotype on African-American male subjects. As Jones explains in the documentary *Dancing to the Promised Land*, "When I was a child and particularly when I was in university in the late '60s and '70s, it was one of the worst insults that one black could hurtle at another, that was, to call him an Uncle Tom." Jones further points out the important distinction between Stowe's Uncle Tom and the black Uncle Tom: the novel, according to Jones, is never anything but a "joke," while Uncle Tom, as a term among blacks, is met with a considerable degree of seriousness and hostility. It is this transferal of affect from Stowe's "good" Uncle Tom to the black "bad" Uncle Tom that Jones's production effectively traces in order to arrive at a conception of the nation where it is no longer possible to think of its heroes without, simultaneously, thinking of its victims. So, while Jones asks the audience a number of explicit questions at a particular moment in the performance, the production as a whole poses a series of other, more implicit questions that can be considered only by putting the show in its specific sociohistorical context. In doing so, the questions can be read as follows: Is it possible to be a hero and a victim at once? If so, how would such a conception revise the standards by which we judge good and bad art?

The phrase *Uncle Tom*, during the so-called revolutionary 1960s—and Bill T. Jones's coming of age as an artist—becomes a term of derision among blacks because it denotes the terms of black male citizenship in the United States. The circulation of the term among black Americans suggests a particular understanding of the conditions of black male citizenship that were developed during the mid-nineteenth century when the ideological parameters of the nation were established by romantic ideals. By romantic I mean not only to suggest the historical period in which Uncle Tom was formed, but also to point to a rhetoric of romanticism that developed an image of the perfect body that essentially excluded the black and/or diseased body. More specifically, as George Frederickson's analysis of nineteenth-century American conceptions of racial stereotypes shows, during the time of Stowe's novel, the ideas of Johann

Gottfried von Herder, a late-eighteenth-century German philosopher, were in wide circulation. Herder's notion of the *Volk* was an important source of cultural national- ism and was used by the American abolitionist movement to establish the particular "virtues" of Africans in order to bring an end to slavery. Fredrickson has usefully termed the logic of this stream of American abolitionism "romantic racialism," a par- adigm that produces the Uncle Tom stereotype of the black male: pious, submissive, willing to sacrifice his life for the safety of his white master and, perhaps most impor- tant, often devoid of sexuality. In Fredrickson's words,

> The image of the Negro as natural Christian received its fullest treatment and most influential expression in Harriet Beecher Stowe's *Uncle Tom's Cabin*. This immensely popular novel, which more than any other pub- lished work served to crystallize antislavery feeling in the North in the 1850s, was also the classic expression of romantic racialism. (1971, 110)

In the mid-twentieth century, the Uncle Tom name becomes a term of disidentifica- tion for African Americans that enables a radical politic that displaces an American nationalist sentiment by explicitly repudiating its operative terms. Moreover, this repudiation of American nationality through a politics of disidentification becomes a touchstone for a new form of nationalism, one that is bound by identity constructions.

Contending with the wide dissemination and influence of the Uncle Tom figure on maintaining the terms of black male American citizenship becomes a central source of inspiration for Bill T. Jones's artistic productions. Again, the explicit ques- tions about the figure of Uncle Tom, most clearly put in the production's "Last Sup- per" scene, where he voices a number of rhetorical questions, function, finally, more effectively as a response mechanism, a response to being called, or merely seen as, an Uncle Tom.

In Jones's capable hands or, more accurately, feet, being called an Uncle Tom becomes, to borrow Judith Butler's terms, a "scene of enabling vulnerability" (1997, 2). To be called an Uncle Tom, as Jones explains in the documentary supplement to *Last Supper*, is "the worst insult one black could hurtle at another." The insult, how- ever, takes on an altogether new dimension when he uses the name to produce a scene of survival and revolution; a scene in which the victim, the object of the injurious name—Uncle Tom—overturns the terms by which he is constituted as a national sub- ject. In taking up the figure of Uncle Tom as a spectacle of late-twentieth-century American culture, Jones particularizes the moment of its utterance and thereby gives Uncle Tom again, in Butler's terms, "a condensed historicity: it exceeds itself in past and future directions, an effect of prior and future invocations that constitute and escape the instance of utterance" (3). Jones's Uncle Tom in retrograde thereby pro- vides a "moving" response to being called or seen as one: a term that is used to disci- pline black male bodies to conform to a romantic ideal that is predicated on racist and heterosexist practices. Through his inversion of Stowe's Uncle Tom as a repository for sentimentalized cultural identification in the first half of the production, Jones establishes the terms of the Uncle Tom figure within a specifically African-American context. In doing so, *Last Supper at Uncle Tom's Cabin/The Promised Land* transforms this figure of cultural identification into one of explicit *disidentification*.[4]

It is this process of disidentification that Jones's work promotes and performs that offends some critical sensibilities. Croce, for instance, had nothing to say about Jones's production not simply because stagings of suffering were "beyond the reach of criticism" but, rather, because Jones uses an artistic medium to unravel the categories of judgment and, more broadly, the constraints of identity categories as such. Whether the critics praise or rebuke Jones's explicitly political intervention through the medium of modern dance/drama, both sides agree that Jones's productions are the necessary outcome of certain social and political movements that unwittingly rarefied identity categories to meet the needs of national subjects who were disabled from participating in its structures and institutions. In this regard, Jones's victim art is the logical consequence of this time in the discourse of the nation, a time imbued with the rhetoric of identity politics. But what Jones does with this rhetoric is ignored altogether. It is one thing to merely represent the logistics of human bodies suffering either from physical or verbal blows; the dance of the naked bodies that concludes Jones's adaptation of Uncle Tom begins to explore the possibilities inherent in the rhetoric of identity politics, which has come under severe attack from the political right. What Jones offers his viewers is the image of figures and names becoming actualized as physical bodies within the logic of the Uncle Tom narrative, and Jones ends up realizing or, at the very least, presenting the audience with a second image that is the dissolution of its logic. As both victim and hero, the name *Uncle Tom* can be applied to just about *anyone*, making it possible to collectivize an otherwise highly individual, and possibly alienating, experience.

By refusing to identify with the Uncle Tom conception of black males in the context of the United States, by effectively unraveling the very terms of its utterance from a nineteenth-century embodiment of a national stereotype to a term of derision among African Americans, Jones embraces the names he is called. Jones takes the names he is given—African American, HIV-positive, gay, artist—to perform what lies behind these names. As his continual representations of death and suffering make clear, behind these names, the names that establish his cultural currency within these times, there is, in Jacques Lacan's words, "the unnameable, with all the resonances you can give this name, that is akin to the quintessential unnameable, that is to say, to death" (1991, 211). In other words, Jones's attempt to represent the necessarily unrepresentable will always result in failure, a form of art that does not—and refuses to—meet the standards of a social establishment that demands an unfailing sense of rigor from its performers that only healthy and nonvictimized bodies can uphold. Jones's production of Uncle Tom embarks upon a critique of artistic standards and critical judgments by failing in its attempt to make the victimized and disabled body visible.

It is no wonder, then, that critics have such a difficult time discussing the content of Jones's productions that deal with this failure and opt instead for a discussion of Jones's art *form*, a form critics have tried, and failed, to dismiss with the label "victim art." What dance reviewers like Arlene Croce find most distasteful in Jones's work is being swindled into feeling sorry for the performers who should be working to entertain its audience in order to justify the price of the ticket. By refusing to discuss the content of Jones's work, reviewers "send a message" not only to artists/performers, but also to "people on the street" who, in Croce's words, "I'm *forced* to feel sorry for because of the way they present themselves: as dissed blacks, abused women, or disenfranchised homosexuals—as performers, in short, who make out of vicitimhood victim art" (55; emphasis in original). The performance of identity, in other words, is only an act of sympathetic identification and, insofar as "contemporary" art goes, we (the audience and critics) refuse to accept art that maintains the terms of an outmoded nineteenth-century conception of sentimentalism.

Texts that fall under the rubric of sentimentalism (and *Uncle Tom's Cabin* is an exemplary instance of the form) are understood as being inherently flawed.[5] At the end of the twentieth century, the term is used both in common parlance and as a literary convention to point out works that indulge the egos of their authors, works that are deliberately dishonest and rely on subjective experiences that can never be tested or proven by way of an objective analysis. Somewhere between the nineteenth and twentieth centuries, the terms of sentimentalism were displaced onto victim art: a shift that has enabled critics to disregard or—just as blindly—to celebrate works of victim art on the grounds of its form alone.[6] Drawing upon the connections between sentimental works of fiction and the production of victim art, Jones uses Stowe's Uncle Tom to make manifest the important differences between these forms. While Stowe's novel is predicated on constructing an identity for blacks that will make them more amenable to whites, Jones insists that such a strategy can only result in failure. Jones produces a successful identity—his own—out of this failure. While the political import of Stowe's novel cannot be disputed, its continued influence within our contemporary moment is not so easy to assess. By placing Uncle Tom on stage in 1990, as both a nineteenth-century literary hero and as a literal embodiment of a racial slur, Jones indicates that blacks—and other victimized bodies of American culture—continue to struggle to find an effective means of representation.

Despite Croce's—and a whole host of other dance/drama critics'—assertions to the contrary, her refusal to participate in Jones's display of victim art is, in fact, the appropriate "viewer-response" to the performance of victim art. In his presentation of victimhood, Jones works to produce a feeling—or, more to the point, a sentiment—of repudiation, rather than sentimental identification, that destabilizes not only the conventions of artistic practices, but also the terms in which certain subjects ("dissed blacks, abused women, disenfranchised homosexuals") are viewed. In viewing these performers of victimhood, the audience is barred from identifying with their experiences. Instead, the audience's response is always held in abeyance, at a distance from the production and therefore *forced* to become aware of its position: a position that is inevitably one of privilege, wherein their bodies are not on stage, a spectacle produced for the sole purpose of entertainment.

Croce's comments, with those of Midge Dector, Camille Paglia, Sid Smith, and Hilton Kramer,[7] who denounce Jones's work, alongside comments made by Henry Louis Gates Jr.,[8] Marcia B. Siegel, and Tony Kushner, who praise and defend Jones's productions—despite their ideological differences—all adhere to notions of artistic value that are stuck in nineteenth-century conceptions of sentimental identification. What reading Uncle Tom in the late twentieth century enables, according to Jones's deployment of the stereotype, is the possibility of recognizing the value of, and perhaps even establishing a whole new set of terms to effectively *evaluate,* victims—on both the stages and streets of the United States of America.

NOTES

1. For an expanded definition of Uncle Tom performances, see Murphy 1994.
2. For a more detailed account of Justice Thomas's assertions of his "victim" identity see Farred 1995 and Ross 1992.
3. The insertion of Truth's address here is particularly relevant to the African-American tradition of "talking back" to the culture of American sentiment. See in particular Mullen 1992, wherein Mullen not only uses Truth's speech as an example of the ways in which Stowe's text "provided an enabling textual model . . . for flegling writers struggling to represent the subjectivity of black women," but also shows that Sojourner Truth's "unwomanly" reputation provided her with the precise means to undermine the terms by which sentiment culture reproduced the terms of her exclusion. In Mullen's assessment, "Sojourner Truth, memorialized as a body with a voice, packs into a concise 'immodest' gesture the ability to shame those who attempt to shame her as a woman" (Mullen 1992, 246).
4. For a particularly trenchant discussion of this concept see Muñoz 1999, in which he locates *disidentification* as a term "meant to be descriptive of the survival strategies the minority subject practices in order to negotiate a phobic majoritarian public sphere that continuously elides or punishes the existence of subjects who do not conform to the phantasm of normative citizenship" (4).
5. Philip Fisher importantly discusses contemporary deployments of sentiment in his comparison between *Uncle Tom's Cabin* and William Styron's *Confessions of Nat Turner.* In "Making a Thing into a Man: The Sentimental Novel and Slavery," he contends that contemporary readers reduce the terms of sentimentalism to "All that is cheap, self-flattering, idealizing, and deliberately dishonest" (1985, 92).
6. See, for instance, Tompkins 1985.
7. See Burch 1997.
8. See Gates 1994.

References

Burch, Steven Dedalus. "Imitation of Life: A Meditation on 'Victim Art.' " *Journal of Dramatic Theory and Criticism* 12.2 (Fall 1997): 121–31.

Butler, Judith. *Excitable Speech: A Politics of the Performative.* New York: Routledge, 1997.

Croce, Arlene. "Discussing the Undiscussable." *The New Yorker*, December 28, 1994, 54–60.

Davis, Angela Yvonne. *Women, Race, and Class*. New York: Random House, 1981.

Farred, Grant. "Take Back the Mike: Producing a Language for Date Rape." In *After Political Correctness: The Humanities and Society in the 1990s*, ed. Christopher Newfield and Ronald Srickland. Bolder, Colorado: Westview Press, 1995.

Fredrickson, George. *The Black Image in the White Mind: The Debate on Afro-American Character and Destiny, 1817–1914*. New York: Harper & Row, 1971.

Fisher, Philip. *Hard Facts: Setting and form in the American novel*. New York: Oxford University Press, 1985.

Gates, Henry Louis, Jr. "The Body Politic." *The New Yorker*, November 28, 1994, 112–14.

Jones, Bill T. *Dancing to the Promised Land*. New York: VIEW Video, 1994.

———. *Still/Here*. First performed: Biennale Internationale de la Danse, Lyons, France, 1993.

———. *Last Supper at Uncle Tom's Cabin/The Promised Land*. First performed: Next Wave Festival, Brooklyn Academy of Music, Brooklyn, New York, 1990.

Lacan, Jacques. *The Seminar of Jacques Lacan, Book II: The Ego in Freud's Theory and in the Technique of Psychoanalysis, 1954–1955*. Trans. Sylvana Tomaselli. New York: W. W. Norton, 1991.

Lott, Eric. *Love and Theft: Blackface Minstrels and the American Working Class*. New York: Oxford University Press, 1993.

Mullen, Harryette. "Runaway Tongue: Resistant Orality in Uncle Tom's Cabin, Our Nig, Incidents in the Life of a Slave Girl, and Beloved. "In *The Culture of Sentiment: Race, Gender, and Sentimentality in Nineteenth-Century America*, ed. Shirley Samuels. New York: Oxford University Press, 1992, 244–64.

Muñoz, José Esteban. *Disidentification: Queers of Color and the Performance of Politics of Cultural Studies of the Americas*. Minneapolis: University of Minnesota Press, 1999.

Murphy, Jacqueline Shea. "Unrest and Uncle Tom: Bill T. Jones/Arnie Zane Dance Company's *Last Supper at Uncle Tom's Cabin/The Promised Land*." In *Bodies of the Text: Dance as Theory, Literature as Dance*, ed. Ellen W. Goellner and Jacqueline Shea Murphy. New Brunswick, NJ: Rutgers University Press, 1994.

Ross, Andrew. "The Private Parts of Justice." In *Race-ing Justice, En-gendering Power: Essays on Anita Hill, Clarence Thomas, and the Construction of Social Reality*, ed. Toni Morrison. New York: Pantheon, 1992.

Sollors, Werner. *Amiri Barak/LeRoi Jones: The Quest for a "Populist Modernism."* New York: Columbia University Press, 1978.

Stowe, Harriet Beecher. *Uncle Tom's Cabin; or, Life among the Lowly*. Ed. John Woods. London: Oxford University Press, 1965.

Tomkins, Jan. *Sensational Designs: The Cultural Work of American Fiction, 1790–1860*. New York: Oxford University Press, 1985.

"It Hurts?": Afflicted Bodies in Beckett's Drama[1]

RUBY COHN

To some extent almost everybody and every body in Beckett's drama is afflicted, at least with discomfort. What is more, some of the bodies call attention to their handicaps, and yet this rarely takes the form of a plea for sympathy. Rather, Beckett exploits corporeal affliction to dramatic ends, and he does so in two main modes:[2] (1) familiar bodies that resemble our own and (2) fragmented bodies that are nevertheless sentient.

Familiar bodies suffer familiar handicaps, and Beckett's first drama is distanced in time but familiar in the affliction it stages. Relying on literary history, his abortive scene of 1940 is entitled *Human Wishes*, after Dr. Samuel Johnson's poem "The Vanity of Human Wishes."[3] Intended to introduce a play set in the eighteenth century, about the septuagenarian Dr. Johnson in love with a much younger widow, Hester Thrale, the "half of a first act" was abandoned before the principals made their entrance. Instead, Beckett presents the actual inhabitants of Dr. Johnson's Bolt Court home—the widowed Mrs. Desmoulins, the ex-prostitute Miss Carmichael, and the blind Mrs. Williams. In spite of being sightless, Mrs. Williams mentions that Mrs. Desmoulins is knitting and Miss Carmichael is reading. Complimented on her perceptions, Mrs. Williams boasts, "I may be old, I may be blind, halt and maim, I may be dying of a pituitous defluxion, but my hearing is unimpaired" (*Disjecta*, 156).[4] Unimpaired, too, is Mrs. Williams's linguistic prowess. She even composes a witty quatrain on her mirthlessness, which she dictates to Miss Carmichael. The latter deceives Mrs. Williams when she affirms that she has inscribed the former's verse lines: "In what will not dry black and what was never white" (157). Beckett invented Mrs. Williams's quatrain and Miss Carmichael's deception for these historical eighteenth-century characters. Mrs. Williams's verse proves to be just another vain human wish, and her blindness evokes no pity from her companions. Nor does she seek it.

In later plays, Beckett exploits blindness more dramatically. On the Act II entrance of Pozzo and Lucky of *Waiting for Godot*, Beckett's scenic direction informs the reader: "Pozzo is blind" (but it does not specify that Lucky is mute). When Lucky stops short at the sight of Didi and Gogo, Pozzo bumps into his carrier, and both fall noisily to the ground, where Didi soon joins them. When all four men are grounded—

a challenge for actors to command audience attention—Pozzo alternates between calls for help and for pity. Yet audience pity is subverted by Pozzo's flatulence, and onstage Didi strikes Pozzo so that he crawls away from the human heap. It is not pity but boredom that eventually impels Didi and Gogo to help Pozzo up, and only then does he proclaim his blindness: "I woke up one fine day as blind as Fortune" (80). Beckett's revised text cuts all but one reference to Pozzo's erstwhile "wonderful sight," and this too subdues audience pity. When Pozzo declares, "The blind have no notion of time" (80), he is simultaneously recalling and denying the tradition of blind prophets, to which Didi alludes. When Pozzo and Lucky leave the stage, they are heard to fall, and yet Didi wonders whether Pozzo was "really blind" (84). His doubt about Pozzo's affliction leads directly to his growing doubt about whether Pozzo was Godot, and soon afterward to his doubt about his own existence—a doubt that climaxes in an image of sight: "At me too someone is looking, of me too someone is saying, he is sleeping, he knows nothing, let him sleep on" (84–85). The audience is the "someone" who is looking at the two friends, of whom one is sleeping and the other is riddled with questions. Blindness, ruthlessly unpitied, is one of Beckett's several tools for sowing audience doubt during night after night of the wait for Godot.

In *Endgame*, blindness is ever-present to the audience. Before Hamm utters a word, his "black glasses" stamp him as blind. Early in the dialogue he informs Clov that his eyes have gone "all white" (94). Clov's eyes are "bad," and Nagg affirms to Nell, "Our sight has failed" (99). Nagg exaggerates, since the sight of the old couple is still in the process of failing, whereas Hamm alone is utterly sightless.[5] Unlike his predecessor, Pozzo, Hamm does not crave pity, but he suggests that Clov obeys him out of "a kind of great compassion" (129). However, the audience has been witness to Clov's lack of compassion. He might have been schooled by Miss Carmichael of *Human Wishes*, for he continually deceives blind Hamm—especially about the black toy dog. Clov tells Hamm that it is "nearly" white, and that it is standing, when in fact the three-legged toy falls over. In his revised version of *Endgame*, Beckett has Clov present the dog's rear to face Hamm, while he affirms that it is gazing at him. Far more insidious than these canine turns are Clov's repeated "No's" to Hamm's question as to whether it is time for his painkiller. The implication of Clov's "No" is "Not yet," until Clov reveals what he must have known all along: "There's no more painkiller. . . . You'll never get any more pain-killer" (127). These lies prepare the play's end, when Hamm, after a final sniff, believes that Clov has left him. However, the son-dog-servant, attired for all weathers, remains on stage until the end of the game. Hamm's blindness has served to sharpen the couple's mutual cruelties.[6]

In *Godot* Didi strikes Pozzo; in *Endgame* Clov hits Hamm with the toy dog, and in *Rough for Theatre I* B pokes A with a pole. Originally written in English as "The Gloaming," Beckett's *Rough* followed *Endgame* by only a few months. In the oral Irish tradition of miraculous cures, Beckett's fragment spurns miracles.[7] His lame beggar happens on a blind beggar with his fiddle, and the cripple suggests that the pair live together and pool their resources, thus alleviating their infirmities. In the final version of what remained a dramatic fragment, Beckett aborts the play midscene, when the lame man, poking the blind man with his pole, threatens to take away his fiddle. After this menace the fragment ends on a scenic direction: the blind beggar "whirls round, seizes the end of the pole and wrenches it from B's grasp" (233). Left to their own devices, the two beggars cannot proffer mutual aid, and no miracle comes to their rescue.

Although none of these plays is realistic, these Beckett characters behave with psychological credibility, particularly with respect to their handicaps. In *Waiting for Godot* blindness contributes to Pozzo's asperity; in *Endgame* it highlights the acrimonious way in which Hamm and Clov are "obliged to each other"; and in *Rough for Theatre I* it helps erode both folk and dramatic tradition. A cruel affliction, blindness in these plays hardens its victims but does not soften its witnesses.

In close chronological proximity to *Endgame* and *Rough I*, Beckett shifted to another genre, the radio play, where blindness is more difficult to perform. In *All That Fall* Dan Rooney is blind and has to be led from the Boghill train station. Upon his wife's solicitous question "Are you not well?" he enumerates his handicaps with relish, climaxing in "No, I cannot be said to be well. But I am no worse. Indeed I am better than I was. The loss of my sight was a great fillip" (192). It is also a fillip for the radio audience, since they share in what has to be verbally presented to Dan's unseeing eyes.

Beckett's second radio play, *Embers*, exploits blindness more subtly. Not only is Henry's father blind, but he is also mute, and on radio a mute character does not exist. Yet the words of Beckett's Henry give credence to the initial presence of his father. To drown the sound of the sea, Henry summons hard sounds, or he imagines conversations with ghosts: "Who is beside me now? [*Pause.*] An old man, blind and foolish. [*Pause.*] My father, back from the dead, to be with me" (253). At first Henry speaks of his father in the third person, but he soon shifts to the second: "That sound you hear is the sea," and the "you" englobes both his father and the radio audience. The "you" is then particularized as the father, in what is tantamount to an exposition. In Henry's fear of sea-sounds, he has resorted to monologue, gramophone, imagined scenes, and invented stories: "Stories, stories, years and years of stories, till the need came on me, for someone, to be with me, anyone, a stranger, to talk to, imagine he hears me, years of that, and then, now, for someone who . . . knew me, in the old days, anyone, to be with me, imagine he hears me, what I am, now" (255). Returning from his Bolton-Holloway story to his father, Henry recalls a paternal taunt: "A washout, that's all you are, a washout!" (256). His father's word triggers Henry's memory of vivid scenes with his wife Ada or their daughter Addie. Ada describes her last view of Henry's father: "I . . . passed him on the road. He did not see me.[8] He was sitting on a rock looking out to sea. I never forgot his posture" (262). When Ada leaves Henry, the latter tries to weave a story around her image, a story that he addresses to his father: "Stands watching you a moment, then on down path to tram, up on open top and sits down in front . . . goes back up path, no sign of you" (263). And there is no further sign of "you" nor of Henry's father, as he lapses back into the Bolton-Holloway story. A difficult play to interpret, *Embers* skillfully enfolds a blind old man into the radio audience, and Beckett also endows a mute character with radio presence. In contrast to Beckett's initial blindness in *Human Wishes*, the playwright's final view of that affliction is subtle, symbolic, and problematic. Of the plays so far examined, *Embers* strays furthest from even Beckett's tangential realism.

Other handicaps than blindness can be quasi-realistic in Beckett's drama. His three longest plays are inhabited by contrasting couples, who are complementarily afflicted. Thus, in Act II of *Waiting for Godot* a blind Pozzo is paired with a mute Lucky, but the first disability is immediately visible to an audience, whereas the latter's muteness is a surprise revelation. When Didi requests that Lucky be ordered to sing, think, or recite, Pozzo replies, "But he's dumb. . . . Dumb. He can't even groan" (83). Didi exclaims, "Dumb! Since when?" and Pozzo replies with a furious monologue that concludes, "They give birth astride of a grave, the light gleams an instant, then it's night once more." Incongruously, blind Pozzo uses light imagery to reach beyond the visible. Lucky lacks this option. Since his Act I monologue is the bravura piece of the play, the audience may unconsciously expect a repetition in Act II, which repeats so many themes of Act I. So the revelation of Lucky's muteness is climactic.

Some thirty years after *Godot*, Beckett again stages a climactic mute. Alone among Beckett's plays, *Catastrophe* is set in a theater. During a rehearsal a director gives instructions for the staging of the Protagonist as a human catastrophe. The Assistant Stage Manager manipulates the Protagonist as though he were a prop, rather than a human being. Rejecting her suggestion of a "little gag," the Director is confident of his actor's muteness: "Not a squeak" (459). This implies that the Protagonist is volitionally rather than physically mute. When the Director is out of audience sight, he imagines the applause at his human catastrophe, which the actual theater audience hears. And the play closes in a mute triumph that Beckett conveys in a scenic direction: "P raises his head, fixes the audience. The applause falters, dies" (461). P has revolted silently against traditional theater decorum whereby we applaud as catastrophe engulfs the suffering protagonist.

In contrast to this ostentatious finale of mutism are Beckett's several handicapped legs—the most frequent affliction in his drama. Prostate trouble is not, of course, centered in the legs, but it is worth noting that the prostate trouble of Henri Krap of *Eleutheria* prevents him from urinating, whereas that of Didi in *Godot* has the opposite effect. Although Beckett's final *Godot* eliminates Didi's "short, stiff strides," almost every Didi-actor develops a distinctive walk for the painful prostate. Maybe Beckett cut references to Didi's gait because it is Gogo who has aching feet, which parallel and contrast with Didi's aching head. In tandem, both friends seek the cause of their discomfort in external objects—boot and hat—rather than in their bodily infirmities. Yet Didi criticizes this in Gogo: "There's man all over for you, blaming on his boots the faults of his feet" (13).

Nagg and Nell of *Endgame* are beyond such blame, having lost their "shanks" in a bicycle accident. Their son Hamm shows little sympathy with their loss since he asks Nagg crudely, "How are your stumps?" (96). Not only does Nagg brush the question aside, but he and his wife "laugh heartily" at the memory of their accident. Truncated images of one another, they contrast with the full-bodied presence of the other pair, but Hamm can't stand and Clov can't sit. It is Clov, the single mobile character of *Endgame*, who is most vocal about his infirmities: "The pains in my legs! It's unbelievable! Soon I won't be able to think any more" (115). On the one hand, this sounds like a non sequitur; on the other hand, we are all familiar with the way physical pain can short-circuit mental activity.

Pain is comparably varied in *Godot* and *Endgame*. In Act I of the former, both friends seek external causes for their respective discomfort. By Act II, however, even this nod to realism dissolves in the abrupt and causeless handicaps of Pozzo and Lucky. Similarly, the two couples of *Endgame* separate in their suffering: Nagg and Nell had a credible tandem accident, but we are offered no explanation for Hamm's paralysis and Clov's "stiff, staggering walk" (92). In "The Gloaming," which became *Rough for Theatre I*, the complementary pair of a blind man and a cripple is dictated by folk tradition, and it needs no realistic explanation. However, *Happy Days* of 1961 still exhibits residual realism beneath its unreal surface.

Happy Days presents the graphic image of Winnie in Act I buried to her waist, and in Act II to her neck. Other than being swallowed by her grave, however, Winnie does not seem handicapped. In Act I her arms, hands, and even her upper torso move at her command, and in Act II her cheeks, lips, and tongue are still responsive to her bidding. It is true that in Act I Winnie declares herself incapable of putting down her parasol, but that might be a failure of will, rather than a physical infirmity. In the main Beckett presents Winnie's mundane and ordinary reactions to her extraordinary situation. She is oblivious of her injuries to Willie—the jab of her parasol and the wound inflicted by her shattered medicine bottle. Winnie's determined optimism even causes her to imply that her condition is preferable to that of Willie: "What a curse, mobility!" (158). Since Willie's mobility is usually invisible to us, we are surprised by his final climactic appearance—"on all fours, dressed to kill" (166). No realistic explanation can encompass Willie's infantile mobility, while dressed in mo(u)rning attire. Monosyllabic, ambiguous of purpose, he is both the climax and conclusion of Winnie's erotic memories. More than the Shower-Cooker couple of Winnie's memory, he is the "last human kind—to stray this way" (157, 165).

Beginning with *Play*, completed in 1963, Beckett changes the way he flays "human kind." Instead of a malfunctioning body part, a fragment of the body becomes an enduring image, while transitory words recall corporeal activity. It might seem that the three urned heads of *Play* simply triple the image of Winnie in Act II of *Happy Days*, "embedded up to neck" (160). However, the ambience is far more stark. Winnie still wears her hat, she is conscious of her facial features, and she responds emotionally to the sight of Willie, whereas the three characters of *Play* have "faces so lost to age and aspect as to seem almost part of urns" (307). In discussing *Play* Beckett mentioned three parts: Chorus, Narration, Meditation. Since three voices speak simultaneously and incomprehensibly in the Chorus, it is the Narration that presents us with the erotic triangle of M, W1, and W2. Although their heads are immobile and impassive, their words tell of coming and going, sitting and kneeling, driving and burning. M and W2 both mention a hand lawnmower cutting grass: "A little rush, then another" (311). And this is the rhythm of the rapid speeches elicited by the spotlight. Tension grows between the eerily invariant stage image of *Play* and the darting spotlight with its concomitant words. This is exacerbated in the Meditation, where the light is said to be "poking and pecking" (312), and where it even interrupts the speakers midsentence. Tension is also aroused between the virtually featureless heads and their words' references to "normal" bodies, climaxing in W1's disparagement of W2: "Pudding face, puffy, spots, blubber mouth, jowls, no neck, dugs you could— . . . Calves like a flunkey—" (310). Although this is brilliantly comic, it is also disquieting in view of the dim stage image. Again and again, the Narration recounts scenes *à deux*, but in the Meditation M has a fantasy of the *three* bodies together in a boat on a river: "I resting on my oars, they lolling on air-pillows in the stern . . . sheets" (314). M's hesitation before "sheets" is the only residue of passion in three immobile heads whose narration is so full of motion and emotion.

Almost the opposite occurs in *Not I* of 1972, where words run parallel to sentience. The audience is focused on a spotlit mouth, whose stream of words demands concentration.[9] Again and again Mouth's monologue refers to a beam and a buzzing, and these two words approximate what the audience sees and hears. The hypnotic mouth and its torrent of words assault the audience so they too may sense "feeling so dulled" (377). Although "she" is said to take a few steps and to hold a shopping bag in her hand, she is almost devoid of corporeal consciousness. She cannot tell her position: "whether standing . . . or sitting . . . or kneeling . . . or lying." Twice we hear "whole body like gone" (380, 382) as the spotlit lips of the actress seem detached from any body, with its affliction of speech. "The flickering of the brain described by Mouth provides a referential parallel with the disjointed and discontinuous verbalisation of the play" (Tubridy in Jeffers 1998, 122). Moreover, we are made conscious of the physical creation of speech by cheeks and jaws, and especially by lips and tongue. Transfixed by the mobile mouth, we absorb the beam and the buzzing in testimony to the power of Beckett's corporeal fragment. Unlike the tension between the bodiless heads and the bodiful narrative of *Play*, the isolated mouth of *Not I* embodies a moving wound.

Four years after *Not I* Beckett staged a bodiless head in *That Time*. He hoped that the two plays would never be performed together since they both resorted to "the same trick."[10] Yet the plays are quite different. The mobile lips of the one contrast with the deathbed head of the other, as the relentless word-rapids of the one contrast with the three different directions of the recorded voice. It is true that both plays stage fragments of a body, but the many evocations of a beam and buzzing underline that very fragmentation in *Not I*, whereas *That Time* resembles *Play* in its tension between a quasi-detached head and words about full-bodied activity. It is often said that in *That Time* the A-voice recalls childhood, the B-voice maturity, and the C-voice senescence, but the pattern is not quite so neat and simple. Again and again the A-voice tells of going *back* in search of his childhood refuge. The B-voice tells of exchanging vows with a loved one while they are positioned *parallel* to one another "like on an axle-tree never *turned* to each other" (391), but the C-voice is obsessed with *"turning-point that was a great word with you"* (390; my emphasis). Back, parallel, and turning are, of course, metaphors, but they also imply full-bodied actions that counterpoint the stillness of the visible old head, before its final toothless smile when that time becomes no time.

Although Beckett probably stages more handicapped or fragmented characters than do other playwrights, he provides virtually no social context for their afflictions. Yet his plays through *Happy Days* often suggest a realistic cause or a credible reaction for the behavior of his people. With *Play*, however, he begins patterned play between a durable stage image and words that parallel or counterpoint it. Through both kinds of affliction Beckett implies the inadequacy of our corporeal equipment for human life on this planet.

NOTES

1. In the wake of Elaine Scarry's *The Body in Pain* and Judith Butler's *Bodies That Matter*, some recent Beckett critics privilege his stage bodies, even at the expense of his texts. Katherine M. Gray's "Troubling the Body" classifies bodies in Beckett's plays as factic, performative, or material: "If the factic body is the familiar vehicle of conventional signification and the performative body the repetitious performance of discourse, the material body is the body evoked by the more radical varieties of performance art" (7). Jennifer M. Jeffers groups a few essays in her *Samuel Beckett: A Casebook:* "Opening up new ways of 'seeing' gender and the stage body is the task of the essays by Derval Tubridy, Karen Laughlin, and Christine Jones" (11). Steering clear of these thickets of theory, I remain characteristically naive in my approach to Beckett's bodies.
2. *Mode* is a multipurpose noun, which I use differently from Gray.
3. The only dating evidence is Beckett's letter of May 21, 1940, to his friend George Reavey, in which he says, "And I wrote half of a first act of Johnson." Yet Knowlson writes, "Beckett's focused research was conducted in Ireland between April and the early autumn of 1937" (1996, 250). Beckett's lapse of three years between research and writing is puzzling.
4. Unless otherwise noted, page numbers in parentheses in my text are those of *Samuel Beckett: The Complete Dramatic Works* (London: Faber & Faber, 1986). My references to Beckett's revisions of *Godot* and *Endgame* rely on *The Theatrical Notebooks of Samuel Beckett*, volumes II and III (London: Faber & Faber, 1986).
5. In an early draft of the play the Hamm character declares that he is blind or pretending to be blind, but Beckett's final version omits the latter possibility.
6. In Hamm's "chronicle" his first-person narrator is not blind. He reads his various meteorological instruments, and he relishes the abjection of the suppliant at his feet.
7. Compare Yeats's *The Cat and the Moon* and Synge's *The Well of the Saints*. Beckett rarely permitted his non-miracle play to be performed. Since his death, however, there seems to be less reluctance on the part of the estate.
8. Since he is blind, Henry's father can see no one. Is this Beckett's oversight, or Ada's? When Henry tries to continue Ada's story, he describes his father as *"looking* out to sea," and this leads me to think that Beckett intended Henry's father to be both sighted and blind, present and absent, perhaps even dead and alive in Henry's imagination.

9.   Although the published scenic direction says the mouth is "faintly lit," every production I
     have seen—including two directed by Beckett—spotlights it.
10. It was the phrase he used to me in conversation. In a letter of July 23, 1974, to me he
     referred to *That Time* as "Not I's little brother."

References

Gray, Katherine M. "Troubling the Body," *Journal of Beckett Studies* (Fall
     1995/Spring 1996).

Jeffers, Jennifer M. *Samuel Beckett: A Casebook*. New York: Garland, 1998.

Knowlson, James. *Damned to Fame: The Life of Samuel Beckett*. New York: Simon
     and Schuster, 1996.

Depression—the Undiagnosed Disability in Marsha Norman's *'night, Mother*

SARAH REUNING

"I was here with you all the time. How could I know you were so alone?"
—MARSHA NORMAN, *'NIGHT, MOTHER*

Marsha Norman describes her drama *'night, Mother* (1983) as "a play of nearly total triumph"[1]—controversial words for a work in which the main character, a divorced epileptic, commits suicide. Despite the play's morbid finale, many feminist scholars have seconded Norman in her belief that Jessie Cates's suicide is a victory. Anne Marie Drew insists that Jessie's death "must not be viewed as a negation but rather as a triumph" (1996, 88), and Lana A. Whited interprets Jessie's self-destruction as "the ultimate act of self-determination" (1997, 72). Raynette Halvorsen Smith even calls Jessie's suicide "a bold act of emancipation" that brings "autonomy" (1991, 287, 279). These critics argue that Jessie wants to control her life and that her suicide enacts that desired control. Essentially, they assert that Jessie achieves something positive by choosing to die. Their interpretation assumes that Jessie has complete control of her mental faculties and that her suicide is a rational act. However, this presumption of rationality ignores the presence of a mental disability. By arguing that Jessie Cates is depressed, I move beyond the common usage of the term *depression* as a synonym for sadness and consider depression as a debilitating illness. While most individuals would agree that Jessie is depressed in the colloquial sense of being merely unhappy, no critic has yet explored Jessie's depression as a mental disorder. Even Jenny S. Spencer, who calls the conditions of Jessie's suicide "naturalistically plausible by clinical standards," fails to view this depression as a disability. I insist we understand depression in its medical context, for in so doing, we discover that Jessie's suicide must be a relinquishing, rather than a regaining, of control. This chapter first recognizes clinical depression as it is manifest in Jessie's life, and second, engages the claims of the critics referenced above who fail to consider depression in their rose-colored readings. I argue that despite Norman's efforts to portray Jessie as a logical individual, Jessie's thinking and behavior demonstrate a mental disability. Thus, her decision to die is not a free choice, but one informed by her illness. For this reason, Jessie's suicide cannot be viewed as the rational conclusion to an unsatisfying life.

Nor is her final act a reclamation of control. In the end, Jessie succumbs to her illness. The most tragic element of Jessie's death is the fact that her depression could have been treated—if only someone had recognized the symptoms.[2]

The National Institute of Mental Health considers depression the leading cause of disability in America and around the world, yet it remains largely unrecognized and misunderstood (NIMH). As a result, any meaningful discussion of this illness must first establish depression as a debilitating condition and dispel certain myths regarding its nature. The Americans with Disabilities Act of 1990 provides the current legal definition of disability in the United States, identifying disability as an "impairment that substantially limits one or more of the major life activities" (ADA). Major life activities include, but are not limited to, "learning, thinking, concentrating, interacting with others, caring for oneself, speaking, performing manual tasks, working or sleeping" (NMHA). "To be substantially limited means that such activities are restricted in the manner, condition, or duration in which they are performed in comparison with most people."[3] Although there are many types of depression, some more severe than others, all forms of this illness substantially affect the quality of life of the sufferer. In *Understanding Depression* psychiatrist Patricia Ainsworth reveals how depression impacts certain major life activities, defining depression as

> a serious, sometimes chronic, and too often terminal illness that clouds the minds of sufferers, robs them of joy and peace, wreaks havoc with their appetites and sleep patterns, and leaves their bodies vulnerable to physical illness and to death, either self-inflicted or as a result of medical illness. (2000, ix)

Given this description, it is clear why the National Mental Health Association considers major depression a "psychiatric disability" according to ADA guidelines.

Legally, major depression is a disability, yet the public often fails to recognize it as such. "Many people . . . wrongly think that depression is 'normal' for older people, young adults, new mothers, menopausal women, or those with a chronic illness" (NMHA). Yet, as the NMHA emphasizes, "depression is never 'normal' no matter what your age or life situation." Another myth claims that depression is a figment of the sufferer's imagination. Contrary to this belief, depression is not just in the mind of the afflicted, but is a real disorder that affects both body and brain. Ainsworth emphasizes the somatic effects of depression, terming it not only a mental illness, but a "total body illness" that does not respond to "motivational lectures" (9, 105). "Telling a severely depressed individual to 'straighten up and pull yourself together,' " continues Ainsworth, "is about as useful and safe as telling a patient with congestive heart failure to take up power walking" (105–6). Ainsworth also attacks the misconception that depression is synonymous with "moodiness": "Moodiness is a transient unpleasant feeling that often occurs in association with some physical or environmental irritant, and is never debilitating. Depression is to moodiness as a hurricane is to a whirlwind (ix)."

The specific tempest plaguing Jessie is major depressive disorder, also known as unipolar or clinical depression. The *Diagnostic and Statistical Manual of Mental Disorders* (DSM) defines major depressive disorder as "characterized by one or more Major Depressive Episodes" (APA 1994, 317). These major depressive episodes consist of "at least 2 weeks of depressed mood or loss of interest accompanied by at least four additional symptoms of depression" (317). A close reading of *'night, Mother* reveals that Jessie meets the above criteria for major depressive disorder by demonstrating a history of both depressed mood and loss of interest extending beyond two weeks. Likewise, Jessie exhibits four of the additional symptoms listed in the DSM: feelings of worthlessness or low self-esteem, decreased appetite, confused thinking, and recurrent thoughts of death with a specific plan for committing suicide (327). Lastly, Jessie manifests two other signs of depression recognized by the *Clinical Handbook of Depression*: withdrawal and hopelessness (Wetzel 1991, 9–10).

Jessie's justifications for killing herself, as well as the frequency with which she ponders suicide, indicate her depressive disorder. Serious consideration of suicide presupposes a loss of interest in life, and Jessie certainly shows no desire to live. She admits to contemplating suicide "Off and on, ten years. On all the time, since Christmas" (721). The exact amount of time that has elapsed since Christmas remains unclear. However, this period greatly surpasses two weeks. Imagining her funeral, Jessie instructs her mother Thelma to ask the mourners "how their garden was this summer or what they're doing for Thanksgiving" (731–32), suggesting that *'night, Mother* takes place in autumn. Thus, Jessie has contemplated suicide continuously for at least eight months. The duration of her depression makes Jessie a candidate for major depressive disorder. The additional signs of depression that she exhibits confirm this diagnosis.

Jessie clearly suffers from low self-esteem. When discussing her divorce, Jessie refers to herself as the "garbage" her husband left behind (727). Jessie believes that she is useless: "You know I couldn't work," complains Jessie, "I can't do anything" (722). She even considers herself a magnet for misfortune: "things fall down around me" (727). Ultimately, Jessie defines her life as the failure to achieve her potential. Contrasting her infancy and her adulthood, Jessie cries, "That's who I started out and this is who is left. . . . It's somebody I lost, all right, it's my own self. Who I never was. Or who I tried to be and never got there. . . . I'm what was worth waiting for and I didn't make it" (731). Norman indicates parenthetically that there is "*no self-pity*" in this speech. Sadly, there is no self-esteem either. Jessie ends her reflection stating, "I'm not . . . very good company" (731).

In addition to causing low self-esteem, Jessie's depression dulls her appetite, destroying her natural desire for food. "You didn't eat a bite of supper," complains Mama after Jessie suggests that they make caramel apples (722). Mama recognizes that Jessie's request for apples is merely a conciliatory gesture and that Jessie is not hungry. "You won't like the apple, either," chides Thelma (726). "It'll be just like the cocoa. You never liked eating at all, did you? Any of it! What have you been living on all these years, toothpaste?" (726). Mama's own sweet tooth highlights Jessie's dormant appetite. As the play opens, Thelma fusses over the "last snowball" (717). "And we're out of Hershey bars," cries Thelma, "and where's the peanut brittle?" (717). Mama relishes food and life. Jessie does not.

Many critics understand Jessie's lack of hunger only symbolically and miss the literal truth of Jessie's illness. In "A Place at the Table," Linda Ginter Brown reads Jessie's decrease in appetite figuratively, arguing that for Jessie and Thelma "Food functions as a complex metaphor" (1996, 75). Thus, Jessie's physical appetite represents a "psychic hunger" (77), for she craves neither life nor food because neither satisfies her soul. Surely Brown's figurative analysis proves accurate. Yet, a more precise conclusion emerges by understanding Jessie's eating habits literally. Jessie has lost interest in food and her scanty diet indicates depression. Additionally, this refusal to nourish her body reflects a suicidal tendency sparked by depression. Jessie directly links her loss of appetite to her impending suicide when she confides,

> I would wonder, sometimes, what might keep me here, what might be worth staying for, and you know what it was? It was maybe if there was something I really liked, like maybe if I really liked rice pudding or cornflakes for breakfast or something, that might be enough. (731)

"Rice pudding is good," interjects Thelma (731). "Not to me," replies Jessie (731). Jessie sees nothing worth eating, and this blindness to healthful food illustrates one way depression cripples the body.

While depression dulls Jessie's appetite, this same illness dulls her mind, leading to confusion. Although Jessie seems lucent during the two hours prior to her suicide, her past is marked by diminished cognitive function. In an ironic affirmation of her mood Jessie claims, "I sure am feeling good. . . . The best part is, my memory's back" (728–29). Mama responds,

> MAMA: Your memory's always been good. When couldn't you remember things? You're always reminding me what . . .
>
> JESSIE: Because I've made lists for everything. But now I remember what things mean on my lists. I see "dish towels," and I used to wonder whether I was supposed to wash them, buy them, or look for them because I wouldn't remember where I had put them after I washed them, but now I know it means wrap them up, they're a present for Loretta's birthday.
>
> MAMA: You used to go looking for your lists, too, I've noticed that. You always know where they are now! (729)

Here, Mama recognizes Jessie's past confusion and the recent improvement in her memory. Jessie attributes this improvement to the phenobarb that blocks her seizures. Indeed, uncontrolled epilepsy probably does account for some degree of Jessie's past confusion, yet depression clearly contributes to Jessie's diminished mental capacity as well. In fact, uncontrolled epilepsy often causes depression, as documented in the textbook *Scientific American Medicine* (Dale 2000, 7). Jessie has gone years without treating her neurological disorder (729). Her history of uncontrolled epilepsy suggests an equally long history of depression. Therefore, Jessie's forgetfulness should not be ascribed to epilepsy alone.

Given the link between untreated epilepsy and mood disorder, it is natural that as Jessie's seizures abate, so does the degree of her depression. Repeatedly, Jessie claims to be "feeling good" (728), which many critics interpret as evidence that Jessie acts rationally. Apparently, if Jessie says that she is feeling well, then she must be thinking well, too. For the most part, Jessie remains calm in the face of death, and the few emotional outbursts that slip past her guard are very quickly controlled. These two elements, Jessie's assertion of well-being and her overall placid demeanor, tend to mask the albatross of depression. Thus, some critics find nothing abnormal in Jessie's behavior, and evaluate her actions as rational. Even the ordinary nature of the evening, aside from the suicide, lends force to these readings. Raynette Smith asserts that on the night of Jessie's death, "Everything is wrong with [Jessie's] life, but no one thing is all that unusual or dramatic" (1991, 284). Smith's argument echoes Mama's summary of events. "There's nothing real sad going on right now," Thelma tells Jessie (721). "If it was after your divorce or something, that [suicide] would make sense" (721). Even though Jessie ends her life on an average evening, these normal circumstances do not necessarily illicit normal behavior. Jessie's mental state at the time of her death requires further investigation.

Jessie kills herself after a period of marked physical and mental improvement. She has not suffered a seizure in over a year; moreover, the side effects of the phenobarb have disappeared. "The double vision's gone," remarks Jessie, "and my gums aren't swelling. No rashes or anything. I'm feeling as good as I ever felt in my life" (728). Jessie even exhibits psychological improvement. As mentioned above, her memory returns. Furthermore, she feels freer to express her emotions, boasting, "I'm even feeling like worrying or getting mad and I'm not afraid it will start a fit if I do, I just go ahead" (728). How has depression determined Jessie's suicide if she claims to be "feeling good" (728)? Despite its superficial irony, the timing of Jessie's suicide fits a common pattern of depressive behavior.

The most dangerous period of depression—the point at which sufferers are most likely to commit suicide—is the term following a major depressive episode (Zirkle 2000). Individuals in the midst of a major depressive episode often lack the energy and confidence to act out their suicidal desires. When this severe depression begins to subside, the sufferer regains a measure of self-esteem, yet, despite noticeable improvement, feelings of depression remain. Whereas the seriously depressed individual lacks the "psychic energy" necessary to kill herself, the recovering individual begins to believe, "I can achieve my goal of suicide" (Zirkle 2000). For this reason, *The Clinical Handbook of Depression* lists "the sudden improvement of previous symptoms of depression" as a "behavioral clue to suicide" (Wetzel 1991, 302). Additionally, the textbook *Primary Care Medicine* urges doctors prescribing antidepressants to "remain vigilant and inquire specifically about suicidal thoughts, even as patients begin to show improvement" (Goroll et al. 1995, 15). Here, feeling good rarely signifies a healthy attitude. Jessie's remark that she "Waited until [she] felt good enough" to kill herself is yet another indication of her mood disorder (718).

In *'night, Mother*, Jessie's phenobarb has the same effect as an antidepressant during the initial stages of drug therapy because it increases her self-confidence—"I'm not afraid"—without relieving her feelings of depression—"I'm even feeling like worrying or getting mad" (728). Jessie claims that she feels as good on the night of her death as she ever felt before (728). This statement proves misleading. At her worst, Jessie suffers from major depression. At her best, Jessie becomes dysthymic, less severely depressed, but depressed nonetheless. Though Jessie exhibits signs of improvement, depression still controls her behavior, as evidenced by her continued and largely self-imposed isolation.

Withdrawal frequently accompanies depression, and not surprisingly, Jessie recedes from society. Although Jessie remains physically capable of leaving the house, her depression creates a mental cage. Instead of going to the market, Jessie has the food delivered, informing the grocery store staff that she will soon be "taking a little holiday" (726). The reactions of Thelma and the staff to this announcement foreground Jessie's reclusivity. "And they [the staff] didn't think there was something funny about that?" puzzles Thelma. "You who doesn't go to the front steps? You who only sees the driveway looking down from a stretcher passed out cold?" (726). The staff certainly recognizes Jessie's habitual introversion: "They said it was about time" that Jessie took a trip (726). While Jessie avoids the public, she also shuns her own family. When her brother and sister-in-law visit, Jessie retreats further from society to the seclusion of her room (720). As Jessie describes death, she imagines suicide as the ultimate withdrawal from society. "Dead is everybody and everything I ever knew, gone" (719).

Isolation for Jessie, as well as for many depressed or otherwise disabled people, is a double-edged sword. Not only does depression encourage withdrawal, but society often excludes those individuals deemed abnormal, reinforcing the exile of these individuals. Rosemarie Garland Thomson accounts for this exclusion in *Extraordinary Bodies*, stating that disability has been constructed by society as the "embodiment of corporeal insufficiency, and deviance" (1997, 6). Thus, "the physically disabled body becomes a repository for social anxieties about such troubling concerns as vulnerability, control, and identity" (6). In *'night, Mother*, Jessie's epileptic body embodies society's fears concerning death, and the resulting ostracization Jessie faces increases her depression. Not only has Jessie been abandoned by her husband and her son, but Thelma's friend Agnes also avoids Jessie's company. Concluding that her seizures scared Agnes away, Jessie asks why Agnes no longer visits. Mama relays Agnes's reason: "Jessie's shook the hand of death and I can't take the chance it's catching, Thelma, so I ain't comin' over, and you can understand or not, but I ain't comin' " (724). Essentially, society, through the fears of Agnes, reinforces Jessie's depressive tendency toward seclusion. Under the weight of her social expulsion and chronic depression, Jessie loses all hope.

Hopelessness proves an incredibly injurious component of depression, robbing the victim of her ability to imagine a happier future. Jessie frequently emphasizes her lack of hope as one of the main justifications for her eventual suicide. "I'm just not having a very good time," sighs Jessie, "and I don't have any reason to think it'll get anything but worse" (721). She does not look forward to her upcoming birthday, nor does she think that she can make a difference in her son Ricky's life. "If I thought I could do that," remarks Jessie, "I would stay" (720). Jessie believes that it is "Only a matter of time" before Ricky becomes a murderer (720). Mama, on the other hand, can envision a brighter future: "Honey, nothing says those calls are always going to be some new trouble [Ricky's] into. You could get one that he's got a job, that he's getting married, or how about he's joined the army, wouldn't that be nice?" (720). Unlike Mama, Jessie cannot imagine her life ever improving. Thus, Jessie defines her suicide as the refusal to hope. "*This* is how I have my say. This is how I say what I thought about it *all* and I say no. To . . . hope. I say no!" (730).

Jessie views her life as ceaseless misery; however, contrary to some critical arguments, this mindset does not validate Jessie's suicide as a mercy killing. Anne Marie Drew, in "And the Time for It Was Gone," recognizes Jessie's hopelessness, arguing that "Jessie cannot look forward with hope" and consequently, "Nothing in [Jessie's] universe makes her believe that time will ever improve things" (1996, 87, 88). Drew correctly identifies Jessie's hopeless state. Nevertheless, Drew, like Jessie, fatalistically concludes that Jessie's condition will never change. Drew sees Jessie in a "world where time is not benevolent and there is no ending in sight" (91). Under these circumstances, Drew insists "suicide can become a triumph" (91), and decides that suicide "is the right decision" for Jessie (94). Drew would do well to remember this adage: suicide is a permanent solution to a temporary problem. No one can predict the future, and while there is no proof that Jessie's life will improve, there is also no evidence that it will deteriorate.

In Jessie's mind suicide appears to be a triumph, yet, for those who recognize Jessie's mental disability, her death can never be a victory. Jessie may see time as unceasingly cruel. However, the critic should not. Time has finally given Jessie and Thelma a night of honest communication, and has brought Jessie's epilepsy under control, giving Jessie the opportunity to get a "driver's license"—in other words, the opportunity for independence (722). These occurrences suggest that time, given the chance, may yet bring mental healing. Time is not cruel to Jessie, but merely indifferent. Unfortunately, Jessie cannot see time as it really is.

The most dangerous effect of depression emerges as altered conceptions of reality, or neurosis. As Alexander Lowen, M.D., explains in *Depression and the Body*, the "neurotic individual is not disoriented, his perception of reality is not distorted, but his conception of reality is unsound. He operates with illusions, and consequently his functioning is not grounded in reality" (1972, 11). Depression distorts Jessie's view of the truth. As a result, she bases her arguments for suicide on misreadings of the world, claiming that if she'd "ever had a year like this, to think straight" she would have killed herself long ago (729). Sadly, Jessie cannot think straight while under the influence of her depression. As Thelma points out, what Jessie conceives to be true and what is true are two different things. "What good would a job do?" laments Jessie (722). "The kind of job I could get would only make me feel worse. . . . It's true" (722). "It's what you think is true!" retorts Mama (722). Jessie concedes. "That's right. It's what I think is true" (722). Clearly, a problem resides in Jessie's thinking, and this problem becomes the crucial conflict of the play. Jessie's notion of reality contradicts that of Thelma and the audience. Tragically, Jessie cannot see her own worth.

"I can't do anything," Jessie complains to Mama. Yet, regardless of this self-declared inadequacy, Jessie demonstrates a capability that underscores her neurosis (722). Jessie has been managing the household for so long that she has to reacquaint Thelma with domestic responsibility. "Be sure you clean out the lint tray every time you use the dryer," warns Jessie. "But don't ever put your house shoes in, it'll melt the soles" (720). Jessie's advice is practical and reflects to her ability to maintain a house: "There's candles and matches in the top of the broom closet, but if the lights go out, just call Dawson and sit tight. But don't open the refrigerator door. Things will stay cool in there as long as you keep the door shut" (721). Jessie's thoroughness indicates her capacity for taking care of herself and others. Despite her melancholia, Jessie anticipates the needs Thelma will have after the suicide. Besides ordering the groceries weeks in advance, Jessie ensures that Thelma's pill bottles are full, and that Thelma will still receive the Sunday paper.

Not only can Jessie manage a household, but her suicide preparations also demonstrate her ability to plan, a skill that shows her effectiveness. To avoid making "a mess," Jessie uses old towels and garbage bags to contain the aftermath of her fatal gun shot (717). Jessie also locks her bedroom door. This act spares Thelma from witnessing Jessie's bloody deed. Additionally, the locked door prevents Thelma from being suspected of Jessie's murder. Jessie takes measures to protect her mother and even helps make her own funeral arrangements, telling Thelma what to wear and which hymns to pick (731). Although some critics consider her suicide preparations a cloaked revenge—Jessie dictates Thelma's future, and in so doing, provides Thelma constant reminders of a child she could not save[4]—Jessie's motives for orchestrating future events are irrelevant to this argument. The fact that Jessie can and does shape her environment illustrates her capacity to act.

For someone who "can't do anything," Jessie proves remarkably organized and efficient (722). Jessie's ability to manage a household and to plan ahead indicate her capability. Despite her arguments to the contrary, Jessie can work. Jessie clearly conceives her own situation inaccurately. As a result, the audience should not rely on her judgment.

As shown above, Jessie's decision to end her life is a misinformed one, and the neurosis caused by her depression has significant implications for the victorious readings posited by many scholars. While some critics erroneously point to Jessie's logic when praising her suicide, others insist that the structure of the play mandates a comic reading. Lana A. Whited expresses reluctance to call suicide a triumph given suicide's "profoundly selfish" overtones (1997, 65). Notwithstanding her hesitancy, Whited declares Jessie's suicide a victory. Whited bases her reading on two factors, Norman's intention when composing 'night, Mother and the definition of tragedy. Both of these factors, however, fail to support Whited's thesis. First, Whited's definition of tragedy and its subsequent application to 'night, Mother begs investigation. Whited asserts,

> Tragedy is, by definition, a work in which the protagonist loses in his or her conflict. Jessie's plan from the very beginning of the play is to kill herself, an act which she accomplishes with perhaps as much deliberation and fore-thought as possible in such a situation. Her goal is to do something which she fully controls, as she has not had control over people dying or leaving her, or even, because she's epileptic, over her own body. (72)

Whited correctly recognizes Jessie's desire for control in Jessie's following speech:

> I can't do anything . . . about my life, to change it, make it better, make me feel better about it. Like it better, make it work. But I can stop it. Shut it down, turn it off like the radio when there's nothing on I want to listen to. It's all I really have that belongs to me and I'm going to say what happens to it. And it's going to stop. And I'm going to stop it. (722)

Like Jessie, Whited views suicide as the means for the protagonist to reclaim control of herself. Whited realizes that, as an epileptic, Jessie cannot always control her body. Still, Whited fails to realize that as a depressed individual, Jessie cannot always control her mind. Despite her negative outlook, Jessie can do something to change her life, to make it better, and to make her feel better about it. She can seek treatment for her depression. Jessie's real antagonist is her metal illness, not her life. If Jessie ultimately were to reclaim control of her thoughts and emotions by fighting her disorder and deciding to live, then 'night, Mother would indeed be a triumph.

Returning to Whited's definition of tragedy, one now sees how the term accurately describes Norman's play. Tragedy is "a work in which the protagonist loses in his or her conflict" (Whited 1997, 72). Although Jessie views her conflict with life, her true conflict is with mental illness. Jessie loses this battle when her depressed mood leads her to suicide. Thus, the dramatic structure of 'night, Mother follows the pattern of tragedy.

In light of Jessie's depression, Whited's assertion about the triumphant form of 'night, Mother fails. What, then, becomes of Whited's reliance on Norman's intentions? In a 1987 interview Norman reveals her own attitude regarding 'night, Mother. Norman does not consider Jessie's suicide a "despairing act" (Betsko and Koenig 1987, 339). "It may look despairing from the outside," concedes Norman, but if "Jessie says it's worth it, then it is" (339). "That's how I see it," continues the playwright (339). "Now you don't have to see it that way, nor does anybody else have to see it that way" (340). Here, Norman denies holding the definitive interpretation of Jessie's life. "Jessie's story is Jessie's story," remarks Norman (340). "It's one that I've written, but it's not one that I have a claim on or can disclose anything else about" (340). Norman wisely realizes that authorial intent does not mandate a particular reading of a given work.

Although Norman did not set out to dramatize mental illness, *'night, Mother* proves a penetrating case study of depression, a "general malaise" that is recognized but misinterpreted by Raynette Halvorsen Smith in " *'night, Mother* and *True West* " (1991, 284). Here, Smith asserts that "universal reasons," not "personal quirkiness" drive Jessie to her death. Smith views Jessie's suicide as "a metaphor for a pervasive modern malaise that manifests itself in real women. This malaise adopts guises such as anorexia and agoraphobia. Contemporary women," warns Smith, "are beginning to exhibit these 'neurotic' behaviors in alarming numbers" (285). Smith correctly links Jessie's actions to other neurotic behaviors; however, she misreads Jessie's malaise as solely metaphorical. Significantly, depression is just as real and destructive as any anxiety or eating disorder. Not only does Smith overlook Jessie's depression, but she demonstrates a very limited knowledge of metal disorders when claiming that women who suffer from agoraphobia do so by choice. Smith takes her argument from Robert Seidenberg and Karen DeCrow's *Women Who Marry Houses*, which asserts that

> Agoraphobics may well be the most completely uncompromising feminists of our times. They will not be placated or bribed by small favors or grants of limited access. Sensing that they are not welcome in the outside world, they have come to terms with their own sense of pride by not setting foot on the land that is deemed alien and hostile. (Quoted in Smith 1991, 286)

In point of fact, agoraphobics do not choose to avoid society out of pride, but rather out of fear, hence the suffix *phobia*. The Anxiety Disorders Association of America emphasizes that phobic individuals are tormented by unreasonable, overwhelming, and involuntary fear (ADAA 2000). Thus the phobic's actions are dominated by the illogical need to avoid normal objects and situations (ADAA). This behavior is shaped by panic, not preference (ADAA). The question of agency in agoraphobia is particularly relevant to Jessie Cates, since she refuses to leave her own home. Before echoing Smith and applauding Jessie for her so-called feminist behavior, we must realize that Jessie's actions are a result of mental illness. Furthermore, they do not challenge, but ultimately conform to patriarchal society. If Jessie is not welcome in the patriarchy outside her home, then the most submissive thing she can do is stay indoors.

Rejecting a seemingly hostile environment, either through agoraphobic seclusion or suicide, may appear to be an act of protest in the mind of the isolated individual; however, this behavior only confirms the suggestion that that individual does not belong in society at large. Susan Bordo acknowledges the futility of destroying the self in "Anorexia Nervosa: Psycopathology as the Crystallization of Culture." Bordo insists, we must recognize that the anorexic's "protest," like that of the classical hysterical symptom, is written on the bodies of anorexic women, and *not* embraced as a conscious politics, nor, indeed, does it reflect any social or political understanding at all. . . . Paradoxically—and often tragically— these pathologies of female "protest" . . . actually function as if in collusion with the cultural conditions that produced them. (1986, 90)

Bordo includes agoraphobia as a pathology of female protest, and to her list I add suicide. In a protest suicide, the woman acts out society's rejection of her body on her body, permanently removing the nonconformant self. This removal acts in collusion with society by rendering the woman completely powerless and silencing her protesting voice. Thelma underscores this phenomenon when she tells Jessie,

Well, nobody's going to be a bit surprised, sweetheart. . . . You know who they're going to feel sorry for? Me! How about that! Not you, me! They're going to be *ashamed* of you. Yes. *Ashamed!* If somebody asks Dawson about it, he'll change the subject as fast as he can. He'll talk about how much he has to pay to park his car these days. (731)

No one will mention Jessie's suicide after her death, and her protest accomplishes nothing.

Perhaps the trend to term Jessie's suicide a triumph stems from a desire to make the best of her horrible situation. Drew concludes her article stating,

We can wish for Jessie that her life view were different. We can wish that like the emotionally deprived David Copperfield, she triumphed over bleak existence. We can grieve that only in death was she free, but Norman's work moves us to an inexorable conclusion. In death, Jessie Cates finds life. (1996, 93)

I do wish that Jessie's worldview were different, that she triumphed over the depression that made her life seem a bleak existence, but I cannot find a triumph for Jessie in her suicide. As shown above, Jessie makes her fatal choice under the influence of a mental illness. The agency ascribed to Jessie by feminist critics proves false. Jessie Cates is the figurehead of a life dominated by depression.

Whereas Marsha Norman sees *'night, Mother* as a "play of neatly total triumph," I find this drama a work of nearly total tragedy. Although Jessie's family recognizes her withdrawal, her loss of appetite, her lack of interest in life, her past confusion, and her neurosis, no one correctly identifies these symptoms as signs of depression. Consequently, Jessie never receives the help she needs to conquer her disorder. When Jessie announces her plan to kill herself, Thelma does suggest that Jessie see a doctor, but this advice proves to be too little too late. In the end, Jessie's disability proves fatal. Far from taking control of her life, Jessie gives in to the dictates of her illness.

Those critics who view her suicide as triumphant succumb to Jessie's irrational logic. Even though Jessie's death remains merely a fictional one, the nature of her demise must be understood within the context of a very real disability. Depression afflicts more than nineteen million adults in the United States alone (NMHA 2000). Moreover, the *Journal of the American Medical Association* considers depression a serious public health problem that is on the rise (Glass 1999). Feminist scholars should pay particular attention to this disorder, as it is the leading cause of disability among women (NMHA), and nearly twice as many women become depressed as men (NIMH 2000). Significantly, only one out of every three women who experience clinical depression will ever seek treatment (NMHA). This statistic becomes increasingly unfortunate in light of the fact that treatment, therapeutic or medicinal, can alleviate symptoms in over 80 percent of cases (NIMH). In other words, large numbers of women never get the readily available help they need. Given the overwhelming number of individuals battling depression, society can ill afford to further ignore this disorder or to romanticize suicide as a positive act.

NOTES

1. Betsko and Koenig 1987, 339.
2. As Herbert Hendin, M.D., points out in *Suicide and Scandinavia*, it is important to realize that not all suicidal individuals suffer from depression and not all depressed individuals are suicidal (13). However, research reveals that "90 percent of people who kill themselves have depression or another diagnosable mental or substance abuse disorder" (NIMH 2000).
3. This clarification of the ADA provided by the Department of Justice: http://www. usdoj.gov/crt/ada/q&a_law.htm.
4. For this reading see Paige and Spencer 1987.

References

Ainsworth, Patricia, M.D. *Understanding Depression*. Jackson: University Press of Mississippi, 2000.

American Psychiatric Association. *Diagnostic and Statistical Manual of Mental Disorders*. 4th ed. Washington, D.C.: American Psychiatric Association, 1994.

Americans with Disabilities Act of 1990. Department of Justice. June 19, 2000. http://www.usdoj.gov/crt/ada.

Anxiety Disorders Association of America. July 29, 2000. http://www.adaa.org.

Betsko, Kathleen, and Rachel Koenig. *Interviews with Contemporary Women Playwrights*. New York: Beech Tree Books, 1987.

Bordo, Susan. "Anorexia Nervosa: Psychopathology as the Crystallization of Culture." *Philosophical Forum* 17 (winter 1986): 73–103.

Brown, Linda Ginter. "A Place at the Table: Hunger as Metaphor in Lillian Hellman's *Days to Come* and Marsha Norman's *'night, Mother.*" In *Marsha Norman: A Casebook*, ed. Linda Ginter Brown. New York: Garland, 1996.

Drew, Anne Marie. "And the Time for It Was Gone: Jessie's Triumph in *'night, Mother.*" In *Marsha Norman: A Casebook*, ed. Linda Ginter Brown. New York: Garland, 1996.

Dale, David C., and Daniel D. Federman. *Scientific American Medicine*, ed. Dale and Federman. New York: Scientific American, 2000.

Glass, Richard M., M.D. "Treating Depression as a Recurrent of Chronic Disease," *Journal of the American Medical Association* 281. 1 (January 6, 1999). Obtained May 3, 2000. http://www.jama.ama-assn.org.

Goroll, Allan H., M.D., Lawrence A. May, M.D., and Albert G. Mulley Jr., M.D., M.P.P. *Primary Care Medicine: Office Evaluation and Management of the Adult Patient*. 3rd ed. Philadelphia: J. B. Lippincott Company, 1995.

Hendin, Herbet, M.D. *Suicide and Scandinavia*. New York: Grune & Stratton, 1964.

Hyman, Steven E., M.D., et al. "Mood and Anxiety Disorders" Section 2. In *Scientific American Medicine,* ed. David C. Dale and Daniel D. Federman. (Note: this section contains information from the May 1995 update.)

Lowen, Alexander, M.D. *Depression and the Body*. New York: Coward, McCann, & Geoghegan, 1972.

Morrow, Laura. "Orality and Identity in *'night, Mother* and *Crimes of the Heart.*" *Studies in America Drama* 3 (1988): 23–39.

National Institute of Mental Health. April 18, 2000, and September 6, 2000. http://www.nimh.nih.gov.

National Mental Health Association. June 16, 2000. http://www.nmha.org.

Paige, Linda Louise Rohrer. "The 'Other' Side of the Looking Glass: A Feminist Perspective on Female Suicide in Ibson's 'Hedda Gabler,' Hellman's 'The Children's Hour,' and Norman's ''night, Mother.'" Ph.D. diss., University of Tennessee, Knoxville, 1989.

Seidenberg, Robert, and Karen DeCrow. *Women Who Marry Houses: Panic and Protest in Agoraphobia*. New York: McGraw-Hill, 1983.

Smith, Raynette Halvorsen. "*'night, Mother* and *True West*: Mirror Images of Violence and Gender," *Themes in Drama* 13 (1991): 277–89.

Spencer, Jenny S. "Norman's *'night, Mother*: Psycho-drama of Female Identity." *Modern Drama* 30 (1987): 364–75.

Thomson, Rosemarie Garland. *Extraordinary Bodies: Figuring Physical Disability in American Culture and Literature*. New York: Columbia University Press, 1997.

Wetzel, Janice Wood. *The Clinical Handbook of Depression*. New York: Gardner Press, 1991.

Whited, Lana A. "Suicide in Beth Henly's *Crimes of the Heart* and Marsha Norman's *'night, Mother.*" *The Southern Quarterly* 36.1 (1997): 65–74.

Zirkle, John W., M.D. Personal interview, April 2, 2000.

"Some Unheard-of Thing": Freaks, Families, and Coming of Age in *The Member of the Wedding*

THOMAS FAHY

Given the popularity of freak shows between 1840 and 1940, their powerful presence in art throughout the twentieth century is not surprising.[1] These shows typically constructed bodies as spectacles by magnifying physical, racial, and/or gender differences through context and juxtaposition[2]: placing dwarfs next to giants, fabricating marriages between fat ladies and skeleton men, dressing nonwhites as exotic cannibals from Fiji, Central America, and Africa, and asking audiences to guess (and in some cases pay extra) to "discover" the true sex of bearded ladies and hermaphrodites (fig. 1). By the end of the Great Depression, however, the physical and economic devastation of the 1930s, developments in medical science (a gradual change toward viewing the deviant body as pathological rather than monstrous[3]), and the popular success of Hollywood films certainly contributed to the decline of the freak show's popularity and commercial success. Several other factors are also important for understanding its artistic applications in the decade following World War II.

Freak shows thrived on questions of truth and humbug: Was the bearded lady really a woman? Could "What Is It?" be half-man, half-monkey? Were Chang and Eng actually conjoined twins? These ploys to ascertain the truth reveal the types of social categories that freak shows both challenged and maintained—rigid boundaries that defined differences in gender (male and female), race (white and nonwhite), and bodies (normal and abnormal). But something in the 1930s began to keep more and more people away from freak shows. Some scholars suggest that these shows had become problematic on moral grounds,[4] but it is unlikely that a higher moral consciousness suddenly began preventing people from buying tickets. Instead, it seems more probable that freak shows were failing to maintain the boundaries between self and other that modern audiences needed in order to look at these exhibits from a safe distance. Although audiences in the late 1930s certainly wrestled with some of the ethical and moral problems of freak exhibits, these concerns were not new to the twentieth century. P. T. Barnum, for example, had assuaged some of these ethical problems decades earlier by aggrandizing certain performers, creating pseudo-aristocratic contexts, and using elevated labels and behaviors to transform the "freak" into a "celebrity."[5] Despite Barnum's savvy, freak shows eventually failed to maintain

Figure 1. Bearded lady and husband. *Becker Collection, Syracuse University.*

the types of boundaries necessary for objectifying and containing difference. And many contemporary writers, such as Carson McCullers, recognized and used this failing as an artistic tool to explore the breakdown of mainstream social categories in America.

This chapter focuses on the ways that Carson McCullers's play *The Member of the Wedding* (1950) uses freakishness to suggest a breakdown in the heterosexual/homosexual binary that American society had been trying to mandate with renewed rigor since the 1930s. On the threshold of young adulthood and faced with making choices about her own sexual desires, the protagonist, Frankie Addams, associates her conflicted sexual desires with the sexually ambiguous freaks she sees at the fair. Recent scholarship has just begun exploring the intersections between freak discourse and queer theory,[6] and I would like to apply these methodologies to McCullers's dramatic adaptation of *The Member of the Wedding*, arguing that significant differences between play and novel enhance her thematic use of freak shows. I will begin by both locating this work in the tradition of Depression-era theater and distinguishing her use of freakishness from images of the grotesque in 1930s drama. Freak shows often get subsumed in discussions of the grotesque and carnivalesque, but recognizing their distinct conventions is important for understanding their role in modern fiction. Lastly, I will consider her link between freakishness and the nuclear family as a critique of compulsory heterosexuality. For McCullers, freakishness is both a reflection of contemporary anxieties about sexuality and marriage, and a means for condemning imperatives that force people to go against their own nature.

Grotesques and Freaks in the Great Depression

In *Rabelais and His World*, Mikhail Bakhtin describes the grotesque in terms of materiality, a "bodily element" that is universal ([1965] 1984, 19). Images of the body are therefore linked with degradation, irregularity, copulation, carnality, defecation, mortality, and renewal. Like the masks and disguises of carnivals, the grotesque, degraded body can be both threatening and terrifying, but only temporarily. Bakhtin points out that the social critiques of the grotesque and carnivalesque are mitigated and, in effect, transformed by laughter. This balance between physical degradation and humor drives Mark Fearnow's study of the Depression in *The American Stage and the Great Depression: A Cultural History of the Grotesque*.

Fearnow argues that theater, film, and journalism in the 1930s tapped into a pervasive sense of the grotesque in American culture. The grotesque, more specifically, was often expressed through images that evoked unresolved contradictions in contemporary society, but these tensions were quickly mitigated, to some degree, by humor:

> The word "grotesque" refers to one's apprehension of an unresolved contradiction among two or more elements in an object. . . . The grotesque object thus operates as part of a social "machine" that transforms vague

anxieties and discordant fears of a culture into forms in which they are represented and mingled with comic elements. Thus reified, these cultural
"nightmares" are rendered less frightening but remain troubling and disrup-
tive of an easy acceptance of "reality." (1997, 12)

The grotesque, in other words, offers a type of containment. It does not dismiss the
problems underlying the social contradictions it raises; it keeps them temporarily at
bay. Many Americans in the 1930s were torn between a seemingly incongruous
past—idealizations and hopes about an American way of life that would help them
survive the struggles of the present—and the radical solutions being posed by the
New Deal. For Fearnow, this contradiction is the primary source of the grotesque in
the 1930s, and successful plays and films of the period combined these tensions with
touches of humor.[7]

The grotesque may have been mitigated by humor, but not when freaks were
concerned. Humor was both less effective and, very often, not present when freaks
and freak shows were employed in works of this period. In John Steinbeck's *Grapes
of Wrath* (1939) and Tillie Olsen's *Yonnondio: From the Thirties*, the freak is a terrifying possibility, embodying the ultimate physical cost of the Depression. Steinbeck's
character Rose of Sharon is frightened that her child will be freakish: "I'll have a
freak!" (537). Similarly, the young protagonist of *Yonnondio*, Mazie, has recurring
dreams about herself as "crooked" and "grotesque," and she eventually sees herself
like Erina, a disabled girl whom the other neighborhood kids mock: "Here comes
freak show, stink show, Miss Sewer from shantylicetown" (120). And Nathanael
West's fiction—though not typically considered Depression fiction—is also perme-
ated with freakish and deformed figures who have tried to escape the ravages of the
economic Depression by moving to New York or Hollywood (places filled with freakish, damaged individuals). In all of these examples, the physical body is the ultimate
cost, a space where the suffering of the Depression can be seen and measured.
Although the freak is often subsumed in discussions of the grotesque, these and many
other contemporary works suggest that the freakish can be understood as having its
own conventions distinct from the grotesque.[8] It has a darker edge—one that cannot
be contained so easily by humor. Humor, of course, is not entirely absent from all of
these examples, but freaks and freak shows primarily appear as terrifying images,
suggesting that the boundaries between self and other (audience and freak) were dan-
gerously fluid. Anyone could become a freak. At a street fair, for example, the masks
allowing people to assume the grotesque are temporary, momentarily applied to
protest social and class hierarchies. But the mask can be put away. As Bakhtin says,
"carnival is not spectacle seen by the people; they live it, and everyone participates
because its very idea embraces all the people. While carnival lasts, there is no other
life outside it" (7). Because the carnival is a "temporary suspension" of hierarchies,
participants do not remain spectacles afterward; the freak, however, is always a spectacle. Once the individual has been constructed and perceived as a freak, the label carries a much more lasting and insidious stigma.

The appearance of freak shows in Depression literature is limited, and when they do occur in Steinbeck and Olsen, for example, they occupy marginal, though important, spaces in the narrative. The presence of freakishness in McCullers's work is strikingly different from that of her 1930s predecessors. Freak shows and freakishness are central to the ways that *The Member of the Wedding* and her other fictional works confront ruptures beneath the surface of white, heterosexual American life. McCullers uses freaks to embody a slippage that threatens sexual categories—categories that postwar America was trying desperately to maintain through family and compulsory heterosexuality. Like a fault line rumbling beneath the surface of a city, freak shows had gotten too close to fracturing some of the categories held sacred in mainstream society. And in McCullers's works, we can see a historical connection among the sexual climate in America, notions of the family, and the demise of the freak show.

Homosexuality and the American Family

To understand the artistic uses of freaks and freakishness in McCullers and the late 1940s and 1950s more broadly, we need to examine the ways that homophobia during the Depression and after the war reflected cultural anxieties about the nuclear family. The freak is not only the despised other, but one without community, without family. Given the increased visibility of homosexuality by the late 1940s, the sexually ambiguous freak was an unwelcome, visible threat to compulsory heterosexuality. It challenged the idealized place of marriage and the family in American society, not by offering a more positive alternative (few would want to trade places with those onstage), but by suggesting other sexual possibilities. Freak shows had always played with social anxieties about sexuality and race, but as these concerns intensified after the war, the freak show was no longer able to maintain the boundaries it challenged. Bogdan attributes the decline of the freak show primarily to competition from other forms of entertainment and to new social attitudes about "abnormality" that emerged from developments in medical science. The medical profession had started attacking freak shows in the early twentieth century, interpreting human differences as pathological: "By the late 1930s, the transformation of those with physical and mental anomalies from curiosities to diseased people was complete" (66). As a result, he concludes that freak shows had become "morally bankrupt" (67), but this may give midcentury audiences too much credit. Instead, I want to consider distinct social and historical factors that contributed to the decline of the freak show, particularly the growing visibility of homosexual culture during the war. By the late 1940s, homosexuality was beginning to be seen as both a political threat to democracy and a threat to the family.

Although poverty during the Great Depression brought many families together, increasing the number of two- and three-generation families under one roof,[9] this dependence on extended family, as well as unemployment, also emasculated many men. George Chauncey explains that "as many men lost their jobs, their status as breadwinners, and their sense of mastery of their own futures, the central tenets undergirding their gender status were threatened. [As a result] lesbians and gay men began to seem more dangerous in this context" (1994, 353–54). This threat inspired greater restrictions on public expressions of homosexuality, and in New York, for example, the repeal of Prohibition became a tool for an increased surveillance of and crackdown on homosexuality.[10] These efforts to criminalize homosexuality—based on stereotypes about "gay" behavior—certainly reflected anxieties about sexual passing.[11] But this persecution would be stalled by the military and social demands of U.S. involvement in the war.

World War II destabilized the family, separating large numbers of men who either volunteered or were conscripted in the war and women who worked as part of the labor force for the war effort: "It uprooted tens of millions of American men and women, many of them young, and deposited them in a variety of nonfamilial, often sex-segregated environments" (D'Emilio 1983, 23). Not only did this separation of families give women new levels of economic and social freedom, but same-sex working environments also opened up greater possibilities for expressing and experiencing same-sex desire. "The unusual conditions of a mobilized society allowed homosexual desire to be expressed more easily in action. For many gay Americans, World War II created something of a nationwide coming out experience" (24). These increased opportunities to explore sexuality did not last long after the war, however, and a new, more insidious assault on homosexuality began.

The social instability of the war years sparked efforts to define stability and security more closely through the family. By the 1950s the heterosexual family—with its implicit whiteness and stabilized gender roles—embodied the financial and social successes of postwar America.[12] After Alfred Kinsey published his reports on American sexuality in 1948 and 1953, however, homosexuality was perceived as much more pervasive and dangerous than previously thought. Kinsey's best-selling study, which was based on individual interviews with over ten thousand white Americans, revealed data that "disputed the common assumption that all adults were permanently and exclusively either homosexual or heterosexual and revealed instead a fluidity that belied medical theories about fixed orientations" (D'Emilio 1983, 35). Not surprisingly, this report intensified anti-homosexual sentiment, and helped establish homophobia as part of McCarthy's anti-Communist persecution in the 1950s. More specifically, since marriage embodied heterosexual imperatives (which were integral to America's image of itself), it was viewed as a sign that one was not a Communist:

> anticommunists linked deviant family or sexual behavior to sedition. The FBI and other government agencies instituted unprecedented state intrusion into private life under the guise of investigating subversives. . . . Some men and women entered loveless marriages in order to forestall attacks about real or suspected homosexuality or lesbianism. (Coontz 1992, 33)

The family had become a much needed symbol for political and social conformity.

This brief history of anti-homosexual policy and attitudes as they were associated with the social need to preserve an idealized vision of "the American family" can help us understand representations of "freakish" sexuality in popular forms of entertainment. Hollywood films in the 1930s, for example, followed a production code that "prohibited any reference whatsoever to homosexuality" (Chauncey 1994, 353). This manifestation of homophobia may also explain, in part, the popular decline of freak shows that featured sexually ambiguous exhibits. While Hollywood adapted to the social pressures of homophobia, freak shows continued to play with gender boundaries, showcasing bearded ladies and hermaphrodites who held a traditional place in these troupes. Their incompatibility with contemporary sentiment (particularly attitudes that equated homosexuality with effeminate behavior and lesbianism with masculine behavior) made these exhibits particularly unsettling and dangerous for audiences. We see these concerns being manifested explicitly in McCullers's dramatic adaptation of *The Member of the Wedding* as both the staging and adult characters present idealized images of marriage as a solution to Frankie's sense of social and sexual freakishness.

Members of the Freak Show

By 1950 Carson McCullers had successfully adapted her 1946 novel *The Member of the Wedding* for the theater. An immensely popular and critical success, this play opened in New York on January 5, 1950, and closed the following year after 501 performances. In addition to grossing $1,112,000,[13] *The Member of the Wedding* was also awarded the New York Drama Critic's Award and the Theater Club's gold medal for best American play that year, and many contemporary critics believed that McCullers would have won the Pulitzer if the work had not been an adaptation. I want to argue that in adapting this work McCullers made significant changes between novel and play to capitalize on the ways a staged production could enact the dynamics of a freak show.[14]

As a young girl, McCullers was captivated by freak shows:

> "Let's skip the cotton candy and hot dogs and save our dimes for the Rubber Man and all the freak shows this year. The Pin Head, the Cigarette Man, the Lady with the Lizard Skin." . . . Lula Carson Smith viewed once more with terror and fascination the midway freaks. . . . The child craved eye contact with these strange withdrawn creatures who sometimes stared at her sullenly or smiled and crooked a finger beckoningly. Yet she dared only to steal oblique glances, fearful of a mesmeric union. (Carr 1975, 1)

Many years later, in a play preoccupied with freak shows and the freakish, McCullers would invoke such images for theater audiences, making them participants in the spectacle on stage. *The Member of the Wedding* would also use these images to present the nuclear family as an antidote for freakish, non-normative behaviors and desires.

The marriage at the heart of *The Member of the Wedding* both defines and shapes twelve-year-old Frankie Addams's struggles to reconcile her conflicted sexual desires with her idealized notions about marriage. Impatient with long summer afternoons filled with card games in the dilapidated kitchen of her father's house, Frankie wants to escape the smallness of this world. In Act I, she meets Jarvis's fiancée, Janice, and decides to run away with them after the wedding: "I know that the bride and my brother are the 'we' of me. So I'm going with them, joining with the wedding" (52). Her hopes that their marriage will somehow give her a sense of belonging begin to break down in Act II. Before the wedding, Frankie gets an orange dress for the ceremony and begins telling people in the town that she will be leaving—as if leaving will provide an escape from her tall, lanky body (which Janice assures her is not too big). Frankie's behavior worries Berenice, the family cook and surrogate mother-figure who decides to tell Frankie about her own obsession with marriage. After a happy, five-year marriage to Ludie Freeman, whose most distinguishing physical characteristic was a mangled and grotesque thumb, she married a series of abusive and unreliable men (Jamie Beale and Henry Johnson) in an attempt to recapture her first love[15]: "What I did was marry off little pieces of Ludie whenever I come across them. It was just my misfortune they all turned out to be the wrong pieces. My intention was to repeat me and Ludie" (79). Berenice uses this story to warn Frankie against doing the same thing with marriage—not to fall in love with an ideal, "some unheard-of thing" (80). Because Frankie feels alienated from her family (her mother died during childbirth, her father is aloof and mostly absent, and her brother has been stationed in Alaska for the war), she fantasizes about the possibilities that marriage offers for companionship, beauty, stability, and family.

Act III begins when the wedding has just finished, and Frankie tries to leave with her brother and sister-in-law. When they refuse to let her come, she storms out of the house with a suitcase and her father's pistol. She gets only as far as the alley behind her father's store (where she briefly contemplates suicide) before returning home. Four months pass between scenes 2 and 3. John Henry has died from spinal meningitis; Honey, Berenice's foster brother, has hanged himself after his arrest; Mr. Addams and Frankie are moving to the suburbs to live with John Henry's parents; and Frankie has become friends with Mary Littlejohn. This relationship, like her friendship with Evelyn Owen before the play begins, temporarily assuages her desire to find belonging through marriage.

In many ways, the staging of the play enacts a type of sanitized freak show—one in which the audience is insulated from the anxiety of looking. Since theatergoers remain in the dark, a safe distance from the gaze of the performer, the drama effectively removes one of the increasingly unpopular dimensions of freak shows—the reciprocated gaze. The fixed setting, the Addams's "ugly" kitchen, also enhances the freakishness of the characters by preventing the audience from seeing an actual freak show; they only hear descriptions from Frankie. As a result, the audience is invited to see those onstage as standing in for the freaks who are repeatedly invoked through language. And just as freak shows relied on the juxtaposition of extremes to construct a performer as freakish, *The Member of the Wedding* relies on this convention to make the bodies of Frankie, Berenice, and John Henry seem more extraordinary.

When juxtaposed with John Henry's smallness (Frankie calls him a "midget") and Berenice's stout black body, Frankie's height, pale-white skin, boyish clothes, and short haircut accentuate her physical freakishness—to the point where she fears becoming a freak: "I am so worried about being so tall. . . . If I keep on growing like this until I'm twenty-one, I figure I will be nearly ten feet tall. . . . Do you think I will grow into a freak?" (28, 30). There is also a performative dimension to Frankie's freakishness. She makes her body appear disproportional by twisting and wrapping her legs around a small kitchen chair to get comfortable, and she acts out her frustration through verbal and physical abuse, yelling at John Henry and Berenice, and "[banging] her forehead on the table. Her fists are clenched and she is sobbing" (40). Her performance, however, is not over, and she immediately threatens to throw a knife in front of Berenice: *"Frankie aims the knife carefully at the closed door to the bedroom and throws it. The knife does not stick into the wall"* (41). Like a failed magic trick, the knife falls to the ground; it is no longer a threatening symbol, nor an impressive act.

The spectacle preceding this moment taps into several traditional freak show conventions as well. After rummaging through Berenice's purse early in Act I, John Henry pulls out her blue glass eye, and she proceeds to place it into her socket—a scene that is absent from the novel (24–25). The stage directions indicate that *"Berenice takes off her patch, turns away, and inserts the glass eye"* (25). Removing the patch draws attention to her damaged body, and turning away to insert it plays with the audience's curiosity to "see" more. Given McCullers's fascination with freak shows, this stage direction is more than a practical "solution" for the actor playing Berenice, who could have simply worn a patch throughout the play. Instead, McCullers uses the type of game-playing typical of freak shows to generate dramatic tension and momentum, and to allay critiques that her novel lacked "a sense of drama."[16] This scene with Berenice's eye is both disturbing and compelling to watch, and, like most freak show acts, it invites questions that remain unanswered: most obviously, How did she lose her eye? Furthermore, its blue color, which Frankie feels is out of place on an African-American woman, also hints at contemporary social tendencies to construct race as freakish.[17]

McCullers's theatrical version does not engage with questions of race as convincingly as does the novel;[18] instead, it primarily focuses on questions of belonging and alienation as they relate to family and sexuality. The strange ensemble onstage— the tall, boyish Frankie, cousin John Henry's sickly small body, and the disabled Berenice—represent a kind of anti-American family, one without the white parents and siblings. Together, these unusual bodies and their abusive interactions suggest that Frankie's confusions stem from not having a more traditional family. She is preoccupied, for example, with her father's aloofness and her brother's disinterest in her: "I wrote you so many letters, Jarvis, and you never, never would answer me" (5). The image of this trio also starkly contrasts Jarvis's marriage, which symbolizes all of the beauty and potential of the nuclear family to be: "They are so beautiful. . . . They were the prettiest people I ever saw" (12, 13).

Frankie's body and age (she is two years younger than the local girls who don't select her as a member of their club) exclude her from feeling accepted by those around her, and she worries that her unusual body will also prevent her from ever getting married, from achieving the social ideal ("some unheard-of thing") of the American family. Berenice explains to her that "the whole idea of a club is that there are members who are included and the non-members who are not included" (22)—a truth that alludes to her own social standing as an African-American woman. The play makes it clear that those who belong are white and heterosexual, and marriage embodies social acceptance and inclusion for those who fit into these categories. Because Berenice equates marriage with comfort and sexual certainty, she uses sexually ambiguous freaks and individuals, such as Lily Mae Jenkins, a local man who "turned into a girl" because he fell in love with another man (57), to reinforce heterosexual imperatives for Frankie. Interestingly, Berenice's racial marginalization has not made her bitter and resentful like her foster brother Honey. Recognizing her own disenfranchisement as an African American, she wants to protect Frankie from being stigmatized for rejecting heterosexual desire. As a white girl, Frankie has access to freedoms and power that Berenice and Honey do not, but Berenice warns her that rejecting heterosexuality will jeopardize the social acceptance and mobility that marriage and family offer.

Several scholars have recently argued that McCullers internalized contemporary attitudes about sexual inversion, believing herself to be a sexual invert.[19] Along the same lines, we can consider her remarriage to her ex-husband James Reeves McCullers in 1945 as another example of her acceptance of certain social norms about heterosexual marriage and the nuclear family. Consider the autobiographical elements of her only other play, *The Square Root of Wonderful* (1957), in which the characters continually struggle with the ways in which their lives do not correspond with images of the ideal American family. The protagonist, Mollie Lovejoy, is torn between her love for her ex-husband Phillip (whom she has married twice) and her new tenant John Tucker. Despite her painful past with Phillip and his suicide in Act III, she associates "family" with happiness and love, as do her son and John, who declares, "I am going to marry your mother! . . . And I am going to build that house, I told you about" (156). The house, which they dream about throughout the play, symbolizes their ongoing quest to achieve some version of the nuclear family. This powerful drive for marriage and family also appears in *The Member of the Wedding* as a force that restricts the possibilities of bisexual desire. Still naive about sex, Frankie links her romanticized notion of marriage to a sense of belonging, not sexual behavior; as a matter of fact, the idea of sex frightens and repulses her: "[other girls] were telling nasty lies about married people" (22). She also reacts vehemently when Berenice suggests that she "make out" with a boy:

BERENICE: Yep, I have come to the conclusion that what you ought to be thinking about is a beau. A nice little white beau.

FRANKIE: I don't want any beau. What would I do with one? . . .

BERENICE: . . . How 'bout that little old Barney next door?
FRANKIE: Barney MacKean! That nasty Barney!
BERENICE: Certainly! You could make out with him until somebody better
                   comes along. He would do. . . .
FRANKIE: Yonder Barney's now with Helen Fletcher. They are going to the
                   alley behind the Wests' garage. They do something bad back there.
                   I don't know what it is.
BERENICE: If you don't know what it is, how do you know it is bad?
FRANKIE: I just know it. I think maybe they look at each other and peepee or
                   something. They don't let anybody watch them. (58–59)

For Berenice, making out with a boy is not about love and romance, but social acceptance, and she believes that Frankie's aversion to heterosexual behavior can be overcome by going through the motions of heterosexual desire with Barney. Berenice also
encourages Frankie to find a white boyfriend because she ultimately needs to be with
someone white to achieve the image of an ideal American couple.

Torn between her refusal to accept this option and her hope that marriage will provide some sense of belonging, however, Frankie recalls her feelings of alienation at
freak shows. Though she fears heterosexual behavior, she is more frightened of the possibility that her body may exclude her from the type of community and sense of belonging embodied in marriage: "I doubt if they ever get married or go to a wedding. Those
freaks. . . . at the fair" (28–29); "Do you think I will grow into a freak?" (30). Though
the novel further magnifies Frankie's isolation by revealing her odd sense of community with these freaks—"She was afraid of all the Freaks, for it seemed to her that they
had looked at her in a secret way and tried to connect their eyes with hers, as though to
say: we know you" (17)—both Frankie and Berenice share their experiences with freak
shows in the play. While the book has Frankie describe the hermaphrodite, the play
relies on Berenice to interpret sexual ambiguity. This narrative shift situates Berenice as
the authority figure on sexuality—a guardian of heterosexual imperatives who teaches
her "children" how to respond to such images: "That little old squeezed-looking midget
in them little trick evening clothes. And that giant with the hang-jaw face and them
huge loose hands. And that morphidite! Half man–half woman. With that tiger skin on
one side and that spangled skirt on the other" (29). Though Berenice says that the
freaks "give [her] the creeps" (29), she never points to the act of looking as a problem;
it is only the image of the hermaphrodite that disturbs her. Berenice's response, therefore, reinforces the link between freakishness and nonheterosexual expression.

Closing the Curtain

Despite this adult-sanctioned perspective on sexuality, Frankie's relationships with
girls are her only source of contentment. The play is framed by her friendships with
two girls—Evelyn Owen (32), who has moved away before the play begins, and Mary
Littlejohn, whom she befriends at the end of the narrative. Mary's clear heterosexual

desires do not offer Frankie much opportunity to experience alternate forms of sexual expression. Instead, she imitates Mary's desires in contradiction to her previous attitudes about Barney. Unlike her earlier reference to him as "that nasty Barney!" (58), she tells Berenice in Act III that "Barney puts me in mind of a Greek god. . . . Mary remarked that Barney reminded her of a Greek god" (116). Though many critics have seen hope in Frankie's friendship at the end of the story, little has changed for her. The only town figures who have broken with heterosexual norms have been marginalized; they are made invisible both onstage and outside the context of the play. And even though Frankie is shocked that she has never seen Lily Mae, Berenice isn't. She understands that the town has kept her hidden from the children. Like the sexual exhibits of the dying stage of freak shows, the implications of her visibility are too dangerous for pubescent children on the verge of making choices about their own sexual identity: normative behavior and desires were at stake; the American family was at stake.

Though freak shows had become an increasingly marginal form of entertainment in the 1940s, associated with bad taste and low culture, understanding some of the cultural forces behind their decline not only says a great deal about modern America but opens up new and important ways of understanding American art. The nuclear family has traditionally been associated with the American Dream, and as homosexuality became increasingly visible, it seemed to threaten society by challenging many of the ideas it held sacred, particularly the importance of raising children in a heterosexual family. The gay body, therefore, had to be vilified and enfreaked to make it seem like an unattractive alternative to heterosexual life. McCullers uses this intersection between freakishness and same-sex desire as a metaphor for criticizing the debilitating impact of heterosexual imperatives on everyone, regardless of sexual preferences. For a young adult poised to make her own choices about sexuality, these imperatives have an insidious overtone. They make sexuality an issue of social control, a way of preserving white, middle-class hierarchies.

McCullers's career as a playwright may have been short-lived, but in this one successful moment, she enacted the dynamics of a freak show in the perfect medium for social critique, the theater—a space that challenged audiences to think about the anxieties and fears that made freaks much safer to look at in the dark.

NOTES

1. Scholars generally agree with Robert Bogdan's claim that freak shows were at the height of their popularity between 1840 and 1940. See Bogdan 1988, 1–21.
2. To reinforce a performer's freakishness, most sideshows also sold cartes de visite and pamphlets offering sensational biographies and questionable medical documentation to vouch for the freak's authenticity.
3. Rosemarie Garland Thomson has argued that "[as] scientific explanation eclipsed religious mystery to become the authoritative cultural narrative of modernity, the exceptional body began increasingly to be represented in clinical terms as pathology; and the monstrous body moved from the freak show stage into the medical theater" (1996, 2).

4. Bogdan, for example, specifically links the decline of the freak show to its association with immoral low culture: "Once the freak show, packaged as rational entertainment, had legitimized and provided a cover for theatrical undertakings; by the forties it had become morally bankrupt" (67).

5. Consider Tom Thumb's popularity in upper-class American society and in Europe. Under Barnum's direction, he had unquestionably become a celebrity (see Harris 1973). For a more detailed discussion of celebrity in modern American culture, see Marshall 1997 and Schickel 1985.

6. Shelly Tremain, editor of a special issue of *DSQ: Disability Studies Queered* (1999), discusses the crucial need for scholars to incorporate sexual orientation and sexual identity into the analysis of disability studies. Successfully bringing together these methods, Rachel Adams has done the only substantial reading of McCullers's fiction that links queer theory with the use of freaks. She is interested in the intersection of these concepts with biography (McCullers's bisexuality) and American consumerism in the 1940s. She situates her argument in some of the social and economic concerns of the 1940s, primarily focusing on the cultural implications of McCullers's language, particularly the use of "queer" and "freak"—a fruitful and important way of bringing together the methodologies of queer theory and disability studies. She does not, however, examine McCullers's dramatic works, and does not assess the historical moment of freak shows in terms of its decline in the 1940s. More specifically, she sees the use of freak shows in *The Member of the Wedding* and *Clock without Hands* as an innovative inversion of the audience-freak dynamic in this entertainment. "In McCullers's fiction, freak shows fail to cement the distinction between deviance and normality, instead calling the viewers' own normality into question through their identification with the bodies onstage, which remind them of their own lonely, uncomfortable experiences of embodiment" (557). I would argue, however, that freak shows had already failed to do this and that McCullers is explicitly using negative social responses to contemporary freak shows as part of her critique of heteronormativity and the image of the American family.

7. As Fearnow goes on to explain, plays that did not incorporate humor into the grotesque quickly failed at the box office. And in some cases, Hollywood completely transformed the original works. The film version of Nathanael West's *Miss Lonelyhearts* (1933), for example, became a comedy (33).

8. Susan Steward, Mary Russo, and Robin Blyn have argued that the freak show is antithetical to Bakhtinian notions of the carnivalesque. As Blyn explains, "unlike the carnival, it is not laughter that overcomes terror in the freak show, but the distance imposed by spectacle, negotiated in the interaction of the barker's spiel with the freak tableau" (2000, 136). I would add to this argument that literary uses of freakishness not only reflect many freak show conventions, but they are also aware of this entertainment's increasing inability to sustain self-other dichotomies. This awareness is a significant part of these artistic uses.

9. See Coontz 1992, 8–22.

10. See chapter 12 of Chauncey 1994.

11. In the United States, racial passing had been an ongoing obsession since the late nineteenth century, as evident in publications by Madison Grant and Lothrop Stoddard, the rise of eugenics, and arts of the Harlem Renaissance (to reference just a few). In *Neither Black nor White yet Both: Thematic Explorations of Interracial Literature* (1997), Werner Sollors discusses some of the "signs" whites used to identify those who were passing, such as a blue

mark or meridian on the fingernails. Similarly, heterosexual society had tried to identify homosexuality based on "effeminate looks and behavior." John D'Emilio and Estelle B. Freedman give an example of a World War II naval officer noticing " 'eye contact' that first alerted him to the presence of other gay men in the service" (1998, 289). See also Katz 1976.

12. See Coontz 1992 and May 1998.

13. See Carr 1975, 330–351.

14. When the play opened at the Walnut Theater in Philadelphia, it ran for four hours, and cuts were needed before it could be presented to a Broadway audience: "Carson had a great deal to say about the cuts. It was *her* play they were getting ready to operate on, and after her last experience with a script doctor, she was zealous in guarding her offspring" (Carr 1975, 339).

15. At the end of the novel, she is also planning to marry T. T. Williams, whom she considers an honest and good man.

16. Biographer Virginia Carr points out that McCullers was inspired to write an adaptation in part because of "Edmund Wilson's remarks that *The Member of the Wedding* was static and lacked a sense of drama" (274). Visually, this "freakish" behavior certainly intensifies the drama.

17. For more on the role of race in this work, see Davis 1996 and Adams 1999. For a broader discussion of the literary and artistic uses of racialized freak exhibits in early-twentieth-century literature see my "Exotic Fantasies, Shameful Realities: Race in the Modern American Freak Show."

18. Davis argues that McCullers, for commercial reasons, diluted her treatment of race in this dramatic adaptation by relying on conventional stereotypes in portraying African Americans.

19. Lori Kenschaft explains that "[Havelock Ellis's] theories of sexual inversion define homoerotic desire as an individual pathological flaw. To the extent that McCullers accepted this model, which she largely did, her vision of the nature of homoeroticism remained that of a soul 'mean of countenance and grotesque in form' " (1996, 227). Kenschaft's essay also briefly links McCullers's portraits of freakishness to these feelings of sexual inversion.

References

Adams, Rachel. " 'A Mixture of Delicious and Freak': The Queer Fiction of Carson McCullers." *American Literature* 71.3 (September 1999): 551–83.

Bakhtin, Mikhail. *Rabelais and His World.* 1965. Trans. Helene Iswolsky. Bloomington: Indiana University Press, 1984.

Bogdan, Robert. *Freak Show: Presenting Human Oddities for Amusement and Profit.* Chicago: University of Chicago Press, 1988.

Blyn, Robin. "From Stage to Page: Franz Kafka, Djuna Barnes, and Modernism's Freak Fictions." *Narrative* 8.2 (May 2000): 134–60.

Carr, Virginia Spencer. *Understanding Carson McCullers.* Columbia: University of South Carolina Press, 1990.

———. *The Lonely Hunter: A Biography of Carson McCullers.* Garden City, NY: Doubleday, 1975.

Chauncey, George. *Gay New York: Gender, Urban Culture, and the Making of the Gay Male World, 1890–1940*. New York: Basic Books, 1994.

Coontz, Stephanie. *The Way We Never Were: American Families and the Nostalgia Trap*. New York: Basic Books, 1992.

Davis, Thadious M. "Erasing the 'We of Me' and Rewriting the Racial Script: Carson McCullers's Two *Member[s] of the Wedding*." In *Critical Essays on Carson McCullers*, ed. Beverly Lyon Clark and Melvin J. Friedman. New York: G. K. Hall, 1996.

D' Emilio, John, and Estelle B. Freedman. *Intimate Matters: A History of Sexuality in America*. New York: Harper & Row, 1998.

D' Emilio, John. *Sexual Politics, Sexual Communities: The Making of a Homosexual Minority in the United States, 1940–1970*. Chicago: University of Chicago Press, 1983.

Fahy, Thomas. "Exotic Fantasies, Shameful Realities: The Freak Show in Modern America." *A Modern Mosaic: Art and Modernism in the United States*. Chapel Hill: University of North Carolina Press, 2000: 67–92.

Fearnow, Mark. *The American Stage and the Great Depression: A Cultural History of the Grotesque*. Cambridge: Cambridge University Press, 1997.

Harris, Neil. *Humbug: The Art of P. T. Barnum*. Chicago: University of Chicago Press, 1973.

Katz, Jonathan Ned. *Gay American History: Lesbians and Gay Men in the U.S.A.* New York: Meridian, 1976.

Kenschaft, Lori J. "Homoerotics and Human Connections: Reading Carson McCullers 'As a Lesbian.' " In *Critical Essays on Carson McCullers*, ed. Beverly Lyon Clark and Melvin J. Friedman. New York: G. K. Hall, 1996.

Marshall, David P. *Celebrity and Power: Fame in Contemporary Culture*. Minneapolis: University of Minnesota Press, 1997.

May, Elaine Tyler. *Homeward Bound: American Families in the Cold War Era*. New York: Basic Books, 1998.

McCullers, Carson. *The Square Root of Wonderful: A Play by Carson McCullers*. New York: Houghton Mifflin, 1958.

———. *The Member of the Wedding: A Play by Carson McCullers*. New York: New Directions, 1950.

———. *The Member of the Wedding*. Boston: Houghton Mifflin, 1946.

Olsen, Tillie. *Yonnondio: From the Thirties*. New York: Delta, 1974.

Russo, Mary. *Female Grotesque: Risk, Excess, and Modernity*. New York: Routledge, 1994.

Schickel, Richard. *Intimate Strangers: The Culture of Celebrity*. Garden City, NY: Doubleday, 1985.

Sollors, Werner. *Neither Black nor White yet Both: Thematic Explorations of Interracial Literature*. Cambridge, MA: Harvard University Press, 1997.

Steinbeck, John. *The Grapes of Wrath*. 1939. New York: Penguin, 1992.

Steward, Susan. *On Longing: Narratives of the Miniature, the Gigantic, the Souvenir, the Collection.* Durham, NC: Duke University Press, 1993.

Thomson, Rosemarie Garland. *Extraordinary Bodies: Figuring Physical Disability in American Culture and Literature.* New York: Columbia University Press, 1997.

———. "Introduction: From Wonder to Error—A Genealogy of Freak Discourse in Modernity." In *Freakery: Cultural Spectacles of the Extraordinary Body*, ed. Thomson. New York: New York University Press, 1996.

Tremain, Shelley. "DSQ: Disability Studies Queered," *Disability Studies Quarterly* 18.3 (March 1999): 166–68.

Young Doctors Come to See the Elephant Man

JOHANNA SHAPIRO

> *We do not see things the way they are.*
> *We see things the way we are.*
> —DAVID PILBEAM, PALEOANTHROPOLOGIST[1]

Introduction

As part of an eight-week, second-year medical student elective in literature and med-icine entitled "Doctor Stories/Patient Stories: The Doctor-Patient Relationship," one session focuses on the experience of disability from the perspective of patients and physicians. We read poetry, essays, and short stories about a range of disabilities, including multiple sclerosis, cerebral palsy, stroke, paraplegia, blindness, deafness, and mental retardation. This year, as an optional supplement to these readings, I sug-gest we read a play, *The Elephant Man*, by Bernard Pomerance,[2] because of its evoca-tive portrayal of the relationship between patient and doctor. Of ten students enrolled in the class, six agree to participate in three successive evening sessions. Most of the students have heard the phrase *Elephant Man* used as a linguistic shorthand, in the words of one student, for "someone really ugly."[3] One student mentions that the Ele-phant Man was someone who lived a hundred years ago and had a terribly disfiguring medical condition. Another student comments he has seen the David Lynch movie,[4] but didn't like it much because it was "black and white." We decide to meet the fol-lowing week.

The "True Story" of the Elephant Man

At our first session, I briefly review with the students pertinent known historical facts regarding the Elephant Man. As source materials, I bring the Michael Howell and Peter Ford biography[5], anthropologist Ashley Montagu's revised third edition of *The Elephant Man: A Study in Human Dignity*,[6] and a 1986 article by Tibbles and Cohen published in the *British Medical Journal* regarding diagnosis. We establish that the so-called Elephant Man was indeed an actual person, Joseph Carey Merrick, who was born in 1862 in Leicester, England, and died in 1890 in London. Probably of normal appearance at birth, he was afflicted with what is now believed to be Proteus syndrome, a progressively disfiguring condition that causes severe dermatologic and skeletal abnormalities, including "macrocephaly; thickened skin and subcutaneous tissues, . . . plantar hyperplasia, lipomas, and unspecified subcutaneous masses; hypertropy of long bones; and overgrowth of the skull."[7]

Joseph was the eldest of three children born to a working-class family. His father owned and operated a haberdashery shop. When he was eleven, Joseph's mother died of bronchial pneumonia, and his father subsequently remarried. Joseph left school at twelve and found employment as a cigar roller. When he became too disabled for this occupation, he hawked his father's haberdashery in the streets. He was mistreated by his stepmother and sometimes beaten. At age fifteen, he ran away from home, but was taken in by an uncle. Unable to support himself, Joseph voluntarily signed himself into the Leicester Union Workhouse. Here he remained for several years. Eventually, at age twenty-two, he contacted a well-known music hall impresario, Mr. Sam Torr, and offered himself for public exhibition as a freak. Torr entered into a contractual relationship with Joseph, forming a syndication of managers who were responsible for the young man's exhibition in various parts of the country, including London.

The surgeon Frederick Treves, whose distinguished career would eventually include becoming a nationally recognized authority on appendectomy, a widely published author, and personal physician to King Edward VII,[8] first entered Merrick's life in 1884. Discovering Merrick at a London side show, he published the first of a series of articles on the Elephant Man in the *British Medical Journal* and presented his case before the Pathological Society of London. Treves then returned Merrick to the streets, where he spent the next two years in exhibition, first in London, then later, when such displays became less acceptable to English authorities, in Brussels. However, official attitudes being no more tolerant in this country, his exhibitor abandoned Merrick, after first stealing his rather sizeable nest egg of fifty pounds. Merrick somehow made his way back to London, where he was able to contact Treves, who installed him in a room of the London Hospital. Although the London, as it was known, was not intended to maintain "incurable" patients, an appeal by the hospital director, F. C. Carr-Gomm, led to a flood of charitable donations that enabled Merrick to remain in this facility for the rest of his short life.

At first assumed to be an imbecile because of his appearance and related speech defects, Merrick was quickly discovered to have normal intelligence. He occupied his time at the London Hospital indulging his passion for reading, building cardboard structures in imitation of the great cathedral St. Phillips, which he could see from his window, and entertaining his "guests," who included many representatives of London's high society. Treves also spent time with Merrick on an almost daily basis. Merrick died in his sleep at the age of twenty-seven. It is believed that the cause of death was compression of his spinal vertebrae due to the dislocation of his ever-enlarging head.

We See Things the Way We Are

In this first exposure to Merrick, it is apparent that the medical students have come to *see*, to *view* Merrick. Not a modern version of the sideshow crowds who came to "gape and yawp" (3), they come more in the spirit of the medical men attending Treves's presentation of Merrick at the London Pathological Society. Their clinical gaze devours the pictures of Merrick's skeleton and other photographic evidence provided in our reference texts. There is some eager debate as to whether, as was originally posited, Merrick suffered from neurofibromatosis or, as is currently the widely accepted view, he was a victim of the more serious and rarer condition Proteus syndrome. This is familiar but intriguing territory, and such discussion makes these students feel like real doctors.

Thus, when at last we begin our reading of Pomerance, the students approach the play with a point of view clearly in place. Confronted with Merrick's monstrosity, they seek refuge in the clinical role of physician. And our reading does not progress far enough to seriously challenge this haven of safety. Having spent much of our time laying down "the facts," we have time only to read a few pages. We conclude at the end of the scene "The English Public Will Pay . . . ," which succinctly defines the physician Treves's goals for his patient Merrick: "Normality as far as is possible" (21). This aim strikes our makeshift cast as a rather humane objective, and in response to my clarifying query, they echo Treves's own words: "What's wrong with that?"

Their reading of these early scenes reflects the students' identification with Treves and their desire to see the physician in a healing, restorative role. Not unlike Treves himself, they have entered medicine to alleviate suffering, to assist and even "rescue" unfortunates. For these students, Treves appears as an ideal role model: he is already financially successful; he has a satisfying home life; and he appears destined for significant professional acclaim. Yet he is also a benevolent physician who donates time to the poor. Thus Treves seems a safe choice through which to understand the unfolding events of the play.

This expectation of Treves as hero and savior colors the students' initial responses. For example, they read Pomerance's sly introductory quote—*"Anyone playing the part of Merrick should be advised to consult a physician about the problems of sustaining any unnatural or twisted position"* (ix)—as straightforward orthopedic advice that places the physician in the position of authoritative expert. Similarly, students justify Treves's decision to return Merrick to continued exhibition after his appearance at the Pathological Society (7) on the grounds that the social responsibility of physicians has significant limits. "The physician can't be expected to fix everything," warn these budding doctors, well aware that managed care may scarcely allow them to fix anything.

In sum, the students view Treves much as, a bit later in the play, he views himself: "curious, compassionate, concerned about the world" (40). They note his enlightened view of Merrick's disability, which eschews superstitious explanations of his condition (for example, exposure to elephants in utero), and avoids person-blame models (Merrick is not responsible for his deformity) (17). Further, when Nurse Sandwich reacts in horror to Merrick's appearance, Treves appears resolutely focused on doing whatever it takes to help his new charge (18). Treves is someone who saves

Merrick from degrading exhibition in freak shows and carnivals, who wants only to "help" Merrick. Aren't doctors supposed to help their patients?

Interestingly, in this introductory reading, little attention is paid to Merrick at all. Merrick, while deserving of our pity, is certainly "other," not-doctor, and perhaps not-quite-human. At best, he is the patient in need of help, indeed the patient explicitly crying out for help (15). Exploited and victimized by almost everyone he encounters, suffering greatly, Merrick simply does not have the resources to effectively intervene in his own life. He is someone clearly in need of rescuing, a patient who desperately requires the benevolent intervention of a dedicated physician.

We See the World according to Pomerance[9]

In our second session, we complete the reading of the play. Since medical students are not stupid, they quickly realize that, at least according to Pomerance, they have "seen" the situation all wrong. In a dramatic shift from their initial expectations, they now perceive Treves as the villain. Instead of materializing as the grateful patient, Merrick reprises the role of victim, but the source of his victimization has changed. Merrick's real oppressor is no longer the showman Ross, who at least has a certain blunt honesty about him, but Treves, whose apparent mercy is really a much more severe cruelty, and who, it turns out, is the worst exploiter of all. The students have discovered the irony in Pomerance's introductory quote, and take pleasure in identifying Treves as someone familiar with *himself* assuming twisted and unnatural positions. Treves has become that worst of all creatures, a *bad doctor*.

What do the students see as Treves's sins? In case we are in any danger of missing the point, Pomerance helpfully outlines the physician's wrongdoings with great explicitness. All at once focused on the dream sequence and the Pinheads' chorus about Empire (59–62, 10, 68), the students learn to see Treves as a colonizer, not of continents but of his patient Merrick. Treves dutifully carries the white man's burden to the world of disability, and requires, with condescending benevolence, that its foremost citizen ape the clothing, customs, and attitudes of his betters. Treves's relationship with Merrick is perceived as controlling, demeaning, and patronizing, that of colonizer to colonized. Students are quick to point out that Treves, for all his elevated language about Merrick's intelligence and sensibilities, seems incapable of seeing him as other than a naif, a child, or even a woman, but always less than a true man, much as white Europeans perceived native Africans or Indians. We begin to think of Treves as "dangerous" precisely because he is an English "gentleman and a good man" (60). Like the British colonizers, he is afflicted with arrogant self-satisfaction, repressed sexuality, and unquestioning confidence in the rightness of his methods and motives. He is, in short, a man incapable of empathy, least of all for Merrick. In fact, Treves is best thought of as a kind of Jack the Ripper (57) who has eviscerated and raped Merrick by totally depriving him of his identity.

Merrick, on the other hand, undergoes no similarly profound metamorphosis. Although he shows some superficial signs of being the grateful patient ("Thank you, sir!" [24]), Merrick continues as primarily victim. If anything, he is judged to be even more profoundly victimized in this new reading. Students recall that the Elephant Man as sideshow freak still retained some autonomy and decision-making about his life, did have a legal contract, and in fact earned a tidy sum. Under the guise of friendship, Treves's exhibition of Merrick to curious scientists and high-society patrons makes him seem little more than a trained pet, and has reduced him to a state of utter dependency. Tragically, Merrick himself seems to succumb to the pathetic illusion that he has become a normal man, when he refuses to return with Ross to the freak-show circuit. "I am a man like others," he proclaims (53), and we are shocked by the facility with which Merrick has traded his identity for an empty mirror.

Merrick as illusion, as emptiness, becomes the theme of this phase of our interpretation. Everything about his life at Bedstead Square strikes us as fake and illusory. The presents he receives from his aristocratic visitors, the silver-headed walking canes, rings, and personal photographs, are simply cruel "props" (39) used to sustain the delusion. We evaluate these "friendships" as counterfeit, stage-managed interactions to assuage the sensibilities of the guests, who have defined civility as being able to view Merrick without fainting. Mrs. Kendal literally is coached by Treves to act out a scripted relationship (29), while the formulaic motions of the other society figures clearly convey their wish only to see their own generosity and large-heartedness reflected in Merrick's gratitude. Merrick's identity has been erased by society's need to make him their mirror ("Who Does He Remind You Of?" [39–40]). And Merrick merits our contempt for having acceded so completely to this desire for conformity. As Treves scornfully puts it, "He is excited to do anything everyone is doing if he thinks everyone is doing it" (64). This is a Merrick we can pity, but hardly admire.

Appropriately, we have become aware of Pomerance's emphasis on the "tyranny of the normal" (9), with Treves cast in the role of tyrant and normalcy the weapon he implacably wields over his most loyal subject, Merrick. We note the ironic observations in the text that the more closely Merrick mimics normalcy, the closer he moves toward death (41, 64). And, in fact, it is normality that ultimately kills him through the intervention of the Pinheads, who place him in a "normal" sleeping position. Merrick, erased and obliterated, ends up the ultimate victim of Treves's misplaced desire to make a "normal" man of him. By the end of the play, whatever might have existed of Merrick's humanity has disappeared, and his death is simply the imposition of the final colonial privilege.

Insights fly fast and furious. But it's time to go home. The students decide to return for one more discussion.

We See More Complex Truths

Despite our cleverness during session two, students come back to the third session troubled. They have thought more about the play, found pieces that don't fit, and seen hints of more complex truths. Pomerance's neat, categorical world of oppressor and oppressed doesn't always add up.

The prod to their dissatisfaction has been the play's preface, which we did not read in our first two sessions. There Pomerance says somewhat vaguely, as though he himself were not sure of the significance, "I believe the building of the church model constitutes *some kind* of central metaphor" (v; my emphasis). We examine the play again, studying all mention of cardboard construction in search of hidden meaning. Then one student locates a statement that, as she excitedly expresses it, "might be what the play is really about!" In the scene titled ironically "He Does It with Just One Hand," referring to his model making, Merrick describes how he first found the courage to begin construction of the cardboard cathedral by realizing that St. Phillips itself was only "an imitation of grace . . . flying up from the mud" (39). Perhaps, the student ventures, this line can help us reinterpret both Merrick and Treves.

Suppose, we wonder, there are no real villains or victims in this play. Suppose there are only questionable heroes, their feet stuck in the mud of cultural blinders, bigotry, and misguided values on the one hand and mind-boggling deformity, societal prejudice, and romantic fairy tales on the other, both struggling to "imitate grace" in their attitudes and actions. Viewed from this perspective, Treves is not simply the benevolent savior or the exploitive oppressor, but a complex, struggling man, besieged variously by ambition and compassion. Merrick is not only a grateful patient or oppressed victim, but also a complex, struggling man, pitiful at times, profound at others.

Our cardboard version of Treves crafted under Pomerance's politically correct tutelage begins to assume greater complexity. As we think more deeply about the physician, we realize that one aspect of the play we conveniently overlooked in our earlier discussion is the fact that Treves's biggest critic is Treves himself. He is no mere caricature of an unreflective oppressor. Before our very eyes, he changes and evolves, developing doubts he assumes himself incapable of entertaining, feeling empathy even as he accuses himself of the impossibility of experiencing this emotion. Toward the end, Treves is "sorry" for his plan urging Merrick toward normalcy (64) and has acquired a disconcerting facility to "see things others don't" (65). He experiences despair and, in a striking role reversal with his patient, ultimately is the one who must beg for help (66).

What has happened to Treves? In fact, he has been profoundly altered by his encounter with the person of Joseph Merrick. We see that the vector of effect in the doctor-patient relationship has not been unidirectional, as we had assumed, Merrick as grateful patient or oppressed victim passively receiving either the benevolent or exploitive ministrations of his physician, but rather bidirectional. In this new understanding, Treves is as influenced by Merrick as Merrick is by Treves. As Montagu and Howell and Ford assert, we begin to acknowledge that the relationship between Treves and Merrick is a complex and multifaceted one. Certainly it contains elements of exploitation and condescension, but it also contains elements of compassion, caring, and commitment.

And what of Merrick? Can he too be understood as an "imitation of grace flying up from the mud"? Merrick, we realize, is no passive victim. Instead, partly through

Treves's agency, over the course of the play Merrick progressively finds his voice, a highly symbolic development for someone initially described as "an imbecile [who] just makes sounds" (11). Further, this reclaimed voice is one that continues to advance and strengthen as the play progresses. Sometimes Merrick uses his voice to claim the mantle of normalcy, as when he tells Ross, "I am like others." At these times, Merrick demands recognition of the similarities he shares with conventional society. Elsewhere, however, his voice challenges Treves's emphasis on rules and conformity. In one witty exchange, he bests his teacher by demonstrating the emptiness of Treves's rule-governed "mercy" (57).

We May Never See "Things as They Are"

It is growing late. We realize we are reaching a stopping point, if not a conclusion. It is time to go home and turn our attention to other obligations, other priorities, other mysteries. We look at the last scene, "Final Report to Investors," and Frederick Treves's last remark: "I did think of one small thing" (71). The hospital director Carr-Gomm is attempting to bring closure to the "official version" of the Elephant Man's story, and he smugly tells Treves it is too late to add anything else. Yet the play invites speculation as to what Treves might have wanted to include. One student suggests that the surgeon intended to say, "It is all a lie. We never really knew Joseph Merrick." The rest of us, however, are not so despairing. We feel we have glimpsed Merrick in many guises, and we wonder if Treves did not also feel he knew Merrick, at least a little.

Perhaps, someone else offers, Treves might have said, "At last I *saw* Merrick," not in the sense of an exhibit, but as a human being. We are still not satisfied. While the initial proposition struck the group as too pessimistic, this one seems slightly oversimplified. We find ourselves doubting whether we can ever truly "see" another. And with Merrick, there is so little to go on. We look at each other in bewilderment. Perhaps Treves really had nothing to add.

Then, another student softly suggests that Treves might have wanted to add the words "I loved him." It is the student role-playing Treves who feels compelled to propose this possibility. As Treves, he asserts that although he may not have understood Merrick completely and at times may have belittled and diminished him, he did have feelings of love for him. Something about this suggestion moves us, and we start thumbing through the play again. There is little direct textual evidence to support this interpretation, but *The Elephant Man* certainly has some important things to say about love. In an exchange with Mrs. Kendal (32–33), Merrick slices through Romeo's narcissistic romanticism (foreshadowing Treves's later self-label of narcissist), in the process showing us someone who, despite the harsh blows life has dealt him, is capable of other-centered love. Later, Merrick demonstrates this love through the trustworthy gaze he bestows on the naked Mrs. Kendal (49). In the subsequent argument between Treves and Merrick about permissible conditions under which to contemplate a woman's nude body, Merrick, so often the "viewed," the recipient of the stares and cruelties of others, implies that unless the physician's clinical gaze, so routinely directed toward vulnerable, suffering patients, is suffused with love, it becomes unbearable (57).[10] Perhaps in the ultimate summing up of the Elephant Man, Treves has seen the importance of gazing on patients with love as well as scientific detachment. Perhaps he has learned that, in fact, he has no choice.

In these final moments, we find ourselves contemplating an open-ended interpretive model that brings us little resolution, and many possibilities. It encourages us to see Treves and Merrick both as flawed, imperfect human beings, two people in mutual and shifting relationship to each other. We have come to see the Elephant Man as only one of many roles Joseph Merrick played, recognizing that he was also dreamer, dandy, and visionary; and that in his story he was ultimately both like and unlike other men. We have come to see that Frederick Treves also played multiple roles, those of scientist, physician, politician, friend, and that all of these roles had importance to him and helped define him. Perhaps most important, we have come to see something about ourselves, for we realize that gazing upon Merrick—and upon Treves—requires appreciation for their complexities and subtleties, humility for all we will never know about them, and above all compassion for the suffering and struggles both men inevitably endured. In our encounter with *The Elephant Man,* we too find ourselves struggling to "imitate grace flying up from the mud."

NOTES

1. Pilbeam, David, 1980, "Major Trends in Human Evolution." *Current Argument on Early Man.* Ed. Lars-König Königsson. Oxford: Pergamom Press, 1980: 261–285.
2. Page numbers in parentheses refer to Pomerance 1979.
3. Graham and Oehlschlaeger 1992, ch. 9.
4. Sparks 1980.
5. Howell and Ford 1980.
6. Montagu 1996.
7. Tibbles and Cohen 1986.
8. Trombley 1989.
9. Graham and Oehlschlaeger 1992, ch. 5.
10. Foncault 1975.

References

Foucault, M. *The Birth of the Clinic: The Archeology of Medical Perception.* Trans. A. M. Sheridan Smith. New York: Random House, 1975.

Graham, P. W., and F. H. Oehlschlaeger. *Articulating the Elephant Man: Joseph Merrick and His Interpreters.* Baltimore: The Johns Hopkins University Press, 1992.

Howell, M., and P. Ford. *The True History of the Elephant Man.* London: Allison & Busby, 1980.

Montagu, A. *The Elephant Man: A Study in Human Dignity.* 3rd ed. New York: E. P. Dutton, 1996.

Pilbeam, David. "Major Trends in Human Evolution." Current Argument on Early
  Man. Ed. Lars-König Königsson. Oxford: Pergamon Press, 1980.
Pomerance, B. *The Elephant Man*. New York: Grove, 1979.
Sparks, C. *The Elephant Man*. New York: Ballantine, 1980.
Tibbles, J. A. R. and M. M. Cohen Jr. "The Proteus Syndrome: The Elephant Man
  Diagnosed," *Bmj* 293 (1986): 684–85.
Trombley, S. *Sir Frederick Treves: The Extra-Ordinary Edwardian*. London: Rout-
  ledge, 1989.

PART II

Acting without Limits: Profiles of Three Physically Disabled Performers

LILAH F. MORRIS

Thirteen years ago Art Metrano was repairing his house when he fell off the roof and broke his neck. He suffered a "hangman's fracture" and was fortunate to be left alive, though paralyzed; this type of fracture is typically fatal. Metrano's physical recovery is replete with significant daily challenges, progressing to far-reaching goals. He lacks full control over his legs, and usually walks with crutches, a tedious and strenuous process. Metrano will have some physical disability for the remainder of his life.

The process for his emotional recovery, however, has been somewhat unusual. Prior to his accident, actor Art Metrano was best known for his "magical" comedy act as "Amazing Metrano" on Johnny Carson's *Tonight Show* and for his role as the belligerent lieutenant in the *Police Academy* movies. During his rehabilitation, Metrano sought emotional strength and survival in the arena he knew best—acting. He almost immediately began writing a one-man comedic drama that offers a personal account of his debilitating accident and formidable recovery process. The aptly titled *Metrano's Accidental Comedy* straightforwardly shares Metrano's vulnerability and uncertainty without asking for sympathy. At the conclusion of the show, Metrano universalizes his adversity: he asks his audience to donate money to help others with similar disabilities.

Many actors who encounter disabling accidents during adulthood follow a course opposite to that of Metrano. Some decide to leave the acting profession, considering their disability an insurmountable hurdle in casting. Others pursue directing, technical, or other "backstage" theatrical positions. Some disabled actors embrace the disabled community and understand their place as a role model within it, while others attempt to disassociate completely, with the hope that their acting peers will learn to forget their disability. Other people with disabilities begin to explore their artistic potentials only later in life, through community theater venues.

Within this chapter I profile three disabled actors whose biographies were compiled through personal interviews conducted in early 2000. Their stories demonstrate only a fraction of the diversity that exists within disabled acting, yet illuminate some important themes. Most actors deal with their disabilities in relation to the cause of their disability (accident versus illness), their level of acting and potential prior to the disability, and the length of time they have been disabled. Sources of support during their initial diagnosis or accident, role models within the acting community, and their personal acting goals are also major influences. Some choose to become teachers and role models for other disabled actors; others pursue acting careers completely divorced from the disabled community.

Despite their differences, these profiles reveal the extent of shared issues between disabled and nondisabled actors. First, both groups face common challenges in the casting arena. The disabled actors profiled all seek access to interesting roles, regardless of whether the character is disabled. Like every other actor, they strive to avoid being typecast. In one sense, acting companies and audiences alike are to blame for wanting to see disabled actors in iconoclastic "disabled roles" that feature the disability. Many people have difficulty relating to a classic character, such as Shakespeare's Hamlet, in a wheelchair. But a "disability" typecast is no different from the buxom, exotic-looking actress who desires the role of the comedic sidekick yet is always cast as the seductress. Clearly, great actors cannot transcend their corporeal forms simply by being great actors; theater is as much about looking the part as it is about playing the part.

Both disabled and nondisabled theater companies also experience funding dilemmas. A majority of the disabled actors who desire community theater involvement have little experience, so extensive training is often a prerequisite to staging any performances. While obtaining funding for some new disabled theater groups seems prohibitively arduous, the majority of mainstream theater companies face similar challenges, and their continued status as a troupe is often questionable from one production to the next.

These similarities bring to light a crucial issue: disabled theater is not *about* disability. Rather, the theater companies that feature physically and mentally disabled actors offer those individuals a challenging, novel platform from which to work. In the majority of community theaters, let alone professional venues, those opportunities are simply and sadly unavailable. Few disabled actors have been able to bridge the gap to gain widespread acceptance within their community acting circles. Many have become inadvertent role models. As pioneers they sought initially only to promote their own careers, yet soon recognized the well-established barriers to their success that have been built by generations of closed-minded audiences.

Prior to presenting the following profiles, it is important to note that these actors represent a small segment of the disabled acting community. They are all physically disabled in a way that prevents them from full use of their bodies, yet all have complete vision, hearing, and mental faculties. One works exclusively with able-bodied theater groups, while the others participate in disabled theater companies. Although all have been involved in a wide variety of theatrical productions, they have worked mostly with previously written material or "mainstream" plays modified to involve disabled actors, as opposed to scripts that explore disabled issues. Despite many of their similarities, the uniqueness of their stories is remarkable; they offer a glimpse behind the curtain of disability into the lives of dedicated, complicated, talented, and inspiring actors.

Thierry

I've had people come up from the audience after some of our productions and say,
"You know, I never really saw the disability. I was so involved in the story and the
acting." And I believe if the actor's really doing his job right, they're not going to
focus on the disability. They're not even going to see it after a while. They just kind
of forget about it and concentrate on what's going on . . . the internal struggle.
      —THIERRY ROGERS, FOUNDER OF IRON HORSE THEATER COMPANY

Thierry Rogers stumbled into acting in his early twenties. Through a public speaking
course during his first year at the University of North Carolina, Greensboro, Thierry
met an actor who encouraged him to enroll in an acting class. Thierry excelled in the
theatrical realm and soon declared an acting major en route to pursuing a bachelor's
degree in fine arts, in theater arts. So many people discover their life's passion by
accident. By pursuing an arena of expression he had never considered, Thierry found
his voice on the stage.
      Seventeen years have passed since the summer after Thierry's junior year in
college. One afternoon, Thierry and a friend were playing with a loaded gun when
an unintentionally fired shot hit Thierry in the back, leaving him paralyzed. During
his convalescence, Thierry resolved to abandon his theater goals. "I didn't think
there would be much of a career in acting being in the chair," Thierry explains prac-
tically. When he arrived back at school the following fall, he changed his major to
psychology.
      Thierry tells his story, now seventeen years later, with the unmistakable wisdom
that only time can bestow. He speaks slowly, thoughtfully, with a deep Carolina drawl.
Two decades ago he may have been furious that fate in one moment unveiled the secret
to his passions and in the next robbed him of the means to fulfill them. Now he is com-
placent, reflective of this time in his life when he wrote off acting as unavailable.
      When Thierry returned to college, he started to drift back to the theater. "There
were a lot of things going on in my head that I needed to figure out," he recalls, "and
the theater has to do with understanding character analysis and different types of per-
sonalities. It tied in to what I was dealing with." He directed Sam Shepherd's *Tooth of
Crime* in UNCG's blackbox theater, recalling, "I didn't see [directing] as a problem in
a chair." Praise received from fellow actors and favorable reviews convinced Thierry
to stay involved in theater. He graduated with a bachelor of arts degree, double-
majoring in theater arts and psychology.
      Although Thierry abandoned acting as his primary occupational interest, he
found other ways to participate in the stage. He eventually moved to New York and
received an M.F.A. in stage direction from Brooklyn College in New York, subsequently returning to Charlotte.
      Despite his experiences in the theater capital of the United States, Thierry did
not participate in stage productions again for nearly ten years. "There were no opportunities for disabled actors in Charlotte. There just wasn't anything going on." It took

Thierry's meeting a Charlotte-based disabled acting group to spark the rebirth of his acting career and his return to the theater.

In 1997, Thierry encountered several physically and mentally disabled people who were interested in acting. None of them had ever been involved in theater, but their enthusiasm for learning motivated Thierry and offered him a way to get back to the stage. Thierry founded the Iron Horse Theater Company with these new actors and began teaching an introductory acting course for disabled people. There was no funding available for this endeavor, so Thierry volunteered his time, teaching in donated space at the Carolina Institute of Rehabilitation.

Thierry had abandoned his pursuit of theater because he felt isolated by his disability and ostracized from the mainstream acting community. Although Charlotte has never been a theater mecca, the number of community theater groups and the community's interest in theater has grown in the last decade. However, there were no disabled actors in Charlotte who had any training. "No one was auditioning. . . . No one was interested. Charlotte didn't know anything about disabled theater companies."

Janet Isenhart, the able-bodied director of the HandiAble Theater Company, changed all that. Sponsored by the Actor's Theater of Charlotte, which Janet also directs, HandiAble was established ten years ago to offer learning and production opportunities for beginning actors. Although HandiAble was founded to make acting available to the disabled community, the company has always been composed of a mix of disabled and able-bodied actors.

When Thierry met Janet in 1997, not four months after he had formed Iron Horse, HandiAble was an established theater company with nonprofit status and a grassroots grant from the Arts and Science Council to teach disabled students basic acting skills. The organization also had secured community recognition and connections. Janet and Thierry immediately recognized that the achievement of their parallel goals could be enhanced by working in tandem. Thierry became the acting coach for the combined groups, concluding with the spring 1999 production of *My Friend the Fox*.

Despite his efforts, Thierry sees the role of a disabled theater company as transitory. His goal has been to increase exposure for disabled actors to make the public recognize the talent that lies within. Ideally, he'd like to give individuals in his group the skills and the motivation to go out and audition with other local theater companies.

One might erroneously assume that the force uniting individuals involved in disabled theater companies is their disabilities. In fact, the bond unifying this group of actors, who all happen to be faced with diverse challenges, is acting. "We're not so much focused on the politics of the disabled," Thierry explains. "There's plenty of that out there. Our point is to concentrate on the acting, the creativity of the theater. Then if [the actors] want to explore [disabled issues], that's certainly fine, but that's not my focus."

Despite this lack of interest in "disabled politics," Thierry recognizes and places high importance on himself as a role model for other disabled actors. He has found that the best way to promote Iron Horse and HandiAble Theater Companies is to start building an audience through children. In addition to performing *My Friend the Fox*,

Thierry and Nancy Bezant, a blind actress, have cowritten another production intended for children. Thierry also has begun to teach acting within the schools. As disabled students are now mainstreamed in Charlotte, Thierry's work is important in helping students understand that the same opportunities available to able-bodied young people are now available to everyone.

Although the theater community in Charlotte is growing, "you can't make a living in theater," according to Thierry. Several of his seven actors have daytime jobs; others rely on social security or Medicare for support. Obtaining funding for his projects has been a major challenge. In addition to avoiding expensive royalties, Iron Horse Theater Company writes its own material to support the talents of its members and to include parts for anyone who wants to participate, including some severely disabled people. Iron Horse has applied for an access grant in conjunction with the Charlotte Parks and Recreation Center. Thierry also has submitted a request for funding to teach three two-week acting workshops at the Metrolight Association for the Blind. This project would help build future audiences as well as recruit new actors. Soon, Iron Horse will be able to apply for nonprofit status. Until then, a lack of funding prohibits the group from offering transportation, a major issue with many of its actors.

Ultimately, Thierry explains, he'd like to put himself out of business. "I know that seems strange," Thierry begins, "but I'd really like to see my people go out and become involved and get cast. Of course, we should be a base that they can come back to and know that they always have someplace to perform." Although there is predominantly stage acting in Charlotte, with few movies or television shows being shot there, Thierry feels that casting for television commercials has become more liberal. Elaine Spallone, an Iron Horse member who was Miss Wheelchair USA in 1998–99, has been recently cast in a commercial and a miniseries. Other Iron Horse actors have auditioned, but none has yet secured a role.

Thierry Rogers's move in his twenties to a city with limited acting opportunities and few disabled actors served to shape his life and ambitions across the next two decades. He has never left the theater, but his personal goals seem to have been usurped by his larger sense of purpose—working to promote other disabled actors. Thierry is building visibility for disabled actors, promoting nontraditional casting, and working through children to teach a generation that talent and creativity lie within. Thierry has created a disabled theater company to catapult his new actors into mainstream community theater. He dreams of a time when casting directors focus on talent, when audiences open their minds and see beyond the person onstage to the character being portrayed.

Chris

> "Is playing Hamlet in a wheelchair hard?"
> "Playing Hamlet is hard. I got the wheelchair down."
> —Christopher Thorton, responding to an
> interviewer discussing his portrayal of Hamlet

The house lights dim, the curtain lifts, and the audience is granted its first view of the palace gates through the contrived Denmark mist. We are introduced to the less-than-dead king, who at this point in the story is merely an eerie presence lurking just beyond these stone walls. The scene quickly changes and we move inside the castle to meet our mourning, bitter tragic hero. The side curtains are pulled aside and Prince Hamlet glides down the stage ramp, coming to a halt just left of center, his seething anger and betrayal lying upon his velvet sleeve. His entrance is quick and dramatic. Although the audience feels as if he has just stormed into the room, with Chris in the lead role, Hamlet never leaves his seat.

Christopher Thorton is a thin, tired looking thirty-two-year-old actor. When he's not performing, he dons a perpetually ruffled hairstyle, which he ascribes to a "bad haircut," atop an unshaven, pale face. Chris seems to conceal his passion for acting underneath a cool, friendly exterior. He is guarded, but perhaps that is more a product of his circumstances than his true personality. Eight years ago a rock climbing accident left Chris unable to use his legs, dependent upon a wheelchair for mobility.

Chris is one of those people who mysteriously moved through childhood and adolescence with precise knowledge of the path he would pursue in life. Because there was no theater program at his New Orleans high school, Chris's acting career wasn't launched until he enrolled in the University of New Orleans as a theater major. His first college performance experiences transformed Chris's childhood musings into tangible goals. After some successful roles, including the coveted part of Shakespeare's Romeo, Chris began to realize that talent, not schooling, was the most essential ingredient to becoming a successful actor. Two and a half years after entering the University of New Orleans, Chris left school and followed his dreams to Los Angeles.

Chris had a few B-movie and minor film acting roles under his belt when he came across the prestigious Stella Adler Academy of Acting. For Chris, the experience of meeting, studying, and interacting with this talented group of actors under the direction of a true role model was pivotal. He recalls his time at the school: "It was a whole different level of acting. It made you want to be more than you were. You go into that class thinking that a movie star is the career to have and you come out wanting to read Chekhov." Chris was twenty-one when he met Stella Adler. He stayed with the school for three and a half years.

At nearly twenty-five years of age, Chris began to recognize the impracticality of his situation. Los Angeles is a city built around the entertainment industry, but the stage stands like a distant, neglected relative to the omnipotent screen and television media. Building a financially solvent lifestyle from a career in theater in Los Angeles is a near impossibility. However, Chris was set on establishing his life in Los Angeles, and despite his love for the stage, there were allures for him in film acting as well. To see one's work reach mass audiences in the way that only film or television can achieve is an appealing vision. So Chris auditioned for television and movie roles while continuing to perform in at least one theater production each year.

In August 1992, shortly after leaving the Stella Adler Academy, Chris fell from a mountain while rock climbing. A spinal cord injury left him paralyzed below the waist.

Unquestionably, the most difficult acting role involves playing a part with which one has absolutely no experience. The obvious tendency, yet the most deadly pitfall, is to base the portrayal on a familiar icon or stereotype without ever uncovering the singularity of the character's situation.

"I couldn't move," Chris recalled of his first few weeks after the accident, "and it feels like you can't do anything . . . like you'll never be able to do anything again. And then the anger and the depression and the misery of it sets in. . . . So much of that has to do with a fear of the unknown because you've never been paralyzed before. The only experience you have with wheelchairs is the image in your head of those people you've seen in chairs, and all of the sudden you're one of them." Chris did not take to his new role immediately. He described writing off acting as something he just couldn't do anymore.

A combination of a strong support network, Chris's fierce personal ambitions, and his already formed reputation as a talented young actor made him recognize that his acting career was far from over. Less than six months after the accident Chris was cast in and began rehearsals for *Waiting for Godot.* The show proved successful, both within the community and for Chris's psychological healing process. The experience also helped Chris regain confidence in his acting abilities and reconcile his new appearance: "I had a really hard time getting on stage after my accident because I thought I looked bad, or just dumb. You just don't feel like yourself. But when I got up on stage again, I realized that the instincts were still there. And everything else just goes out the window."

The motivation for the production of *Hamlet* described above, in which Chris played the young prince, performed by the neophyte Joanne Linville Ensemble at Hollywood's Lillian Theatre in early 2000, originated in a classroom. In spring 1999, Chris read a scene from *Hamlet* for a class of Joanne Linville's, his former acting teacher. By chance, Chris met a group of actors who were trying to figure out how to become a theater company and stage their inaugural production. According to Chris, they proposed staging a production of *Hamlet* with Chris cast as the prince. "They really handed me this great part," recalls Chris. "They loved the scene, and they essentially decided to build a play around it. It was a real gift to me." He is very quick to add, "It was never about the wheelchair at all. The theory is that you don't decide to put on *Hamlet* and then look for a Hamlet. You wait until a Hamlet presents himself. And Joanne, God bless her, felt that I was at a place age-wise and development-wise to play Hamlet. It really had nothing to do with the chair."

Despite Chris's attempts to distance his acting from his physical limitations, he alone appeared on advertisements and on the program cover with his wheelchair in profile, staring out at his audience. As an explanation for this choice of representative photographs, he simply repeats the obvious: "If you take a picture of me, unless it's a headshot, you're going to see the wheelchair." However, this icon of a wheelchair-bound prince introduces the audience to a new conception of Hamlet. The young Dane whose tragic flaw lies in his inability to act is so emotionally disabled that the wheelchair becomes merely a physical manifestation of his intellectual drama. From the moment he first speeds down the ramp to center stage to denounce vehemently his father's murder and his mother's hasty marriage, Hamlet appears to be not just mentally, but physically ill. His skin is pale, and at points his torso appears to be held up only by the chair.

Despite the potentially novel intellectual interpretations surrounding a wheelchair-bound Hamlet and the opportunity for a disabled actor cast in such a classic role to serve as a role model for other disabled actors, Chris repeatedly attempts to divorce himself from his wheelchair, in effect to sever the link between his body and his mind. Although Chris read countless theoretical discussions about approaching the role of Hamlet, he claims that the theater company never discussed the fact that this Hamlet was in a wheelchair. This omission, although somewhat understandable in light of Chris's reluctance, is still striking from a group of dedicated, intellectually motivated, professional Hollywood actors.

Although he has had some success in television and movie roles playing disabled characters, he explains that being typecast to play a disabled person lacks challenge. Chris has never played a disabled role in theater, which he credits to the medium's openness. "It's much more interesting to me to play somebody who's in a chair, but dealing with everything but." To Chris, this is the most formidable task of his own life: "The truth of it is, after a while your life is not about [being disabled] anymore. . . . It's just another part of your routine, but your life doesn't revolve around it." It is apparent that Hollywood feels constrained by this image, and the majority of successful screen and television writers portray disabled people in roles in which the disability is tantamount.

Chris has chosen to focus his career on pursuing acting opportunities within mainstream, rather than disabled, theater companies. He explains, "There are people who do such admirable things for the disabled community. . . . The flip side of working within the disabled community is that your entire life revolves around the disability." Instead, Chris believes that his particular contributions, like playing Hamlet four nights each week, are just as essential to the disabled community as any advocacy work with which he could be involved. "I could start a disabled theater group that would produce its own *Hamlet*, and you'd see that a disabled person can play Hamlet, but I think it's more potent if I went out and did it in a completely nondisabled group and I was given the part for reasons that had nothing to do with the wheelchair." The awareness for the disabled community, he explains, will always come as a result.

Chris's immediate goals involve melding writing and acting. He strives to create the character of which he constantly speaks—the physically disabled guy who is dealing with everything life brings *from,* not *through,* a chair. A few years ago Chris wrote, coproduced, and played the lead in a successful short film that whetted his appetite for filmmaking. In the last eight years his theatrical acting career has continued at much the same pace and progress as it had prior to his accident. Hollywood, however, has not been so inviting. Chris feels that only through writing parts for himself will he be able to play challenging movie roles.

In Chris's eyes, acting was the thing he was born to do. It is clear now that acting is Chris's life force. The Los Angeles theater scene that embraced Chris when he first

Disability as
/ab-/normal to
scale
pop.
cultur

arrived twelve years ago has rendered his wheelchair invisible. In late 1999 it handed him any male actor's role of a lifetime, the part of the young, betrayed, emotionally incapacitated Danish prince. Hollywood, thus far, has not been so open-minded. Art doesn't always imitate life; it often creates for it a new truth. Bodies on the silver screen are examples of this contrived reality—always too beautiful, too thin, and unobtainable. And disabled characters as written are first and foremost disabled, but that is not reality—that is Hollywood's version of the story. Perhaps if Chris's writing is successfully produced he will have the opportunity to place disabled characters in roles that have never before been accessible.

Robin

I've noticed that in television, in movies, and in theater, the disabled character is always either completely pitied or a total superhero. I keep thinking, "We're just like everybody else. We're not all good or bad. We're not all superheros, either."
—ROBIN DAVIS, FOUNDING MEMBER OF CENTER STAGE PLAYERS

Despite her current ambitions, in her youth Robin Davis never considered acting as a career choice. In fact, it is possible that Robin never thought much about pursuing a "career." Robin has muscular dystrophy, a degenerative genetic disease characterized by progressive weakening of the muscles that control movement. Although she has worked sporadically at various low-skill jobs, investing in a career is complicated at best when she never knows the course her disease will take or the new limitations the following day might bring.

Robin is a charming, upbeat woman who, now thirty-two, speaks with a clear, articulate confidence about her experiences. When she was nineteen, Robin participated in the inaugural acting class at the Center for the Physically Limited, in Tulsa, Oklahoma. She initially enrolled in the course only to support the teacher's efforts, but Robin soon recognized the enjoyment that acting brought her. She quickly sought out ways to pursue her ambitions further.

Robin gained confidence in her performance abilities through the support of her acting coach and a gradual awareness of her innate talents. She became one of the five founding members of the Center Stage Players, a disabled theater company based at the Center for the Physically Limited. It was soon apparent that the group needed community involvement to progress. After a successful show in collaboration with a local theater company, the Center Stage Players opened auditions in an attempt to expand beyond a "disabled group" into a community theater company.

When Robin first began acting, she was excited primarily by the unique opportunity it offered her—the invigoration she experienced doing something that she had always believed was inaccessible to her. After a few years with success in playing small parts, Robin began searching for more challenges.

Robin speaks plainly about her physical limitations. She acts from an electric wheelchair because she is unable to use her legs, has little arm movement from her elbows to her shoulders, and is unable to lift anything over a pound. Because she has full motion in her head and neck, Robin relies a great deal upon facial expressions to convey her characters' emotions.

As any actor should be, Robin is also keenly aware of her limitations onstage. "I enjoy comedy, but I find the comedies a lot harder for me because there's a lot of physicality involved," Robin explains. "With drama I can use my facial expressions and my voice a lot better." However, Robin resents the disability typecasting that occurs in local theater companies: "Outside the center, all the roles I've played have been disabled characters. And while I'm grateful for the opportunity to act outside the center, I'm looking for more open-mindedness. Just because I'm disabled doesn't mean that's all I can play."

In the last few years, Robin has acted in several classic plays, including a small role in *1918,* the part of Helena in *A Midsummer Night's Dream,* and the grandmother in *Grapes of Wrath.* Robin most recently played a role in a two-person cutting of *The Exercise* at a competition with the Oklahoma Community Theater Association (OCTA). The scene won second prize for best performance, and Robin and her acting partner both received best acting awards. She had similar success with the OCTA's 1991 competition, at which she received a second prize and another best acting award.

Despite the level of acting Robin has achieved, she still feels limited by the constraints within her theater community. While local theaters are typically accepting of a disabled person playing a disabled character, they have not yet opened their doors to the possibility of nontraditional casting. And at the other end, while the Center Stage Players always offered a home to Robin, she does not feel consistently challenged by the opportunities available. The Center for the Physically Limited is designed for all levels of disabilities, and the acting program has sparked widespread interest; thus, it has been difficult to maintain its appeal among the more advanced members.

In addition, there are definite audience stereotypes associated with a production billed under the Center for the Physically Limited. "We advertise that we're putting on a play," Robin explains, "and the audiences in Tulsa seem to get it into their heads, 'Oh, isn't that cute. . . . We'll go watch them do their little show.' They don't give us the credit for being serious actors."

The Center Stage Players is able to recruit new audiences through Tulsa's Summer Stage, during which all of the community theater groups stage performances at the Performing Arts Theater. In the most recent Summer Stage, for instance, the Center Stage Players performed Lee Blessing's *A Walk in the Woods,* which chronicles the relationship between an older Russian diplomat and a young American diplomat in the off-hours during a peace conference in Geneva. The billing for the performance describes how it "deals with weighty issues ranging from the difficulty of communicating across generations, languages, and nationalities to the impact of one person's work on matters of global significance." Participation in Summer Stage lends the Center Stage Players legitimacy. As little is mentioned about the mixed disabled and nondisabled cast, and the play is performed among other community works within the context of a community theater group, Summer Stage audiences may regard the Center Stage Players more seriously.

Although they mostly perform mainstream, previously written material, the center has, on occasion, worked within the "disability genre." In 1990, disabled center members and teachers collaborated to write *Shade,* a series of comedic scenes about life as a disabled person. The mixed disabled and able-bodied cast that toured *Shade* around Oklahoma and Arkansas sought to make audiences more comfortable with disabilities. For example, one scene featured a disabled boy who fell out of his wheelchair, depicting the panic that ensued among the nondisabled bystanders. Able-bodied people chaotically attempting to help this boy (one woman frantically suggests, "Call 911!") seem ridiculous as his small voice gently insists that this is a common occurrence; he is perfectly capable of getting back in his wheelchair. *Shade* asks audiences to laugh along with disabled people at the everyday issues they encounter. Initially, Robin explained, audiences were wary of this type of comedy, afraid of laughing *at* disabled people. "Once the ice was broken," she recalls, "they loved it."

Robin has also been involved in a number of center productions that were written for actors with full physical movement. Robin and another wheelchair-bound actor performed *Dancing the Box Step.* A choreographer helped the pair develop a "dance" routine that involved coordinated wheelchair movements. A swordfight in *A Midsummer Night's Dream* was staged by an actor who had sword experience from the University of Tulsa.

As an advocate for disabled actors, Robin performed at a disability conference in Seattle, Washington, in 1992. She relished in the opportunity to connect with other disabled actors nationally, but her primary goal has been intracommunity work. She feels that her most important personal accomplishment has been to inspire other members of the Tulsa disabled community to become involved in acting.

As Robin begins to branch out from the center's productions to pursue other community acting opportunities, the center is having difficulty finding actors and securing funding for its theater program. More severely disabled people are attending the center, and there is a dearth of actors ready to perform onstage. Grants are dependent upon having a certain ratio of disabled to nondisabled actors, which is challenging to maintain with so many disabled actors with low skill levels. Unfortunately, most funding agencies do not consider the fact that the Center Stage Players' backstage crew is comprised nearly exclusively of disabled people. Robin is concerned about the survival of Center Stage Players, even within the next year.

In an attempt to be accepted into other community theater companies, Robin began her first formal acting training in fall 2000, attending junior college acting classes. This enables her to perform in plays associated with the college, adding acting credits in plays totally separate from the center. "I'm not looking for anything professional," Robin explains. "I'd really just like to have the opportunity to do more community plays."

Along with Robin, many other center participants have only sporadically held full-time employment; government funding does not offer incentives to work. Therefore, many people depend upon the center's activities for much of their daily stimulation. Acting has offered Robin and others intellectual challenges, excitement, and new skills. The Center Stage Players developed to give new disabled actors a place to perform in exciting roles that they would not have access to in community theater. Perhaps Robin's ambition and courage will not only inspire other actors, but bridge the gap between a disabled acting group and mainstream community theater.

Disabled theater companies are about creating a space for developing talent in individuals who are not accepted in mainstream arenas. The "disabled genre" of writing that I uncovered has much more to do with creating interesting, non–disability-focused characters that can be played by disabled actors rather than with dissecting "disabled issues." Of course, I have offered here a minute sampling of the American disabled theater community—three physically disabled, wheelchair-bound actors. There is a large network of disabled theater groups in communities across the United States that range from offering opportunities for creativity to severely mentally or physically disabled adults and children, to allowing some of the most talented actors an open stage on which to shine.

Ideally, as Thierry Rodgers described, disabled theater companies will put themselves out of business. For that to happen, centers and community groups that interact with disabled people need to continue to offer acting courses and to give new actors a chance to participate in productions. The mainstream theater community and audiences alike need to open their minds and recognize that disabled actors, like all other disabled people, do not define themselves by their disability. When audiences see Chris play Hamlet, perhaps they will begin to recognize that the majority of classic characters, just like most people, have disabilities. Perhaps they will learn to look beyond the chair and open the doors to talent and beauty.

Two-Act Play

NANCY BEZANT

Can a blind actor play a role as well as a sighted actor? Troubled by what seemed to be my coactor's increasing fear of falling off down stage, I again question my philosophy that a blind person such as she could act equally as well as any "normal" person.

Annie was playing a page in the children's play we were working on and she had great attitude in her voice, yet it appeared that she lost confidence in her mobility during the move from the rehearsal space to the professional stage. Naturally, concern for Ann prompted changes to be made to her blocking. Unfortunately, the space she worked in became smaller and smaller and her cohort, the villain, became meaner and meaner, pushing her around to get her into position. It was a director's nightmare.

It was Annie's nightmare too, more so. Ideally a blind person prefers a generous amount of time to get comfortable with change. After all, the surroundings must be mapped out by memory, quite a task. Nevertheless, it is common for actors to transfer from their prep locale to the professional arena just prior to a show due to the high rent needed to pay a well-established theater auditorium for its use, in this case perhaps a thousand dollars a day, base. Therefore, a request for extra time there to perfect acting skills would have been unreasonable. However, at the onset, when I emphatically requested that our practice area (a warehouse floor) be marked off to mirror the performance area, the only accommodation made was the introduction of chairs for entrance markers, but they were easily moved out of place. The "stage" remained vaguely defined. Since our director was the sweet-and-sour type, it was difficult to tell whether she was being impudent or merely lacked empathy when she repetitively stated she would have someone measure the stage, but waited until the end of our practice to tell us it was close in measurement. Undoubtedly, she simply relied on her own judgment for the space, having worked in the business for ten years, because the sighted could make the minor adjustments; for the sightless it would continue to be a source of anxiety, one of many. I considered the matter to be the director's "blind spot," as well as a miniature reflection of society as a whole, where perhaps a direct hands-on (if you have them) learning experience involving the handicapped is the best source of education.

Blind spot or no, our director did take us on a personal tour of the auditorium in advance. So, I bit my lip and bore it during the scant dress rehearsals when the entire cast, made up primarily of disabled actors, warily worked their new surroundings, especially around the four-foot drop, where quick recovery from an accidental fall would be impossible for most. Daunted by close calls, Annie would say, "I'm not worried so much about falling. I'm worried about how fast you're going to pick me up when I do." Even given statements like that, I predicted that Ann would regain her confidence before long. Instead her aplomb waned until she was very upset. Fellow actors encouraged her. I touched her warmly, assuring her that she was doing great and would continue to do so. Annie made it through her first professional stint; her performance was terrific, but she was shaken.

What went wrong? I am certain that I had the right philosophy about the blind actor; after all, I am blind myself. Beyond that, this was a handicapped-friendly theater company. In fact, it was the second company I'd worked with whose outreach targeted disabled artists.

The first was headed/directed by a gifted paraplegic who would say enthusiastically to a potential newcomer, "We take able-bodied or disabled-bodied," a term I thought awkward at first. It was working with this company that I would learn more about disabilities than at any other time. It was during that time that I realized something else.

I well remember the birth of our little theater group in the city. Introductions unveiled an already talented group. We played theatrical games, mostly improvisation, and we got to know each other through those games. Then we were guided through cold readings, skits, and plays. With thought, our director gleaned our fears by having us try a piece the way he visualized it but listening and working with us when we needed to do something differently. Thus, my mind was prepared to maintain a certain level of confidence while I worked. I saw that same mindset in the other members. We learned about ourselves; we learned about each other. We pushed ourselves; we pushed each other, always respectfully. It was done with the kind of respect only an artist can yield while working a sculpture, foreseeing the summation of the assorted materials. At least that's the way I envisioned us—as *art*. For we were partially made of chemicals, plastic, metal, fabric, and wood. Also, we had colorful backgrounds, exciting experiences, and shining accomplishments. Together with the able-bodied members, our theater company added some unique dimensions to the stage.

Furthermore, for many disabled dramatists, there is a glasslike infrastructure within us that is rarely exhibited. It is tempered by experience and acceptance of one's limitations but is fragile and may at times require restoration work. Like the "fourth wall," which is an acting term for the invisible wall between an actor and the audience, between the story and reality, it is either accidentally or tastefully exposed. Similarly, this inner wall exists between an actor and his or her handicap, between mind and reality. It is the difference between a dictionary definition of *handicap—a mental or physical disability; a disadvantage or deficiency; a hindrance*—and the implied definition—*problem, what problem?* In other words, faith to overcome any obstacle is the core concept.

So, within that concept, any barrier to the mind or body must be bypassed. I say "bypassed" rather than "ignored" because I'm not one of those handicapped individuals who live in a constant state of denial. To be sure, that is the way some people cope with their disability. However, it strikes me as funny to hear anyone say that they do not consider themselves handicapped, then list complaints or seek sympathy. I also shake my head when a search is made for new words to describe a particular impairment. For example: in mental health, the language has changed from retarded, to mentally challenged, to exceptional. No matter the name given, the negative stigma is reattached by uneducated or insensitive people.

The stigma is there; work around it. The obstacle is there; work around it. The handicap exists; do your best work within it. If it requires the use of others, so be it. It is not a sin to use assistance if it is required or even if it makes activity less stressful. Once I had a coactor in a wheelchair lead me safely off stage. To the audience it may have appeared that I was pushing her, when in reality she has no handlebars on her wheelchair because she doesn't like to be pushed. She gave of herself to make it easier for me.

Just as it is not a sin to use assistance, it is not a crime to make a mistake onstage due to the nature of one's handicap. If the inner wall is broken momentarily, make peace with reality and move on; the audience will go there with you. Besides, more often than not it is the one making the error who notices rather than the audience. If I may quote one of my directors, he said, "Ninety percent of the time, ninety percent of the people do not realize when a mistake has been made." That is comforting information, particularly since I have made my own share of mistakes due to the nature of my handicap. I must commit so much to memory, including sound and touch, that one can imagine the consequences that may result from the simplest of changes. Since change in live theater is inevitable, I try to prepare for it wherever it is most likely to occur. If my placement in a scene is critical, then I may count my steps before planting rather than using a general feeling for the number of steps. I may have to determine the speed at which I approach an object or person so that if I miscalculate it won't become a bowling event. Also I must ask myself what are the risks to my personal safety. However, no amount of preparation will eliminate disorientation, which is as much a mental challenge as a physical one.

Interestingly, a major cause of disorientation is a change in sound. Traveling sound waves bounce off solid objects. Therefore, any change in my location presents a new acoustical arrangement of those waves.

In one play I assumed the role of a runaway teenager with a baby. We had changed locations to an outdoor venue when previous to that there were walls to contain and reflect sound. Now the sound traveled away from us, and though my coactor was not many steps away, it seemed like a million miles, and I didn't know how to get back to her, although I had performed the play several times in a couple of locations. Covering, my attentive coactor called me back by asking me to show her the baby.

Once during the rehearsal of another play, the acoustics were good but all of the actors in the wings were unusually quiet. I had been using them subconsciously as a guide. Now in the silence I was turned around, and I left off stage at an improper angle, putting me right in their midst. I asked, "What are you doing over here?" Then a sick feeling came over me as I heard the play continue. My director wasn't aware of the puzzle in my head. My husband, who played opposite me, knowing me well, explained it to him while I was still in my state of confusion.

With the variety of experiences such as those, I could dig for the answer to the question of what went wrong for Annie, the page, in the children's play we were working on. She was facing the same enemy as I: change. The stage hands kept moving the rock that she was supposed to position herself on. Because of this, the villain had to pull her around and push her down onto it. In a different scene, the page was to meet the villain down stage under a special, but Annie couldn't find the light, so the villain had to assist. Of course, down stage was already a concern for Annie, as she didn't want to find herself lying on the floor below, in embarrassment. These things were excusable because of the nature of her handicap. Moreover, I knew this was only part of the battle waging within her: she was discouraged when she received criticism from the director; she had received bad news that a friend had passed away; she had serious health problems as well as family problems. I was amazed how she worked through it all. What a strong inner wall she had! Later our director gave her some encouragement when she told Annie that she did a wonderful job for her first time. No truer words could have been said.

It was a real pleasure working with Annie, and if anything went wrong it was that she copied me by not using a cane or guide dog while working. The option to use such aids is always open, particularly for those dangerous situations like the edge of the stage, though assistive paraphernalia has its own set of problems. Regardless, we fooled most of the people most of the time. So can a blind actor play a role as well as a sighted actor? Yes, yes. Annie and I each acted in two parts; one was the character we portrayed and the other was a sighted person.

An Interview with James MacDonald

THOMAS FAHY

James MacDonald has lived in England for over thirty years and is currently a writer-in-residence at Exeter University. As a playwright, MacDonald has struggled to get his work about disability published and produced, finding British theater and the public reluctant to accept disability as a topic for art. This response to disability theater—drama written and performed by disabled people—reflects an ongoing discomfort with visible difference. Most audiences see the disabled body on stage as something that requires explanation and justification, and in a similar way, they often question the value and quality of work produced by the disabled. In these ways, the stigma of disability takes precedence over the art itself. Both society's unwillingness to accept difference and inability to move beyond the physical as a standard for judgment are focal points for MacDonald's writing. He often explores the ways that disability intersects with differences in sexuality, class, and ethnicity through characters who struggle to find social acceptance and a sense of belonging outside of the disabled community. His most recently published plays include *As Russia Goes (Left-Handed Enterprise* and *Kleptocrats)* and *Balance Is Stillness,* in this volume. I began the interview by asking him to talk about his background as a playwright.

JM: I was born in Chicago, grew up in France, and have lived for the past thirty-one years in England. I have been writing plays since the early 1960s, although my stuff wasn't staged until 1980. Two associations have been watersheds for me. Peter Thomson, Professor of Drama at Exeter, retiring this year, is a first-round judge in a student play competition. He short-listed six of my plays while I was a student and has been my most consistent supporter ever since. After my play *Too Many Monkeys* was staged in Edinburgh, I sent the script to Margaret Ramsay [the celebrated play agent here]. She took me on, as it were, and advised me to strengthen my contact with the Exeter drama department. I'm there as a kind of writer-in-residence, as others are at similar institutions.

If none of my plays has enjoyed a major production, most of them after 1980 have had some kind of performance, usually with a combination professional/drama student cast.

Since most working playwrights in England live at or near the poverty line, my own relative lack of success may not be completely atypical. I have been working with a professional director for five years now, and it is a shame that theater in Britain, for all its reputation abroad, is so precarious.

TF: As a disabled playwright, what difficulties have you had getting your work published and performed? Why do you think this is? What are some of the obstacles facings those who write about disability?

JM: How long, really, is a piece of string? I have had considerable difficulty getting my plays put on. The vexing question is how far this has had to do with disability. And I take the word to refer to people's response both to me as a disabled person and to the subject of disability in plays.

And, generally speaking, I would say further that this has to do with how receptive people are to the mere fact of disability. This may strain your credulity, but twenty years ago, disabled people weren't widely visible in British society. They weren't being educated, so how could they even begin to assimilate? I know this from the number of times I, as a cerebral palsied person, was mistaken for a drunk and the amount of difficulty this created over the whole of my life. I had difficulty finding accommodation, for instance, and in freely entering a restaurant or shop. If I managed to convince the relevant people I was, indeed, "disabled," I still had to deal with *that*.

British society overall hasn't been good about dealing with *difference*. If it was, disability would be recognized, first of all, for what it is, and then dealt with humanely. If people can't even acknowledge it, how can they engage with it to overcome the problem? We are still dealing with the differences thrown up by class barriers, so others—sexual, ethnic, and physical—must be some way off being addressed. Things have improved. Disabled people are now generally visible at least. But being accepted remains a future stage of progress; how far in the future I don't know.

In terms of plays about disability (my own for the moment), their reception has rather fallen in step with people's attitude toward disability. I was told that two, for instance, were "too depressing" for transfer beyond the fringe, although both reflected my life and my experience of being disabled in Britain. Maybe it remains for able-bodied writers to write about disability, because *they* know what the able-bodied market can bear. But it all adds considerable pressure to one's efforts simply to write for performance.

TF: Have you seen any changes in these attitudes in the last few years? Have plays that address some of the social, cultural, and political dimensions of disability become more mainstream? Are they at least beginning to reach a broader audience?

JM: Not plays, no. The most mainstream plays about disability that I know about were written by able-bodied writers . . . and earlier than in the last decade. Disabled *issues* are beginning to be raised on network television. The BBC and the commercial networks have had disabled "slots." But I doubt very much that these programs are being made by disabled people. All right, perhaps no disabled person is qualified to make them. But neither are disabled people being trained. How, then, can they enter the mainstream?

Several years ago, a television company approached me about a short play I'd written with a disabled theme. The idea was that they would mount a production of it—which would have given it a wider audience than any theater play ever has. Of course, I accepted. When the line crew came down to discuss the project, though, the producer suddenly had the notion of doing a profile on me instead—not only that, a profile about my floppy marriage at the time. This was *really* what people wanted to know about, she said. It smacked of tabloid journalism, to me, again with the able-bodied dictating a life. I wasn't even going to be featured as a *writer*—and that was the whole point, to *me*—my "able-bodied" play. (Does it surprise you that I turned them down?) The network has somewhat mended its ways since then. Recently they did feature five-minute shorts by disabled filmmakers. But this should have happened years ago, before the experience of my play.

I think theater groups need to win a few fringe awards before their work is shown at what would be called "mainstream" theater venues. Some do tour, and some attract the collaborative interest of people like Steven Berkoff. In the States, I believe, Robert Wilson has used disabled performers in his work. And I approve of that. I'd far rather been seen as an artifact than as "disabled." But that's still at several removes from disabled companies generating their own work and becoming mainstream thereby.

TF: What directions do you hope disability theater will take in the next decade? How do you think they could increase their viewership?

JM: I would hope that disability could gain the kind of presence that other minority interests and issues have. This might well result in a "ghetto" of disabled drama. But at the moment there is still too little disabled drama of any kind. Progressive theaters, providing spaces for young people, might just as readily extend their facilities to disabled groups. They advertise pushing back frontiers, being daring. It might be "the final frontier" for these Young Turks of today's theater to bring in a troupe of disabled performers. It's bound to happen sooner or later. But, for the time being, they're still celebrating their accommodation for the disabled audience.

While I think of it, there is an established form of theater that targets the disabled as participants. It's called "drama therapy" and it shouldn't be used to substitute for work by bona fide disabled groups. "Disabled theater" I take to be work by accomplished theater people who happen to be disabled. They exist "in industrial numbers," I think. A blind drama student I know graduated from university this past June—with a first, as though anybody thought she'd get anything less. She's so accomplished a performer that she could appear sighted in a role. She played Mrs. Warren without difficulty. She and all others like her need to be given the chance, that's all.

TF: In regards to your most recent play, *Balance Is Stillness,* I noticed that you use sexuality to critique some of the binaries (homosexual/heterosexual and disabled/nondisabled) that prevent people from accepting difference. Could you comment more on the intersection between disability and sexuality in *Balance* and in your works more generally?

JM: I think the two leads in *Balance Is Stillness* use their sexual orientation to form a bond with the children in their care—possibly seeing the difference as their "disability." And the binaries you mention are there, certainly. A trigger binary for me (as far as I can interpret my own work) is innocence and experience toward an inquiry into how much society will accept. To see this in sexual terms, the carers' sexuality is depicted as being almost prepubescent, in keeping with the care of toddlers. Both are loving and lovable, reflecting difference in its most acceptable form. The gray area surfaces when disability develops into something autonomous, proactive, adult and threatening, and the sexuality becomes predatory and carnal. It's bound to happen as surely as these kids are bound to grow into adults. The inquiry was into what people do about the change. It changes them in the process, as the play shows, I hope.

There is a genre that seems to equate sexual deviation with physical deformity. Carson McCullers is one exponent. The work of Ramon Vaille-Inclan touches on this in play form. A play by John B. Keane, called *Sharon's Grave,* also investigates this association. I am aware of it, though not in my work as a whole, and I wasn't conscious of it when I wrote *Balance.* Which isn't to say that it isn't there.

TF: Some of the issues you raise about sexuality and the "dangers" of expressing nonheterosexual desire in front of children remind me of Lillian Hellman's *The Children's Hour.* Did you have this or any other works in mind while writing *Balance*?

JM: Lillian Hellman has been the longest-standing influence in my writing life. I thank you for bringing her up. Ironically, though, *The Children's Hour* is my least favorite Hellman play, and I wasn't conscious of it when writing *Balance.* Again, that doesn't mean there aren't similarities. My Emma's manipulative skills may well resemble Mary Tilford's, for instance, and she disturbs the lives of two nice women as Mary does Karen's and Martha's. I don't really see *Children's Hour* as being about forbidden love, however. What's exposed rather is manipulative evil, I think, not a secret shame. Of course, I could be wrong. But Hellman's screenplay for the first film version didn't mention lesbianism. There again, sexual awakening comes into it. But maybe it's only a coefficient for the larger focus of manipulative power, a recurring theme in Hellman's work. Hellman admitted she couldn't write love scenes, and in the play itself, someone says love ought to be "casual." It isn't that in the play—it's very messy. And I think I can see what you're getting at with my play. Emma has sexual drives, and she isn't meant to—she's meant to be uncomplicated, "angelic," like the kids. So, yes, both plays present situations where responsibilities are hived off.

One other way in which Hellman has influenced all my work (and I hope it's true of *Balance*) is with her practiced belief that playwrights shouldn't dislike any character. Working playwrights know this, of course, but she stated it precisely, and, along with her influence generally, this is something I've taken with me throughout my writing life. It's true, isn't it? The longer characters are onstage, the more sympathetic they become, because the more you are seeing the world from their standpoint, however flawed they may be. I liked the world I was writing about, liked the characters and the issues they were struggling with. Why bother with them else? Feminists might disagree. But I love women and love writing about women. Assuming they're real enough in this play, their ways of coping with the problems were engaging to me—because *they* engage with them. I wanted very much to set this inquiry in a world I could care about, not one which provoked my anger. That has a lot to do with why I wrote the play and where Hellman's influence has affected me consciously.

TF: As a playwright, how do you see your work fitting into drama of the late twentieth and early twenty-first century?

JM: For the last decade, new British drama has been dominated by what I call "in-your-face" plays . . . influenced by Tarantino, I think. My plays, I'd say, are less angry, less head-on, perhaps. I've been very influenced by the Russians, including those who are writing at the moment. The shock is there, as you might expect, given post-Soviet events. But there is also a quirky, reflective tone that's distinguished Russian drama from its beginnings. I buy into that, and I think the influence is evident in *Balance Is Stillness*. British drama is altogether harsher. People feel dislocated, postmodern, if you like. Perhaps a really shocking play including all the things we've talked about will emerge in the next few years. It's certainly due. If there is such a play, perhaps the ground underneath will shift sooner than I anticipate. I wouldn't be surprised or disappointed. Perhaps this volume [*Peering behind the Curtain*] will help pave the way. I'm delighted, anyway, to contribute to it; thank you.

Balance Is Stillness

A PLAY BY JAMES MACDONALD

Characters

Frances
Katha
Emma
Louise
Maire
Pigeon
Deirdre
Incidentals

A "special needs" center in the West Country.

Act One

The stage is deep and necessarily sparse, representing a "pool," a physiotherapy unit, and, latterly, two domestic settings. Flats represent doors. Set props consist mainly of disabled children's aids.

> *Young women's voices in unison sing a children's round,*
> *as the lights come up gradually on a "swimming pool,"*
> *represented by a pit.*

> > *Puffa train*
> > *Puffa train*
> > *Noisy lit-tle puffa train*
> > *If you're going to the sea,*
> > *Puffa train, oh, please take me*
> > *Puff puff puff*
> > *Puff puff puff*

The voices trail off in a peal of laughter as the lights rise to discover four
women in the pool ringing a fifth with joined hands and rapid movement.
FRANCES, 32, is the leader. She has the liveliness and fun of a child.
There is affectionate mischief in her social intercourse. KATHA, 33, is the
adult version. Her mischief, for instance, registers as harmless skepticism.
LOUISE, 40, is an older "mate," entering into the spirit of this collective
but otherwise fixed in a more recognizable world. MAIRE, 21, is Irish.
EMMA, 29, is the woman in the middle. She is leggy, physically, emotion-
ally, she's "bruised." The reasons for this unfold in the action.

FRANCES: Faster . . . faster. Now the other way. *(To MAIRE.)* We've got to try to create more and more turbulence, you see? *(To EMMA.)* While *you've* got to
try . . . *(giggling)* . . . to keep still.
LOUISE *(mock bark):*   Keep still now!

MAIRE stops.

FRANCES *(giggling)*:   Not *you.* You've got to try to keep *up.*
MAIRE: Oh, Christmas pudding, I'll niver git it.
EMMA: Balance is stillness.
FRANCES: Right, balance is stillness.
MAIRE: It's not, you know, it's several packets of I-don't-know-how.
LOUISE: That's why you've come on this course.
FRANCES: What's the first thing we know about water?
EMMA: It's better with your clothes off.
KATHA: It's better with Bushmills.
MAIRE: Hey, I know about that.
FRANCES: In relation to swimming, what? *(A beat.)* It *holds you up. (Taking hold of*
EMMA. Presumably this next bit would be done with wires.) If I take my friend
Emma here . . . and I try as hard as I can to push her down, she comes again.
LOUISE: Like a bad penny.
KATHA: Or a champers cork.
EMMA: Why can't I come up as me?
FRANCES: Shh. Can anybody tell me why?
MAIRE: Oh, you're looking to me for the answer?
FRANCES: She's *balanced. Buoyant.* In any kind of motion. So the first thing to tell
disabled kiddies learning to swim is the *water* . . . is a *friend.* There's no magical
formula. The disabled can swim as well as anybody else.
LOUISE: Look at Emma.
EMMA: Do you mind?
FRANCES: Emma came to us as a student . . .
KATHA: . . . and tomorrow she's going to teach you.
EMMA: So watch it.

FRANCES: Some of our best swimmers are disabled, you know.

MAIRE: Oh, I know, I know. It's jist I don't know that I can. You know.

FRANCES: Can what?

EMMA: It's easy.

LOUISE: Easy peasy.

FRANCES: Do you want to have a go now?

MAIRE: A go at . . . ? Oh, no, I couldn't.

FRANCES: There's just time before we have our tea.

MAIRE: What, in the middle, you mean?

FRANCES: I mean leading us.

MAIRE: You're niver serious.

EMMA: You won't drown us.

FRANCES: Come on, chuck, you sock it to us.

MAIRE: Do you think I dare? Look, I haven't a notion.

FRANCES: What have I been going on like this for? *(Reaching out for MAIRE'S shoulder. Laughing.)* Come back here. Where do you want us?

MAIRE: Why? You're not thinking of leaving?

FRANCES: You're the gaffer.

MAIRE: Oh, jeez, no.

FRANCES: What do you want us to try first, entry?

MAIRE: That's a good one.

FRANCES: Well . . . what?

MAIRE: Everybody in.

FRANCES *(giggles)*: Not like that.

LOUISE: We've got to get out to get in again.

EMMA: . . . you grummit.

FRANCES *(arm around MAIRE, giggling)*: You're a bit useless, aren't you.

MAIRE: Oh, I tell you I am, altogether.

FRANCES: Here, I'll be your guinea pig. Make way.

FRANCES gets out and lies prone at the edge.

Now what?

MAIRE: Oh, dear, I suppose . . . roll over.

FRANCES: *I* can't roll.

MAIRE: Oh, dear. Can you not?

FRANCES: I'm hemiplegic. You've got to roll me over.

LOUISE mutters "Roll Me Over . . ."

MAIRE *(crossing to her)*: You're not ticklish anywheres, are you?

KATHA: Get on with it!

FRANCES: You're going to need more than one to do it. Go on, delegate.

MAIRE: Righto, erm . . . you *(EMMA.)* . . . and . . . do you want a go? *(KATHA.)*

EMMA: Where do you want us?

MAIRE: Shh. Don't muddle me now. I'm jist after getting the hang of this. Right, you go that side of her . . . and put your hand under her . . . *(To FRANCES.)* . . . is that right, under your back?

FRANCES: I'll tell you when I'm in pain.

MAIRE: Sure, there's nothing stopping your mouth, is there.

KATHA *(laughs)*:   You're right about *that,* "chuck."

EMMA *(to KATHA)*:   She's a not complete looney, is she.

MAIRE: What? I mean she's not playing speech impaired! Not—

KATHA: No, she'd never convince us of *that.*

FRANCES: Shut up, you lot. *(To MAIRE.)* Carry on with the demonstration.

MAIRE: Oh, no, *you're* demon—

FRANCES: What do you do now?

MAIRE: Eh?

FRANCES: Where do you want Emma?

MAIRE: What's that? Oh, yeah. *(To EMMA.)* You come this side . . . er, no, the other.

EMMA: Make up your mind.

> As EMMA crosses to KATHA'S side of FRANCES, her clubfoot is noticeable.

MAIRE: That's right . . . and you put your hand under . . .

FRANCES: . . . under me bum, come on.

MAIRE: Right, her dur-rear.

FRANCES *(laughs)*:   Me what?

LOUISE: Perhaps that's what they call it, her side of the water.

MAIRE: No, we call it bum just like everybody else.

EMMA: We've all got one.

MAIRE: Oh, yeah, mine's like the House of Kilkenny, I know.

KATHA *(sotto voce)*:   I think it's lovely.

FRANCES *(laughs)*:   What's the House of Kilkenny?

EMMA: It's the size of her bum.

MAIRE: Right, now, into me arms now.

FRANCES: Not yet.

LOUISE: Watch it!

KATHA: Emma!

> EMMA has pushed FRANCES in before MAIRE is ready. Both scream. MAIRE loses her balance and goes backwards. FRANCES grabs hold of her.

FRANCES *(with a laugh)*:   Are you all right?

KATHA: Well, that was clever, I don't think.

EMMA: What?

LOUISE: Too much clowning about.

FRANCES *(trying to joke)*:   Perhaps you should have been the swimmer. *(A beat.)* Are you sure?

MAIRE: Yeah, I'm fine.

KATHA *(to EMMA)*:   What were you playing at?

EMMA: I wasn't playing . . . she said she was ready.

KATHA: Well, was she? *I* didn't tell you to. We're meant to do it together.

EMMA: *I* know.

LOUISE: You should have done it then, shouldn't you.

KATHA gets out and goes through the door marked "Boys."

FRANCES *(with MAIRE)*:   Here, rest by the side.

MAIRE: No, I'm all right, really.

FRANCES: It's tea-time anyway. *(Generally.)* She says she's all right. Soup and sarnies up top. And afterwards, we have a film. *Safety in the Water.*

LOUISE: Sounds appropriate.

FRANCES: Oh, yes, one more thing.

EMMA: Not another lecture. *(She goes through the door marked "Girls.")*

FRANCES: As you'll have noticed, we only have girls on the course. So you're free to use either changing room.

LOUISE *(tries to open the boys' door)*:   No, we're not . . . this one's locked.

FRANCES: Oh, sugar. *(Crossing to it.)* And I don't have the key.

KATHA *(from behind the door)*:   Just a minute.

FRANCES: Kathie?

LOUISE: Let us in.

FRANCES: Are you all right?

KATHA: I'll be out in a minute.

MAIRE *(trying to stand but can't)*:   Ow.

FRANCES crosses immediately toward her.

LOUISE: It's silly-beggars time, is it. *(At the girls'.)* Come on, Emma, open up.

EMMA *(from behind)*:   It's open.

FRANCES: Can you help me, please, Lou?

LOUISE crosses to them and gets the other side of MAIRE.

MAIRE: Oh, jeez, it's painful.

LOUISE: If it's sprain, you'll have to have a refund. You could probably claim damages from us.

MAIRE: Oh, sure, it's niver that bad.

LOUISE: You don't know that. Emma deserves a good hiding.

FRANCES: It wasn't all her fault, Lou.

LOUISE: Whose was it, Mr. Moon's?

FRANCES: It was my fault really. I started it.

LOUISE: Stop trying to take the blame.

MAIRE: No, look, I'll show you I'm all righhht. *(She's in pain.)*

FRANCES: Maybe we should get a stretcher.

MAIRE: Both of me legs are asleep.

FRANCES: That sounds more like cramp. Can you shift your weight?

MAIRE: Jist give me another minute now.

FRANCES: Careful.

KATHA has come out by now, dressed. She crosses to the women.

KATHA: Is it serious?

FRANCES: We think it may only be cramp.

LOUISE: Doesn't mean it isn't a lesson.

FRANCES: I think I want to change up at school anyway.

LOUISE: I'll help you then.

MAIRE: No, really, I think I can manage on me own.

LOUISE: You leave it to us, love.

KATHA *(crossing to the girls')*:   Emma? Can you pass us everybody's clobber?

EMMA: Everybody's?

LOUISE: I'll get it. *(She crosses to the Girls'.)*

FRANCES: I think Emma could do with some sympathy, Lou.

LOUISE: Ooh ahh. Her feelings are hurt.

FRANCES: She didn't mean it.

LOUISE: That's it, careless. She never means nothing.

KATHA: What's your problem, Louise?

LOUISE: Me? I have no problems. I just don't say sorry for what I haven't done.

MAIRE: If we're speaking of penance, maybe *I* should be the one.

LOUISE: You and Franny can say Hail Marys, I'm a Prodi dog.

MAIRE: That's all right, I forgive you.

FRANCES *(laughs, arm around her)*:   You're a card, though, aren't you, Maire. Come
    on. I think you're lovely. You won't give up on us, will you.

MAIRE: Sure, I'm not gonna sue you, what for?

LOUISE *(joining in)*:   What shall we give her, Fran, a victory lap?

MAIRE: You can pass us me bag. Give us yours as well. I fancy meself as the trolley.

KATHA: I'll bring Emma.

FRANCES *(laughing)*:   Most people get cramp only *after* they eat.

FRANCES and LOUISE carry MAIRE off.

KATHA: Emma? *(EMMA comes out, still in her swimsuit. She's been crying.)* Don't
         you want to get dressed?

EMMA: I didn't mean it.

KATHA: I know. Franny knows, too.

EMMA: Louise doesn't.

KATHA: Oh, well. You don't expect any different, do you? She's the wife of a rozzer.

EMMA: What does *that* mean?

KATHA: Everything's black and white to her. Do you want me to brush your gor-
         geous hair?

EMMA: Isn't gorgeous.

KATHA *(with a brush)*:   Says you.

EMMA: I want you to tell Louise to bog off.

KATHA: You've a wee chip on your shoulder, haven't you?

EMMA: Wouldn't *you* in my place?

KATHA: Well, yes, I suppose so. And yet I don't think you should, you know. I think
         you're far better that.

EMMA: Is that why you wouldn't change with me?

KATHA: I don't change with anyone else. And that's more to do with me, not with you.

EMMA: Franny and Lou wouldn't either.

KATHA: They were looking after Maire. You mustn't think that everything you're a
         part of comes down to you and what you see as your problems. That's more your
         problem than anything you actually do to people.

EMMA: I matter that little, you mean.

KATHA: No, now stop it. That's silly. And you know it is. I mean, for example, these
         swimming courses. Too few people signed up this time. That's why Franny was
         making an effort.

EMMA: That's how she always does it.

KATHA: All right, but it's not how she behaves when something goes wrong. Louise
         could be worried for her more than she's angry with you. You never thought of that,
         did you. I'll bet it's the truth. Are you going to tell me I don't know Franny's moods?

EMMA: Louise resents the time I spend with you and Franny.

KATHA: So? That's still her own hang-up, not yours. *We'd* tell you if you were in the
         way, don't worry. We wouldn't even have you around.

EMMA: You have to, because of my placement.

KATHA: That's the school—work. That's nothing to do with these weekend courses.
         Of which I'm getting a bit sick of myself. So that's *my* angle on what went
         wrong just now. And even then I don't think it was very much. The Irish lass did-
         n't seem to notice.

EMMA: She was hurt.

KATHA: No, she wasn't. She was fine. Everybody but you has forgotten it by now,
         and you better had, too, before it turns into your fault. If you're going to work
         here, you can't be so sensitive. It won't help the kids, will it. You're normally
         very good. I've been meaning to tell you. This is probably the time for it.

EMMA: Are you going to make it permanent then?

KATHA: I can't tell you that. I'm not allowed. And I don't know myself, for sure. It's Franny who recommends anyway, and then it has to go before the board. *(A beat.)* I can tell you one thing you might find a comfort, I don't know.

EMMA: What?

KATHA: Promise to keep it to yourself?

EMMA: Go on, tell me.

KATHA: You can probably guess anyway.

EMMA: Guess what? Kath-a.

KATHA: All right, the reason why I always use the changing room on my own.

EMMA: Well?

KATHA: All those naked bodies, crammed in together. You're not the only one with hang-ups.

EMMA: That's a hang-up?

KATHA *(stops brushing her hair)*:   I tell you . . . I nearly go wild.

> *Fade.*
> *In the darkness, FRANCES'S voice is heard reading from an adapted children's story.*

FRANCES: . . . Then Pooh turned to Piglet and said with a tearful moan, "But I can't get across to the other side . . . *I don't know how to swim.*" "Well aren't you the silliest bear that ever tasted honey," said Piglet with the broadest grin. "Of course, you're going to swim across. I'm going to *teach* you."

> *Women's laughter once more, and the lights come up partially on a section of the sleeping quarters, up right. EMMA is discovered making tea.*
> *KATHA comes on.*

KATHA: Hey, have you any idea of the time?

EMMA: I couldn't sleep. You mean I woke you?

KATHA: No, I'm too used to my creature comforts, I think. Dunno how much longer I can hack these weekends in a kid's camp bed.

EMMA: Not to mention the changing rooms.

KATHA: Watch it.

> *They smile at each other.*

   Well, let's have it then.

EMMA: Are you sure? It's not Horlicks, you know. You're not likely to get back to sleep.

KATHA: You neither. *(Grins.)* Shall we run away together?

EMMA: I'm taking the session this morning . . . that's if Lou doesn't stage a walkout.

KATHA: Oh, please. This is a fine way of making our Irish cousin feel at home. She already told me she thinks most of the English she's met act like they live in a cave.

EMMA: She didn't seem to be that way about us.

KATHA: No, I didn't say she was thinking of *us*. I think in general, before she met *us*.

EMMA: Franny thinks she's adorable.

KATHA: Yes, well, she is.

EMMA: Kath-a.

KATHA *(grins)*:   Did you know the Irish drink the most tea in the world? More than the Chinese.

EMMA: Does that mean I should pour Maire a cup?

KATHA: It's just a statistic, you dafty. It doesn't mean anything more than it means.

EMMA: I want to go home.

KATHA: Like I said, shall we sneak off?

EMMA: No, I don't. Home's the last place I want to go.

KATHA: Come here, you softie.

EMMA: Softie, dafty.

KATHA: You need your sleep. *(She cuddles her.)*

FRANCES comes on.

FRANCES: Kathie? What you doing?

KATHA: Em got up to make the tea.

FRANCES: Is it time yet?

KATHA: Isn't she good?

FRANCES: All by yourself, Emmylou?

EMMA: Don't associate us.

KATHA: Oh, don't.

FRANCES: What? *(Yawns.)* I was thinking of Emmylou Harris.

EMMA: Who's she?

FRANCES: Yank singer. *(Yawns.)* Bit too early in the morning. I haven't wunked up.

KATHA: I'll say you haven't. "Wunked"?

FRANCES: I'm never sure which it is, so I made up me own.

KATHA: At four in the morning—what else would you do?

FRANCES: Is that all it is? I think I'll go back.

LOUISE comes on.

LOUISE: Have you lot lost all your sense of proportion. What is this—midnight bean feast?

FRANCES: Sorry, Lou.

KATHA: It's closer to dawn.

LOUISE: It's closer to one in the morning!

KATHA looks at EMMA'S watch.

KATHA: You're wearing it upside down.

FRANCES *(giggles)*:   Oh, for St. Piteous's sake.

LOUISE: You may well laugh. I was about to ring Brian. Tell him there'd been a break-in.

KATHA: He's not on desk duty tonight, is he?

LOUISE: He's never on anymore—he's CID.

KATHA: Oh, that's right.

FRANCES: He wouldn't need to know anyway. We've had the new security alarm installed. Direct line to HQ. *(Yawns.)* I meant to tell people locking the pool.

LOUISE *(yawns herself)*:   I'm getting too old for this lark.

KATHA: I just said that. *(To EMMA.)* Didn't I. *(Yawns loudly.)*

LOUISE yawns again.

EMMA: Oh, for God's sake.

FRANCES *(arm around LOUISE, laughing)*:   Come on, Wheezie.

LOUISE: I think we'll have to make these Day Release jobbies.

FRANCES: It's not that bad. *(LOUISE groans.)* It's not as bad as looking after Patrick Nugent for a weekend.

LOUISE: Years ago, that. I was still in me prime.

FRANCES: What are you now?

LOUISE: In me dotage. I'll be needing a Zimmer frame soon.

EMMA: *You* said it.

FRANCES: No, you're not—you've just got primer. Remember Shits and Squits?

LOUISE: Oh, lor', yes. Shits and Squits and Jimmy Riddles.

FRANCES: Jimmy Riddles, that's right.

EMMA: What?

LOUISE *(laughing)*:   . . . and a still, small voice calling out, "Franny?" God, I haven't thought of that in years.

EMMA: Whose Jimmy Riddle?

LOUISE *(laughing)*:   Piddle.

EMMA *(anticlimax)*:   Oh.

KATHA *(to EMMA)*:   This is all about Fairacre.

FRANCES: We used to have to have to take some of the kids to Fairacre Farm for Whitsun. And Mr. Showleigh used to tell us, before the first time, "Be on the lookout for Shits and Squits and Jimmy Riddles."

LOUISE: That was his term for . . .

EMMA: . . . I worked it out.

LOUISE: . . . bodily spills in the night.

FRANCES: And one night—I think it *was* the first visit—Patrick Nugent . . . you remember him, don't you, Kathie? Spinabiff farmer's lad.

KATHA: I remember this story, too, by heart. Don't let it take all night.

FRANCES: Unlike Patrick.

LOUISE: "Franny?"

FRANCES: "Yes, Patrick, do you have to go?"

LOUISE *(trembling small voice)*:   "I think I've gone."

FRANCES: . . . the first time, I think about midnight, wasn't it, Lou?

LOUISE: The first one was, yeah, midnight, just gone.

FRANCES: So Lou and I get up, get Patrick up, out of bed, change the bedding, wash Patrick, get him back into bed, ask him, "Are you sure you're all right now, Pat?"

LOUISE: *(trembling, small voice)*:   "I'm sure . . . I'm sorry."

FRANCES: He was ever so embarrassed.

LOUISE: Didn't stop him going, though, did it.

FRANCES: No, because then, about two later, that same voice again . . .

LOUISE: "Franny?"

FRANCES: "Yes, Patrick . . . You awake, Wheeze?"

LOUISE: *Three* times altogether.

FRANCES: . . . the last time just after five.

LOUISE: By then it was nearly time to get the other kids up.

FRANCES: No, I don't think we bothered to get Patrick down again after the last time . . . let him fall asleep in his wheelchair.

LOUISE: Did we get him dressed?

FRANCES: Yeah, I think we got him dressed, put a blanket round him, and left him there.

LOUISE: He had no more jammies anyway.

FRANCES: No, that's right. Oh, but that was a night and a half.

LOUISE: Like fire-watch, during the war.

KATHA: You can remember, can you, Lou?

LOUISE: My father can. He was over at Wyvern Barracks.

EMMA: I have to go to my *grandparents* to hear stories about the war.

FRANCES *(joking)*:   This is the one against Hitler, you know, not the Boer War.

EMMA: Yeah, I know.

LOUISE: Your parents remember the war, surely. Winnie, in his homburg and boiler suit? You ask them. I bet they can.

EMMA: I can't very well do that, can I.

LOUISE: Why not?

KATHA: Lou.

LOUISE: Oh. I've done it again. I just wasn't thinking, Em. I'm sorry. Johnny Hobnail Boot, I am. Sorry.

A pause.

KATHA: She's apologized, Emma.

EMMA: Yeah, I heard her.

FRANCES *(arm around her)*:   Come on, Emmy. Beddy-byes. You have to do your
    stuff in the morning.

EMMA: *This* morning.

FRANCES: Don't remind me. I could sleep for the rest of the course.

LOUISE *(small, tearful voice again)*:   "Franny?"

KATHA: Oh, no, we're not going through that again!

EMMA: If my post is made permanent, would I have to go to Fairacre?

FRANCES: You don't fancy it, eh?

EMMA: Not the way you tell it.

LOUISE: Oh, Patrick left years ago.

FRANCES: Yeah, his son's with us now.

EMMA: His son?

FRANCES *(laughs)*:   Who do you think I am? Goodbye Mr. Chips?

    The alarm goes.

LOUISE: Oh, lord.

FRANCES: Kathie?

KATHA: Could it be like a car alarm?

FRANCES: Someone's got into the building!

    She's about to investigate when MAIRE comes on.

MAIRE: Oh, look, I really am sorry.

FRANCES: You mean it was you?

MAIRE: Feel like a fool on me fourth birt'day. I was after going out for a walk.

FRANCES: But the door's trip-locked, I told you.

MAIRE: I know, I'm that much an ej'ut. I forgot altogether.

EMMA: This time you can't say it was me!

KATHA: It looks like we've got Patrick's *daughter.*

MAIRE: Paddy who? Me own dad's a Thomas. *(They laugh.)* What? Where's the
    joke?

FRANCES *(laughs, collapsing against her)*:   Oh, you're priceless.

    Fade.
    Dogs bark in the distance as the lights come up on an area representing
    FRANCES and KATHA'S cottage deep in the Devon countryside. The
    women, minus MAIRE, are drinking mulled wine.

FRANCES: Well, team! What was the point of it all? Eh? What's the point? as they
    say.

LOUISE: What point? And who's *they* with their hat off?

FRANCES: You know—the *point* of it all.

LOUISE: You God-bothering again? Evensong finished an hour ago.

FRANCES: I go to mass.

LOUISE: Ah, that's it . . . been tippling communion wine.

KATHA: No, this is her dad's.

LOUISE: Bernard make this, Fran?

KATHA: Good, isn't it.

LOUISE: It's strong.

KATHA: I keep after him to teach an evening class.

LOUISE: Oh, I don't know. All the students would have to be breathalyzed.

FRANCES: I thought we were meant to be debriefing.

EMMA: I'm in favor of that!

> *KATHA pokes her, giggling.*

> Get off!

FRANCES: What about it? No debriefing?

LOUISE: What's there to say? We were marvelous, as per usual.

FRANCES: If we were, why didn't more people sign up?

LOUISE: All right—we were rotten?

FRANCES: That's what I say. What's the point?

LOUISE: Well, we sharpened our skills.

EMMA: Or our claws.

LOUISE: We met Maire.

FRANCES: We met Maire. *She* was marvelous, wasn't she, Kath? She was an absolute panic.

LOUISE: I bet the police thought so, too.

FRANCES: Apart from that.

KATHA: She'd be very good with some of our kids.

FRANCES: Wouldn't she just? I can see her with someone like Cassie. She'd really make her relax in the water.

EMMA: Cassie's mine.

FRANCES: Yeah, I know, Em. I was just saying.

EMMA: Cassie's due a home visit this week. I'm dreading it.

FRANCES: You'll be fine. What's that got to do with Maire? *(A beat.)* Do you think she had a good time?

KATHA: "I feel a fool on me fourth birt'day."

FRANCES *(laughs)*: What's that?

KATHA: Yeah, I think she didn't want to leave.

FRANCES: Do you really? That's a relief.

LOUISE: Is she staying in Devon?

FRANCES: She's on a job placement, like Emma.

EMMA: Do you want to give her my job?

FRANCES: No, I don't. *You've* got your job.

EMMA: I was joking.

A pause.

KATHA: It was a joke, Fran. Come on.

LOUISE: It was a joke . . . and this was a weekend away. Same as a Murder Weekend.

FRANCES *(bursts out laughing)*: Same as *what*, Wheeze?

LOUISE: Well, same sort of thing. You know what I mean.

EMMA: I know what you mean exactly.

FRANCES *(crosses to EMMA)*: I certainly hope that was a joke!

LOUISE *(rising)*: Well, I'm not going to wait to find out. *(As she starts off.)* I'll say this for it, Franny. It's weekends like this that make me remember how much I miss working here.

FRANCES: You miss the Patrick Nugents of the world?

LOUISE: I mean it. Being with you lot takes years off me. I'd forgotten how good that can be.

FRANCES: You were marvelous, too. You were. *(Going with her to "the front door.")* If you're serious, I'll speak to Sid about it.

LOUISE: Well, I would think about it, after this weekend. Thanks. You going my way, Emmy?

EMMA: No, I'm stopping here *(To KATHA.)* . . . aren't I?

KATHA: You are, indeed.

LOUISE: Well, I'll love you and leave you, in that case.

EMMA: Yeah, that sounds like you.

KATHA: Shush. *(To LOUISE.)* Bye-bye, Lulu. Thanks.

LOUISE goes off.

EMMA: "Lulu"!

KATHA: What's the matter with it . . . *(Grinning.)* Eh?

EMMA: You're getting as bad as Fran.

KATHA: Well, she's Franny's friend.

EMMA: Let her say it, then. *(Mocking.)* Franny and Emmy and Lulu . . . I want to squit!

KATHA *(teasing, maybe tickling her)*: Like Patrick Nugent.

EMMA: Get off!

KATHA: All right, then. *(Pointedly putting her hands in her lap.)*

EMMA: What did she mean about working here?

KATHA: Feel threatened?

EMMA: No, I mean when did she work here, doing what? And what's she doing now?

KATHA: Ambulance driver.

EMMA: Is she qualified?

KATHA: What a question! Of course, she's "qualified." She has to be.

EMMA: A lot of them aren't. That's been a big problem in the health service, recently.

KATHA: Well, Louise isn't part of the problem. Don't be bitchy.

EMMA: I wasn't. Only thinking what she could have done here.

KATHA: Or insecure either. She worked as a physio aid. She's not after your job. And Franny's not thinking of offering it to her. She's *not* qualified for that . . . and you are, long as you don't have a hang-up about it. I told you yesterday. I don't want to keep telling you.

EMMA: You threatening to give me the push?

KATHA: No, I'm threatening for you not to push. There's no need for it atall, as Maire might say, so stop it.

FRANCES *(returning)*:   Stop what, Kathie?

KATHA: Stop hogging all the wine. *(Reaching for the wine.)* This was our Christmas present from your mum and dad.

FRANCES: No, it wasn't. They gave us the ski holiday. *(Laughs.)* They'd never stop at a bottle of homemade wine . . .

KATHA: Good though it is.

FRANCES: . . . brilliant though it is. *(Laughs.)* What you on about?

KATHA: Well, then it was for my last birthday, and I say she's had enough. So stuff it.

FRANCES: Ooh, isn't she mean.

EMMA: She's horrid.

FRANCES: Why are you so horrid, Kath?

KATHA: I'm a mean-minded, tight-bottomed cow.

FRANCES *(giggles)*:   Kathie.

KATHA: And you both love me for it. I'm off to bed. *(Rises.)* Louise says she feels young round us.

FRANCES: Maybe she does. What's wrong with it?

KATHA: Not a thing. I just think I'm getting too old.

FRANCES: No, you're not. I'll tell you when that happens, chuck.

KATHA: Too old for a kiddy's cot, anyway. *(To EMMA.)* I don't know why you want to bother with our sofa.

EMMA: I'll tell you, if you like.

KATHA: Can it wait till tomorrow?

FRANCES: That's a point. Do you want to ring up your husband?

EMMA: No.

KATHA: That's that then.

EMMA: Do you know what he whispered in my ear the other night?

KATHA: No, of course not, how could we?

FRANCES *(laughing)*:   D'you reckon we're old enough to know?

EMMA: . . . that I was the most frigid woman he'd ever been out with.

KATHA *(brightly)*:   Oh, did he really? That's *nice. (Loaded, not sarcastic.)*

FRANCES: Kathie. What a thing to say. *(To EMMA.)* For him, too. Does he often say things like that?

EMMA: He says that next time round he wants a "whole woman."

FRANCES: Eugh. Not exactly sweet nothings at bedtime. That'd put me right off.

KATHA: Make me put him right *out*.

FRANCES: Is that what we do with him?

KATHA: I'd gizzard him first.

FRANCES: John Wayne Bobbit.

EMMA: Who?

FRANCES: No, never mind. *(A beat.)* All couples have rows though.

EMMA: Not those kind.

FRANCES: My mum and dad. Me brother. He's been married twice.

KATHA: Emma's right—not those kind of rows.

FRANCES: I don't mean to be unsympathetic.

KATHA: Well, then, don't be. Neither sets of parents rowed like that, ever. I don't imagine hers did either. Did they?

EMMA: I only remember them as loving.

KATHA: Exactly. *(To EMMA.)* He's a definite looney, your old man . . . and the sooner you're shot of him—

FRANCES: Has he hit you ever?

KATHA: That doesn't matter.

EMMA: No, he "doesn't hit cripples."

KATHA: There, you see? He doesn't need to physically "hit" her.

FRANCES: Have you been to someone, like your minister, or Relate?

KATHA: What's the matter with you? This isn't a case for God-bothering. For God's sake.

FRANCES: I just know in my heart it's a sin.

KATHA: A lot of our kids are from divorced parents.

FRANCES: Of course, I'm not saying it's *their* fault.

KATHA: And Emma's in the same double bind.

FRANCES: As our kids?

KATHA: It's not *her* fault, is it?

FRANCES: It's too much for me this time of night.

KATHA: Oh, grow up. Live a little beyond your bedtime, for once.

EMMA: Look, we're all tired. *I* want to go to bed. I didn't mean to get you arguing.

KATHA: We're not arguing.

FRANCES: Aren't we? I dunno what you'd call it.

KATHA: Facing up to a problem.

FRANCES: Whose?

EMMA: I just know . . . whatever I do . . . that I wouldn't have been able to live this past year . . . the accident and everything.

FRANCES: I know.

EMMA: I mean they were my *parents* . . . Louise talks about hers.

KATHA: Louise sometimes needs a lobotomy.

EMMA: No, but yours. Franny's dad making mulled wine. Paying for a trip to the Alps.

KATHA: On the other hand, we can't keep everything out of earshot.

EMMA: No, you shouldn't keep any of it out. It's wonderful, that's what I'm saying. My brother, when he got the news, drove his Rover through the Sainsbury's shop front. Was that very clever?

FRANCES: Understandable.

EMMA: But wrong. They charged him with criminal negligence, as though he'd been driving my parents' death car.

FRANCES *(arm round her)*:   Don't think about it.

KATHA: Why the hell shouldn't she? *(To EMMA.)* What on earth were they thinking of? Didn't they have all the facts, the circumstances? Didn't you try to explain?

EMMA: You haven't twigged, have you. No, of course, you're both too kind.

KATHA: Sod that.

EMMA: I won't sod it. I can't. Without the two of you . . . helping me . . . making me feel whole again . . . human . . . I'd be just like my brother.

> *A pause.*

FRANCES: We feel the same about you.

EMMA: You can't. You haven't been through the same thing. But you've done it just the same. That's what's so marvelous about *you*.

KATHA *(whispers)*:   You can sort her out?

FRANCES: Yes, but—

KATHA *(starting off)*:   We'll talk more about this, Em. I promise.

FRANCES: But . . .

KATHA: But what, Franny? I'm knackered.

FRANCES: Nothing, I'll see you in there.

KATHA: I'm glad we know you, Emmylou. Night-night to you both.

> *She goes off without kissing FRANCES goodnight.*
> *Fade.*

Act Two

The doors now represent a physiotherapy unit within the primary school.

> *FRANCES'S voice is heard from behind the door as the lights come up gradually.*

FRANCES *(very slowly)*:   I put my finger heeeere. Where is it? Where's my finger? No, Adrian, not in my eye. That would *hurt. Ow.* On my . . . *(Laughs.)* No, not *in* my nose. Oooh. Horribubble.

Lights up full on EMMA with a splint. KATHA comes on, presumably from her office.

KATHA: I always suffer with Franny on hand class days. Job getting Adrian anywhere near his nose.

EMMA: My kids are lovely.

KATHA: What, all of them? Who's a lucky girl then?

EMMA: It's the parents that need sorting out.

KATHA: Well, the kids *and* the parents. Eh?

EMMA: In here . . . *(Taps her head.)* In the upper storey.

KATHA: Occupational hazards of the fledging Occupational Therapist.

EMMA: What? What are they?

KATHA: Oh, what we just said—you work on the kids in the lower storey, the parents in the—

EMMA: . . . and what does "fledgling" mean, failing?

KATHA: . . . means what you are, dear—new.

FRANCES *(giggling)*: Adrian, what on earth are you doing now?

KATHA: I showed him a book, and he set about trying to *eat* it.

EMMA: His mouth's too small.

KATHA: He had to *nibble* at it.

Katha is working on cardboard cutboards with big scissors.

EMMA: Are you still planning to make pastry with them?

KATHA: Oh, some time, I suppose . . . I dunno when.

EMMA: I dunno quite how either, they'll think it's modeling clay.

KATHA: That's the tactic I'll use.

EMMA: I'll give you a hand when you do.

KATHA: Shall we do it in our kitchen . . . so they can be snowmen?

EMMA: Let's set a date.

KATHA: All right, but it'll have to be after Christmas.

EMMA: Your birthday? Franny told me.

KATHA *(smiling)*: All right, you're on.

A pause.

EMMA *(with her work)*: This is the third splint I've made Cassie. Her mother keeps ringing up to complain.

KATHA: What's the matter with it?

EMMA: The matter with it? Her mother.

KATHA: Did you tell Franny?

EMMA: And she told Cassie's mum.

KATHA: And Cassie's mum just won't be told. *(Giggles.)*

EMMA: Do you know her? *(Imitating a Devon accent.)* "You wants 'em to wear it *all* the time? Her be crippled fer life then." I dunno how she expects her not to be, without it. What do these people expect?

KATHA: You didn't tell her that, did you?

EMMA: I should have done.

KATHA: No, but did you?

EMMA: I can't remember. Why?

KATHA: Well, I don't know her mother, but I've had her *dad* on the phone to me all morning. So you must have said *something* she got the wind up about.

EMMA: Franny talked to her.

KATHA: But *he* mentioned you.

EMMA: I never met the man. After her, I don't want to, thanks.

PIGEON, a physio of about 50, comes on.

PIGEON: I thought it was you, Katha.

KATHA: Oh, sorry, Pigeon. Were we too loud?

PIGEON: It was you I wanted. You know Jamie is one of the ones down for assessment this afternoon.

KATHA: Yeah?

PIGEON: Well, *I'd* like to have him instead. We've started this new conductive physio course, and—

KATHA: . . . he could do with it, sure.

PIGEON: Could you clear with Sidney?

KATHA: Oh, I see. You want my permission. Can't you see Sid yourself? We have fifteen others. I'm sure he won't mind.

PIGEON: I'd rather ask you.

KATHA: Fine, but it's his idea. *(A beat.)* Oh, go on, go ahead.

PIGEON: I wouldn't want to get you in trouble.

KATHA: You won't. You take Jamie.

PIGEON: I don't really know Sidney, strange as that sounds.

KATHA: I know what you mean, though.

PIGEON: Well, it wasn't like this in Mr. Showleigh's day, was it?

KATHA: We were smaller then, too.

PIGEON: We could liaise all we needed with teachers, them with us. Now it's all going through channels, I don't know.

KATHA: And the channels are usually blocked.

PIGEON: Well, they needn't be. We have a whole set of outpatients we didn't used to have, and yet Franny and I never clash. If she needs to switch times or I do, we just say it, and, there, it's done. I sometimes think Sidney Aldermost wants a requisition order—"Attention Sidney Aldermost"—just to take a child from a lesson for half an hour. It's ridiculous.

KATHA: Well, he's new, and he needs to feel involved.

PIGEON: He's been here three years. He'll remain new at ten with that kind of silliness.

KATHA: I'm working on it, Pigeon.

EMMA: I didn't know you saw outpatients, Pig.

PIGEON *(after a moment)*:   I never said I did. *(Back to KATHA.)* You and Franny run the school between you, everybody knows it. It might give Sid a shock to find it out some time.

KATHA: Might give me the sack, too. He means well, love.

PIGEON: I've no quarrel at all with what he means, thank you very much. *(Stops, smiles.)* Well, hark at me. *(Turning to go.)* Thanks, very much.

EMMA *(after she goes off)*:   She said that twice. *(Stifles a giggle.)*

KATHA: Shh. You need to watch that.

EMMA: What?

KATHA: Slow down. She has a point.

EMMA: I dunno what you—

KATHA: Calling her "Pig" like that. Are you barmy?

EMMA: Franny calls her that.

KATHA: "Pig*let*" . . . see the difference? And even then, they've known each other for years. And that's Franny. Nobody else'd get away with it. *I* don't know her that well.

EMMA: Pigeon itself is a stupid name.

KATHA: I dunno where *that's* from.

EMMA: Reminds me of droppings.

KATHA: What if we all called *you* "Enema." *(Tickling her.)* Watcha, "Enema."

EMMA: Get off!

KATHA: I think I'll do it . . . whenever you step out of line.

EMMA: Right, boss.

KATHA: I'm serious.

EMMA: You do and I'll hand in me notice.

KATHA: What notice? You're on placement.

EMMA: Ooh, are you dressing me down?

KATHA *(giggles)*:   Am I *what*?

EMMA: Shut up. Are you tickling me off? You can't anyway.

KATHA: Yes, I can—I'm the Deputy Head.

EMMA: . . . of the school, and I'm physio. Franny's my boss.

KATHA *(joking)*:   I'm the boss of everybody in the place. Except Sid, and you heard what Pigeon said.

EMMA: That's why you stick up for her. She's your groupie.

KATHA: I stick up for her because she's right. Do you know, I caught him taking forty winks the other afternoon? Right there in his office.

EMMA: That's disgraceful.

KATHA: He covered it well, but now I have something on him . . . when I need it.

EMMA: *You're* disgraceful as well. Whole blinking place is corrupt. I'd better leave before you have something on *me*.

KATHA: I already have.

EMMA: Like what?

KATHA: Cassie's dad.

A pause.

In some ways it's probably a good thing Sid doesn't know what's going on.

EMMA: What are you trying to do, freak me out?

KATHA: I just want you to watch yourself . . . for your own sake.

EMMA: So I'll call her Penelope Jane from now on. See? *I* know.

KATHA: I knew it, too. I just forgot. That doesn't matter.

EMMA: Yes, it does.

KATHA: . . . in itself, in isolation, that doesn't matter a dickie bird. But it's part of a whole, and that matters a lot, yes. It's the whole reason you're here. Are you with me? You're the newest member of the staff—

EMMA: I'm on trial.

KATHA: . . . you want to be staff.

EMMA: We're back to the swimming course, are we? You said that was different.

KATHA: It is. And again it's not.

EMMA: Make up your—

KATHA: I didn't want to mention it.

EMMA: You didn't, *I*—

KATHA: Cassie's father, I'm talking about.

EMMA: I dunno him! I talked to the mother.

KATHA: And the dad talked to me about it.

EMMA: "All morning." I didn't do anything.

KATHA: I said that to get your attention. He *was* upset. He wanted Sidney, but I managed to get there first. That's what I mean, it's a good thing—

EMMA: But I was right.

KATHA: That's as may be.

EMMA: *Franny* said so. She told the woman herself.

KATHA: But that's Franny.

EMMA: No, it's not, it's bloody unfair.

KATHA: Keep you voice down. They're from Devon, for God's sake. You're a bolshy-tempered Essex Girl.

EMMA: . . . and "disabled."

KATHA: Most of them are still back in 1953—they've just watched the coronation.

EMMA: I don't believe anybody nowadays . . . we're all on Internet!

KATHA: You'd be surprised.

EMMA: Even people like them have a telly.

KATHA: But they know bugger all about splints and physios and "conductive education."

EMMA: They sent her to school.

KATHA: That's the law, but it's all witchcraft to them. Their daughter's bewitched, she's "afflicted," and this is all a form of ritual bloodletting to them. The dad probably wants her dead anyway. She's the one that wants Cassie saved.

EMMA: Why is he bothered then?

KATHA: You frightened his wife half to death.

EMMA: All I said was the truth.

KATHA: He doesn't see it like that. He doesn't like hearing it from *Franny*, but from *you*—

EMMA: . . . someone else who's "afflicted."

KATHA: . . . a noisy Essex Girl, I said.

EMMA: We *are* back at the swimming course.

KATHA: We're back to yesterday afternoon.

EMMA: Franny entered the pool seconds early, that was all. But because it was me, with my wonky foot—

KATHA: You didn't kick her in.

EMMA: . . . an issue is made.

KATHA: Only in your head. Like I told you. Like I'm telling you now—

EMMA: What? You're telling me I risk the sack.

KATHA: If you don't watch yourself, yes.

EMMA *(starting off)*:   I'm going to see Franny.

KATHA: Why? Don't disturb her hand class. It's not that important.

EMMA: Oh, sod off.

KATHA *(crossing to her quickly)*:   Shh, shh, shh. Calm down. Come here. Come . . .

KATHA has her in a comforting embrace that gradually develops into fondling.

You're all right, aren't you?

EMMA: I'm miserable.

KATHA: Why, because of the work?

EMMA: . . . when you tell me things like that.

KATHA: You haven't been listening. You're fine. You don't want to tell Franny, do you? *(Fondling her.)* Do you?

EMMA *(laughs)*:   No, I bloody don't.

KATHA *(smiles)*:   You sure now?

EMMA: You better watch your step, Katha.

KATHA: No, I'm telling you you have to watch yours. You don't need to worry about anything else. I can handle Franny . . . Sid . . .

EMMA: . . . Cassie's dad.

KATHA: Well, I did. I can handle them all.

FRANCES *(her voice, getting nearer)*:   . . . and tomorrow we'll work on your toesies.

The women separate. FRANCES comes on.

FRANCES: Handle who, Kath?

EMMA: Were you listening?

FRANCES: What? I heard you . . . just now.

EMMA: Did we disturb you? I'm sorry, Fran.

FRANCES: No, you didn't "disturb" me, but like Adrian "disturbs" me. D'you think it's deafness as well? He doesn't listen . . . *that's* really most of his problem.

KATHA *(looking at EMMA)*:   Oh, yes.

EMMA *(laughs)*:   Are you saying I'm really autistic?

FRANCES: Better not be. My timetable's full. *(Slumping down on her chair.)* God, I'm knackered . . . and it isn't even eleven o'clock. Who've we got to handle?

KATHA: Apart from our esteemed Head?

FRANCES: Yeah, I know about him and his "assessment." Load of rubbish. Who else?

KATHA: Cassie's dad, since you mention it.

FRANCES: Oh, '*im.*

KATHA: You know this kerfuffle about Cassie's splint?

EMMA: I was right, too, wasn't I. She has to wear it all the time.

KATHA: It's the way you put it across.

FRANCES: *I* told him that.

KATHA: And he accepted it?

EMMA: How?

FRANCES: I said we needed his advice about muck-spreaders.

EMMA: This is serious . . . come on.

FRANCES *(Devon accent)*:   "Ooh, ar. You sees, the problem with compost, m' dear. Am all down to *soyance* . . ." *("Science.")* " 'Tis all a question of courtship with *nayture.*"

KATHA *(to EMMA)*:   Devon farmer . . . didn't I tell you?

EMMA: I'm going out to milk a cow.

KATHA *(laughs)*:   Worm a bullock or two while you're at it.

FRANCES: Is that it then, sorted?

KATHA: Pigeon saw me just now.

FRANCES: About Jamie?

KATHA: I said it was all right.

FRANCES: 'Course, it is. Sid'll never know the difference.

EMMA: She also said you and Katha run things round here.

FRANCES: Sometimes wish we didn't. I'm washed out. It isn't true anyway. Board of Governors *run* things . . . and Sid's got a seat on the board.

EMMA: And why haven't either of you?

FRANCES: I'd rather put me feet up come five o'clock. The board always meets after eight.

EMMA: Billy says he wants a divorce.

FRANCES *(jokes, giggles)*:   Does that mean *you're* free in the evenings?

EMMA: Means I'm out of a home.

FRANCES: Shall I put your name forward?

KATHA: Quiet, Fran. *(To EMMA.)* Seriously? *(A beat.)* Why can't *he* leave?

EMMA: I won't stay where I'm not wanted. She's in my bed!

KATHA: He's got a bird? Then you kick her out. That's your right. He's taking advantage. You want me to do it?

FRANCES: Kathie, don't interfere.

KATHA: This has nothing to do with religion, damn it. Emma's our *friend*.

EMMA: But what can you do?

KATHA: Show him we know our matrimonial law, for a kick-off. He's committed adultery—the law's on your side. And he knows it. He's trying it on.

Internal telephone rings. FRANCES answers.

Don't stand for it, Emma. I'm telling you.

FRANCES: Shh. Quiet a minute. *(Into receiver.)* What was that, Sid . . . ? Yes, she is . . . She's right here.

EMMA: What's he want?

KATHA: Nobody, nowhere, says the wife has to leave.

FRANCES: It's a fuss about nothing.

KATHA: Are you listening to me?

EMMA: No, I'm not. What's he want, Fran?

FRANCES *(ringing off)*:   I better talk to you.

EMMA: What's he want?

FRANCES *(on her feet)*:   He's just heard about Cassie Williams.

KATHA: Who from? But we sorted that out.

EMMA: I better go with you.

FRANCES: No, I have to deal with it. *(Exasperated sound.)* You stay here . . . listen to Kathie.

EMMA: *My* head's on the block.

FRANCES: No, it's not. Just leave things to us. Between us we'll see you're all right.

Quick fade.
Lights rise slowly at the sound of FRANCES'S voice as she addresses a Board of Governors meeting. Scenically, she's upstage, with her back to the audience, addressing people who comment and question off-stage. Simultaneously, a group of women, EMMA among them, are preparing teas and coffees for the guests. The other women are LOUISE, PIGEON, and, latterly, KATHA.
It should be assumed that the women can't hear the meeting and that although they speak afterward, their scene takes place simultaneously.

FRANCES: Er, where was I? *(Slight laugh.)* Oh, yes. I've been allocated this certain sum of money "to be used as I see fit." Well, what can I say? On the one hand, it's ever so generous . . . thanks. But on the other, I'm Oliver Twist. We could use this sum annually, and that's if I'm not being greedy. We can all find a lost dog a home.

VOICE: We're talking about money, aren't we?

FRANCES: Yes, I know it.

VOICE 2: Let Franny speak.

FRANCES: I'm not being flip about money, believe me. In the end, it's for you to decide. And I wouldn't act without your approval, whatever it was "I saw fit" to do.

VOICE 3: We only ask to be consulted, duck.

VOICE 2: She's consulting us now.

FRANCES: Right, I want it clear we're discussing the matter. Fair enough? We could always use new equipment, but I've been told that's another fund. This additional sum is to be used for "additional resources." Any chance you could be more specific? What did you have in mind, exactly? Another school outing, like Fairacre Farm?

SIDNEY (*his voice*): Go on and tell us what you decided, Fran.

FRANCES: With your permission, all right, I will. It's not really up to a salary for another full-time member of staff. That's my only dilemma really. We do need one, at least that's what I'd like. Or we pay a part-timer a fraction of this, and what do we do with the rest? More part-timers just mean more clutter, to me. I'd far rather have one full-time member I knew I could rely on, as part of the team. There's little movement among my staff, and I welcome that. I think it's better for the kids. Makes them safer to know they grow up with us, come back to see us, and frankly, I like working with those I can trust.

VOICE 1: We're with you so far.

VOICE 4: We're ahead of you.

SIDNEY: Let's do this in turn.

VOICE 4: She wants another full-timer. Where'd we find the cash?

FRANCES: There is a way with the money you've given me . . . with this. That's what I want to discuss with you. If we got someone on the A scale . . .

VOICE 4: She'd be a trainee.

FRANCES: She's been training with us already . . . on placement.

VOICE 1: Oh, you already have someone in mind?

FRANCES: An OT. She's been with us since August . . . she's up for review, and I'm for recommending we make the post permanent as long as . . .

VOICE 1: . . . as long as the money's there.

FRANCES: This money.

VOICE 4: And what about next year?

FRANCES: Well . . .

VOICE 3: Hang on a minute. Who's this we're talking about?

VOICE 4: Doesn't matter *who* . . . it's *how* and how *much*.

VOICE 2: And her name wouldn't be Emma Swannows, would it?

VOICE 4: Doesn't matter about her *name*.

VOICE 2:   She's not that disabled lass you've taken under your wing?

FRANCES: She's a trainee.

VOICE 1:   She's disabled?

VOICE 3:   I thought you were talking staff.

FRANCES: She *is* staff. She's a trainee OT.

VOICE 1:   But she's disabled.

SIDNEY: What's that got to do with it? She's been working at the school, as a regular member of Franny's staff.

VOICE 1:   And you knew about this, George?

VOICE 2:   I'd heard something about it.

FRANCES: I think I can focus on your concerns. Disabled workers in the NHS is almost an unknown phenomenon.

VOICE 1:   And with good reason.

VOICE 4:   Mostly they need care themselves.

FRANCES: I know.

VOICE 1:   Mostly they lived in hospitals . . . a drain on the public purse.

FRANCES: If you'll permit me a minute to make the case, please. Thanks, Sid. First, the question of money. Emma's case is the strongest of all, in a way. She's entitled to claim placement money permanently, unlike—I hate the term—able-bodied workers. So that takes care of the finance. And then there's her physical condition. She's "disabled" only in name. She has a full case load already, believe me. And I couldn't recommend her if she didn't do the job. Well, she does, admirably. And she has a rapport with the kids that any of you would find touching, I'm sure. They take to her in a way I couldn't begin to match. That's another way she's an *advantage*. And, between ourselves, it'd do her good.

VOICE 1:   Do *her* good, did you say? Who's this we're helping here, Emma?

FRANCES: It would do us all good, I meant to say.

VOICE 4:   We're do-gooders, as it is, helping the children. You want us to now help the members of staff?

VOICE 1:   We're not Social Services, love.

Calls of assent.

But I'd like to go back to the money for a moment. You say she'd be funded by disabled charity, have I got that right?

FRANCES: Partly.

VOICE 1:   Partly right or—?

FRANCES: Partly funded by disabled charity. It's standard practice.

VOICE 1:   Yes, but, love, *we're* a disabled charity ourselves. Looks to me like your friend Emma knows when she's onto a winner. She's collecting twice. Seems to me it's a case for some committee on standards and ethics to consider. That's the review issue where this lady's concerned.

Lights up on the women. LOUISE comes on with her swimming bag.
EMMA and PIGEON are making tea and coffee.

LOUISE: No swimming this week?

PIGEON: Committee meeting.

LOUISE: Oh, sugar, I forgot.

PIGEON: I did, too.

EMMA: I didn't forget.

LOUISE: You wouldn't. But why are you here? Oh, you're the tea lady. That's right.

PIGEON: That's what I'm roped into doing.

LOUISE: What happened to what's-her-name, Georgie? She still work here?

PIGEON: It's all change now, Wheezie. It's all contracted out now. Never know, one
    day to the next, who's bringing the dinners, what we're having . . . and how
    many is always a bit of a Lucky Dip. Oh, don't get me started on kitchen staff.

EMMA: We know what they're sending at least.

PIGEON: That's right: chips.

LOUISE: Chips with everything, eh?

PIGEON: . . . with cottage pie, would you believe?

EMMA: Pizza.

LOUISE: That's what kids eat, though, isn't it.

PIGEON: Exactly. That's why they should never have contracted out.

EMMA: No, *don't* start, Pigeon, please.

PIGEON: With our own staff, the meals were always well balanced, always varied,
    always on time. And Georgie took well care of this kind of thing.

LOUISE: More than that. We took her to Fairacre with us.

PIGEON: . . . as part of the family, I know.

EMMA: Will you two stop living in the past?

PIGEON: And you don't want to know the redundancy deal Sidney got her to agree to.

EMMA: Then don't tell us.

LOUISE: You're wrong, Em. I do want to know.

PIGEON: Three weeks.

LOUISE: Three weeks' *pay* . . . ? And no *pension*?

PIGEON: To begin with. She wasn't entitled to it. Hadn't been here long enough, so
    he said.

LOUISE: That's ridiculous. She'd been here years.

PIGEON: Just short of the number—ten—according to him. He said she'd only been
    paying in for three, so she wasn't entitled, in any case. Fortunately, she went to
    Katha about it, and Katha, I guess, had a quiet word.

LOUISE: So she got it in the end?

PIGEON: She got *something*. But she shouldn't have been *sacked*. That's the Alder-
    most Regime. Life under Himmler, I call it. He even had the cheek to present
    with a P40. She thought it was a gift voucher, at first.

EMMA: Silly moo.

PIGEON: What?

EMMA: Sor-ry.

LOUISE: You weren't here in Mr. Showleigh's time. If you had been, you'd know just how sad that is. You, especially.

EMMA: Why me . . . why especially?

LOUISE: Oh, nothing.

EMMA: No, you said something personal.

LOUISE: A slip of the tongue. You know I'm always doing it.

EMMA: You're always riding me, yes. Why?

PIGEON: Ladies.

LOUISE: I'm not always riding you . . . it's just me.

PIGEON: Hey, ladies.

LOUISE: I meant nothing by it, believe me . . .

PIGEON: . . . except you don't know how nice it could be.

LOUISE: Exactly.

EMMA: That's all I ever hear. Mr. Showleigh this . . . Mr. Showleigh the other. Mr. Showleigh's my Uncle Mac.

PIGEON: He did get Uncle Mac down here to visit the kids. Remember, Wheeze?

EMMA: Oh, St. Chrispin's sake.

LOUISE: Emmy's too young to remember Uncle Mac.

EMMA: We're back to the war, are we?

LOUISE: Postwar. The Beatles.

EMMA: I should well think my mother was too young.

PIGEON: And you've had your own problems with Sidney, haven't you, Em.

EMMA: No, I haven't. Just what have *you* heard?

PIGEON: Same as we all have. That's all I meant. You wouldn't be part of the team if you hadn't.

LOUISE: No secrets in places of work. Don't you know that? You *are* young.

PIGEON: Just that all ours used to be pleasant ones.

EMMA: I'm going to *scream*.

LOUISE *(crossing to her)*:   Steady on, chuck.

PIGEON: What did I say?

EMMA: It's my appointment they've come to consider tonight. And Sid's a member of the board.

LOUISE: . . . see now why you're keen to defend him.

EMMA: No, but he's bound to raise the business with Cassie Williams. That's the trouble.

PIGEON: Shouldn't think so—that was weeks back.

EMMA: It's part of my review. They've been in there for hours. They must be discussing it.

LOUISE: What business is that?

EMMA: Oh, please don't.

PIGEON: It's nothing, pet.

LOUISE: It must be nothing . . . or Franny would have told me.

EMMA: It was meant to be confidential.

PIGEON: You'd have already got the sack.

LOUISE: She tells me everything worth knowing.

PIGEON: Emma had words with a parent, that's all. It was taken the wrong way.

LOUISE: We've been through this ourselves, haven't we, Em. Taking things the wrong way.

PIGEON: We've all been through something with parents—they're the visiting constabulary.

LOUISE: . . . wouldn't put it that way meself.

PIGEON: Eh? You know what I mean.

LOUISE: . . . should think so and all. My Brian's constabulary.

PIGEON: But parents and teachers, parents and school. It's an unholy alliance whatever you do. Here more than most places. Unlike most, our kids come "protected." We're the wicked world, in most parents' eyes. That's *why* I go on about Sidney. He proves their point. But even before Sidney, with Franny backing me up every move . . . I've had parents telling me everything about their darlings, and in the process everything at all about my job. I can't tell you the number of times I've had to bite my tongue saying, "Which physio course were *you* on?" Franny now makes it a point to have as many as can attend classes in this new conductive approach. And don't they create Merry Hell about that! You know what I'm talking about, Em. You've heard them. Far worse than Farmer Williams created.

LOUISE: What did he say?

PIGEON: I dunno for sure.

LOUISE: Bet I can guess.

PIGEON: Have you met him?

LOUISE: You're treated to Licorice All Sorts as a rozzer's wife. Old lags' wives are the worst. You want to hear about *my* life sometime.

EMMA: I've had a twin packet of me own.

LOUISE: I can appreciate that.

EMMA: Did Franny tell you *that*?

LOUISE: Doesn't need to. I can see for meself. You've what we once called a strawberry mark on you, Em. There's no use denying it's there. Your friends and the world's angels will do their best to pretend it isn't, and see the rest of you for what it is. But, let's face it, there aren't that many of them, though maybe my view is more biased than most.

PIGEON: Being a rozzer's wife.

LOUISE: I have me own doubts, though. *I* think angels are only in heaven, and your friends—Christmas—nobody ever has enough. If you go through life with more than a couple, you've been truly blessed, in my book. Franny's been both friend and angel to me.

PIGEON: . . . and me. I'd do anything for her.

LOUISE: 'Expect we all would . . . that's why we're here.

PIGEON: She'll make up for the Farmer Williamses of the world for you, Emma.

LOUISE: She does her best to . . . I'll say that for her. I could say a lot else besides. She's a wonder.

>   *A pause.*
>   *Noise from the meeting, and KATHA comes on.*

EMMA *(rushes toward her)*:   Have they decided yet, Katha?

KATHA: Decided what? Hallo, Lou. Fancy seeing you here.

LOUISE: It's swimming club night. I forgot.

KATHA: Oh, yeah. Any bickies going?

PIGEON: Jammy dodgers.

KATHA: Franny's faves, those. I keep trying to get her to buy Garibaldis, but she says they're more like cheese bickies. Which they aren't, are they? You're partial to Garibaldi, aren't you, Em?

EMMA: I'm not thinking about biscuits.

KATHA: Not jammy dodgers, I agree. Not worth thinking about.

LOUISE: The kids like 'em.

PIGEON: They're for Franny's sweet tooth.

LOUISE: They're probably here for the kids.

KATHA: Don't believe it. They're here for Franny. She's an absolute piglet about bickies. Excuse me, Piglet. *You're* not.

EMMA: Katha!

KATHA: What!

EMMA: What have they *decided*?

KATHA: About what? I haven't been in there . . . so I wouldn't know, would I.

PIGEON: How long are they likely to be?

KATHA: Meeting started at what, eight?

PIGEON: Half-seven.

KATHA: Oh, not much longer now, I should think. It's gone nine. Is that why you're waiting?

PIGEON: I stayed here to serve teas and coffees . . . Franny asked me.

KATHA: Oh, I should bunk off, if I was you, Pigeon. They don't deserve waitress service. I'm sure Franny didn't mean you to do that.

PIGEON: I don't really mind.

KATHA: I'm sure she would, if she knew. I think she'd be ever so, you know, ever so *Franny*. I'd take her home in tears. You go off now. You and Lou have a drink at *the Beacon*. I'll see to the meeting.

EMMA: I'm staying.

KATHA: Emma and me will see to the teas. 'Appen we'll join you, if it's before closing.

LOUISE: *I'd* like to get off. Franny don't know I'm here.

KATHA: We won't tell her.

EMMA: Will you tell *me* . . . ?

KATHA: No! I heard it was about the pool anyway.

EMMA: Oh . . . bullocks. It isn't.

KATHA: It's swimming club evening.

LOUISE: An hour and a half? Perhaps it's about a new filter. That could cost a few thousand, I suppose.

KATHA: Easily.

PIGEON: We could do with it, mind.

LOUISE: I know we could. I remember saying to Franny on the last swimming course, "We wanna make certain somebody don't catch something."

PIGEON: And the way disease spreads in this place . . .

LOUISE: P'haps it's not as ludicrous as it sounds. 'Bye-bye, you two.

PIGEON: Oh! Yes, goodbye!

KATHA *(laughing)*:   We'll probably follow you out.

> *LOUISE and PIGEON go off.*

They're a pair of happy campers, aren't they?

EMMA: *I'm* not.

KATHA: No. You're neither camper nor a pair. You're unique.

EMMA: I'm bloody cross, too.

KATHA: You're *shirty. (Laughs.)* Even without your shirt.

EMMA: You've never seen me without my shirt . . . not likely to neither.

KATHA *(mischievous grin)*:   I wouldn't say that. You might want to take it off for me sometime.

EMMA: Unlike you me.

KATHA: Oh, I don't know about that.

EMMA: . . . in the changing room.

KATHA: That's in front of *others*. I might well do it . . . just for you.

EMMA: Oh, yeah? When, exactly?

KATHA: Oh, sometime. *(She giggles.)*

EMMA: All right—what was all that rubbish about a new filter for the swimming pool?

KATHA: Oh, that? That was rubbish.

EMMA: The meeting was never about that.

KATHA: I know.

EMMA: Then why did you say it was? The meeting's about me, isn't it.

KATHA: Of course.

EMMA: You rotter. Why'd you pretend it wasn't . . . tormenting me like that?

KATHA: I wasn't tormenting you, on purpose. You idiot. That was for Pigeon and Lou's sake.

EMMA: But they know. I already told them.

KATHA: What do they know? They know bugger all. So do you, for the moment.

EMMA: Do *you* know?

KATHA: I have an idea.

EMMA: So tell me! Why didn't you *tell* me?

KATHA: All right, but if you think I was going to tell *them* . . . Pigeon's the Enid
Sharpels of school, and Wheezer is Franny's best mate.

EMMA: I thought you were.

KATHA: . . . she's also your natural enemy. If she thought you put Franny on the
spot, she'd be down on you like an articulated lorry. And she can drive one. You
know what I mean.

EMMA: Have I been made permanent?

KATHA: First I want you to know what's involved here . . . and then I need to know
where you stand.

EMMA: I stand nowhere unless I've a job here. Have I?

KATHA: That depends on you.

EMMA: You're wrong, Katha. It depends on you and Franny.

KATHA: . . . and on you. On your attitude, your level of commitment, let's say. I
need to be dead sure about that.

EMMA: What do you mean? Yes, of course, I'm committed.

KATHA: But to what?

EMMA: Will you stop playing twenty questions with me? *I* need answers. One, in
particular.

KATHA: There are others as well.

EMMA: Only one that I'm bothered about. Did Cassie Williams come up?

KATHA: Not specifically, so far.

EMMA: Then I'm out of the woods.

KATHA: You already were, about that. Like I told you. Doesn't mean there aren't
problems about your appointment.

EMMA: But that was the only problem.

KATHA: They're still in there. You're not a snug bunny as yet. They're still talking . . . and all about *you*.

EMMA: They don't know me that well. You make me feel I'm on *trial*.

KATHA: Got it in one, chuck. That's just what you are . . . When I looked in just
now, one silly fart even called for a public inquiry. He thought you might be on
the fiddle.

EMMA: But *how*? The money's crap.

KATHA: Maybe that's why he's suspicious.

EMMA: Jesus, Mary, and Joseph! I'm meant to be a witch one day, a crook the
next . . . you tell me, "Don't be so *sensitive*."

KATHA: That's right.

EMMA: Whyever not?

KATHA: Like I said . . . he's an old fart.

EMMA: What are you telling me for?

KATHA: . . . think you should know what's involved.

EMMA: Why? Why do I need to know? What if I don't want the job anymore? I
don't need to know then, do I. I'm not sure that I do, after all.

KATHA: Of course, you *want* it. What are we doing here then? What're *you* going to do instead?

EMMA: At this point I don't really care.

KATHA: Don't you . . . about me and Franny? *(A beat.)* So it was all a lie then . . . everything you said about how you felt about us. We're not friends at all. We're just the latest mod cons to you. Main Chance Mary and her latest mod cons.

EMMA *(tearfully)*: Why are you doing this to me?

KATHA: I told you—to test your commitment.

EMMA: I dunno what that means!

KATHA: Yes, you do. Think about it.

   A pause.

   (speaking quietly): I want you to listen to me, Em. Remember I told you to trust me?

EMMA: I—

KATHA: No . . . listen. You've got the job, if you want. All right? Whatever they may say, the board believe Franny. They'll follow whatever she says. They pretend they're in charge, but in reality, they'd be lost without her . . . and the sharper ones know it, I think. She'd become dangerous if she realized just how much power she has. But she still throws up in the mornings before work, from nerves. So I guess there's no danger of that. Are you with me so far or not?

EMMA: Yes, so far. You mean there's more?

KATHA: There's everything more . . . are you kidding me?

EMMA: Go on then.

KATHA: Franny does . . . whatever *I* tell her to do.

EMMA: So *she* doesn't want me at all.

KATHA: Of course she wants you. She's in there pleading her heart out for you. You're what she wants most for her kids . . . those pitiable creatures that don't have an earthly idea of being of you. She still wants you for their sake. That's what's going to finally persuade the board. Okay? *(A beat.)* I want you, too.

EMMA *(grinning)*: What it is to be in demand! I've never known it before, Katha. I've always been last in the queue.

KATHA: Shh. I know.

EMMA: Oh, sweetheart! *(Moves to cuddle her.)*

KATHA: So you're up for it?

EMMA: What? Yes!

KATHA: Are you? There're going to be problems. I'm not quite sure how they'll work out.

EMMA: But with Franny behind me . . .

KATHA: I'm not talking about Franny now.

EMMA: What *are* you talking about?

KATHA: You know. Say it. Say you don't know what I mean. And then tell me for
real that's not what you want. *(A beat.)* Is it?

EMMA: I'm excited . . . a bit terrified actually.

KATHA: I know.

FRANCES comes on.

FRANCES: Sorry to keep you, Em. You didn't tell her, did you, Kath?

KATHA: Tell her what? Look—jammy dodgers.

FRANCES: Oh, crikey. That'll have to wait.

KATHA *(with the plate of biscuits)*:   Go on, they'll never know.

FRANCES *(taking one)*:   Fingers and toesies crossed, I think we're in with a shout.
They want to see her, Kath. D'you think it's a good sign?

KATHA: More than two hours is a good sign. *(Of the biscuits.)* Another for luck.

FRANCES *(with her mouth full, to EMMA)*:   You just have to agree with everything
they say. Don't worry if it sounds daft. I'll do the hard bit, all right?

EMMA: You're the boss, Boss.

They go off, FRANCES'S arm around EMMA.

KATHA *(low)*:   Oh, Franny.

Fade.
Children's voices singing the carol "Little Donkey" bring the lights back
up. The scenic arrangement is the same. This time, though, the off-stage
audience are the school's disabled children, and the staff are competing in
a fancy-dress competition at the Christmas party. "Out front," MAIRE, as
a leprechaun, tells the kids a story. Inside, LOUISE and DEIRDRE, a
friend her own age, prepare festive snacks, dressed for the occasion
though not in fancy dress. PIGEON is there too, though not at the moment.
She's also dressed up.

MAIRE: Right now. There's this Englishman, Scotsman, and the leprechaun—me
second cousin twice removed, if you want the full stretch of it—and were each
of them staring into this great hole in d' ground. And the Scot addresses d' others wit' a grin, and he says, "Me ancestor MacTavish is buried in yon hole in d'
ground. Our kin go back twenty generations." "I am awfully sorry to correct
you, old chap," says the English in reply. "Awfully sorry, indeed, I'm sure. But
I'm afraid this hole to which you refer as your province"—"Ma own province,
you say?" says MacTavish. "I hain't said a word about colonization"—". . . is
ectually . . ."—this is the Englishman now—". . . is ectually the ancestral seat
of my own people, Wellington Boot." "We're not talking wardrobe, hoots
mun," says MacTavish. "What you going on about a Wellington boot? Y'act as

though you dug the hole this morning, and haim telling you . . . haim telling you . . ." "It's been here the while." "The fact is"—this is *me* blood and bone speaking now, the leprechaun, whose name doesn't matter, since he's not there to claim any kin. But he says in a voice as firm as your man the Irish Magistrate himself—"I can vouchsafe the hole was niver there atall until four o'clock yesterday morning. Sure I put it there meself to keep d' evil spirits away." "What spirits would these be?"—MacTavish. "You're non talking aboot non else but d' demon drink." "A boot? A boot?" cries the Englishman in highest dudgeon. "I tell you, there are three hundred down there, and they're all Wellington, mark my words." "No, haim telling you . . . haim telling you . . ."—Mac-Tavish—". . . you've mistaken dis hole for Culloden or some such . . ." "And you know where y'are? You're in *Wales* . . ." says me cousin at last. "In Wales?" says d' udder two. "It's as plain as dis hole in d' ground. Sure there's a leek looking up at us. Don't you see him? What's that? Sure he's saying, 'Me name's Jones.' "

Lights up on the women.

DEIRDRE: Are you working here now or not?

LOUISE: No fear.

DEIRDRE: Damn. I thought you could tell me the gossip.

LOUISE: That's why I'm not working here. I still help Franny with swimming club, but I wouldn't work here for double the money.

DEIRDRE: Well?

LOUISE: I can't tell you, Dee. It wouldn't be fair to Franny.

DEIRDRE: But I wanted to ask about this new OT.

LOUISE: Shh.

DEIRDRE: Oh, dear. She's not working out?

LOUISE: They can't sack her, too. That's the problem. She's just been made permanent. At least not before her probationary period runs out . . .

DEIRDRE: But if she was that bad, why make her permanent?

LOUISE: It's personal, Dee. That's all I can say.

DEIRDRE: You rotter—I thought we were friends.

LOUISE: No, it's not you. I *can't* say. I'm not supposed to know. Nobody saying anything. Franny hasn't . . . to me. Just try to pretend nothing's happened.

DEIRDRE: Since I don't know what has, there's no need to pretend. Such a shame, though.

LOUISE: It's so sad . . . and so silly.

DEIRDRE: I don't call it "silly" when a disabled girl is perceived as causing trouble in the workplace. There are so few of them, it's bound to reflect on others.

LOUISE: It's not because she's disabled.

DEIRDRE: Well, but isn't she? It must do.

LOUISE: I'd better not say any more.

DEIRDRE: I'm on her side, though, whatever's happened.

LOUISE: You don't know the circumstances.

DEIRDRE: Whatever they are. Nobody's perfect. We all do all sorts of mistakes, every day . . . nobody does a thing about it. Let a disabled girl make just one, and she's finished.

LOUISE: This isn't about her *work*. I told you, this is per—

DEIRDRE: Then there oughtn't to be any problem. I'm serious about this, Louise.

LOUISE: I shouldn't have said anything.

DEIRDRE: No, *I* asked *you*. I'm glad that I did, too.

LOUISE: Just don't say anything to Franny, tonight anyway . . . with the kids here and everything. I shudder to think how this has affected *them*.

DEIRDRE: You're becoming darker and darker about this.

LOUISE: I know. I'm sorry.

DEIRDRE: I expect Franny will tell me herself. We're going to be on a conductive ed course in Great Yarmouth the week after next.

LOUISE: I *want* her to talk about it to someone . . . I think she should. Just that she won't talk to me.

DEIRDRE: I expect that's professional. Feels she can only talk about it at all with another head physio.

LOUISE: Yes.

DEIRDRE: Oh, it's bound to come up, because I want her advice about a trainee *we're* thinking of making full-time. *She* has cerebral palsy.

LOUISE: Don't use Emma as a guide.

DEIRDRE: But I have to . . . there are so few.

LOUISE: Emma Swannows isn't disabled.

Noise from the party as FRANCES comes on in a trainer's kit.

FRANCES *(laughing)*:   She's a caution, that girl. I tell you, Wheezie. She ought to do comic relief. The kids are in stitches in there . . . all over Wellington Boot.

LOUISE: She's not wearing green wellies, is she?

FRANCES: It's her story . . . ooh, mini sausage rolls. Yum. *(Eating one.)* You make them, Dee?

LOUISE: Pigeon did.

DEIRDRE: Were we meant to bring a dish? *(To LOUISE.)* You never said.

FRANCES: Oh, no, there's masses left. *(Another bite.)* Should think we could donate some of it to comic relief.

LOUISE: Why'd you take off that dress, love? It looked gorgeous.

FRANCES: Never feel meself wearing formal.

LOUISE: Ohh, I'll have it.

FRANCES *(giggles)*:   Think you'll fit it?

LOUISE: Not a chance. It's just right on *you*.

FRANCES: Have to get in me cosi. Don't worry, I'll wear it again.

DEIRDRE: Never reckoned you were *haute couteur,* Fran.

FRANCES: I'm not—it's just a dress. Seen Katha about? We're doing our Nellie the Elephant.

LOUISE: Not for a while.

FRANCES: Emma's Long John Silver.

LOUISE: Yes, that fits.

DEIRDRE: How *is* Emma, Fran?

FRANCES: Dunno yet. Haven't seen her since five.

DEIRDRE: I mean how's she working out?

LOUISE: Deirdre.

FRANCES: Fine. Emma's fine. You know she was made permanent.

DEIRDRE: And how's that working?

FRANCES: All right, I think. Better than. The kids love her.

DEIRDRE: Oh, they do. Oh, that's good.

FRANCES: I think they do. Why? You haven't heard anything different, have you?

DEIRDRE: No, how would I hear? I'm in Middlemoor.

FRANCES: 'Course you'd have to ask Emma. She seems happy, don't you think, Lou?

LOUISE: I never see her except swimming club. Then we don't say very much.

FRANCES *(to DEIRDRE)*: They rub each other the wrong way.

DEIRDRE *(eyeing LOUISE)*: Oh, *that's* it.

FRANCES: Ever since the last weekend course. That all you got against her, Lou?

LOUISE: She's all right. As Franny says, the kids take to her.

FRANCES: You don't know that yourself, do you. As you said, you're not here.

LOUISE: This is becoming monotonous.

FRANCES: Me Bible says never pass judgment on someone.

LOUISE: Good, that lets me out of the fancy dress.

FRANCES: Oh, I wouldn't let you judge the fancy dress. Em'd be bound to come last.

LOUISE: Maybe she deserves it.

FRANCES *(to DEIRDRE)*: You see there? Rank prejudice.

DEIRDRE *(eyeing LOUISE)*: I'll do it, if you're stuck for someone.

FRANCES: Would you? It's only for the kids really. Expect we'll decide by show of hands. You can be MC, though, if you like . . . you know, introduce us.

Noise again as MAIRE comes on.

There's the real star anyway. You're marvelous.

MAIRE: D' you think so? D' you reckon they liked it?

FRANCES *(giggles)*: Where did you hear that daft story? It's wonderful.

MAIRE: Wonderful nothing—it's out of me own head. Sure it's only a bit of stereo-type rubbish. Like this carry-on. *(She means her outfit.)* Don't you know lep-rechauns is only a bit of tourism. Much more authentic as Molly Macguire or Catherine Houlihan.

LOUISE: Keep your politics out of it.

MAIRE: These are national heroes, you know.

FRANCES *(giggles, hand on MAIRE'S shoulder)*:   Do you know where you are? In south Devon . . . and they're six years old.

MAIRE: I'd be better as old Farmer Giles, you're saying.

FRANCES: No, I'm saying you're better as you.

DEIRDRE: Oy, are you going to tell me what I'm meant to be doing . . . as MC?

FRANCES: Eh? Just go out and announce us. Where is Katha, though? I've got the cosi already. But she's got to be the top half.

> *Noise and PIGEON comes on.*

PIGEON: The kids are getting fairly excited.

MAIRE: Me own doing, I suppose.

PIGEON: Aren't you dressing up, Franny? You're the only one they're waiting for.

DEIRDRE *(in fun)*:   Cheat. It's decided before she goes out.

LOUISE: It's not her fault she's popular.

PIGEON: Popular, what, as yourself, Fran?

FRANCES: No, as Nellie the Elephant.

PIGEON: Nellie's already out there.

FRANCES: What! She can't be. I've got the costume right . . .

> *She rushes out.*

DEIRDRE: Hey! I'm meant to be judging the thing. *(Follows.)*

MAIRE: Here we go again. *(Follows.)*

LOUISE: That's torn it.

PIGEON: What? Aren't you coming, Lou?

> *LOUISE and PIGEON look at each other.*
> *Lighting shift.*
> *The subsequent tableau features KATHA and EMMA as Nellie the Elephant, increasingly playing to the crowd as the kids' approval grows. In the midst of this, DEIRDRE calls out, "The winners—by unanimous verdict—Emma and Katha. Nellie the Elephant. Take a bow, ladies." But instead of bowing, they get out of costume and embrace in a way that becomes increasingly private.*
> *Lighting shift back to the women.*

DEIRDRE: That was a bit OTT, don't you think?

PIGEON: What, Dee?

DEIRDRE: In front of the children? I'd say it was.

PIGEON: I don't suppose anyone noticed.

DEIRDRE: Of course they did.

LOUISE: Why? What happened?

PIGEON: Oh, nothing. Emma and Kath acting silly, that's all. *(To DEIRDRE.)* It's all in fun, Dee.

LOUISE: Nobody'd do anything to hurt the children . . . you ought to know that.

DEIRDRE: Well, yes, I know, but . . . what a display.

LOUISE: You don't stop your dog scratching himself in front of your kids, do you?

DEIRDRE: What? That's an animal.

LOUISE: People see what they're made to see.

FRANCES comes back on with MAIRE.

FRANCES: That's the secret. You should have come on last.

MAIRE: Ah, sure, they deserved it. What was the prize now?

FRANCES: Box of chocs? We don't usually have *prizes*.

MAIRE: There now. 'Tis all in fun.

LOUISE: Franny's friends give her prizes in presies. She gets more than the other combined.

MAIRE: So you don't really mind not winning like.

FRANCES: You can't win if you don't take part. Besides, I did win, in a way. Nellie frequently wins, so I'm well pleased, me. I didn't lose, put it that way.

LOUISE: Oh, Franny.

FRANCES: What? Come on, Maire, my lovely. *(Giggles.)* You up to sorting out the mess?

MAIRE: Oh, ay. Swimmin' lessons, fire drill, cleaning detail . . . I'm your man all right.

PIGEON: The more of us do it, the sooner we can get off home. I have yet to buy our Christmas tree.

DEIRDRE: I can't understand Kath and Emma.

FRANCES: Can't you? Emma's happy, that's all. This is the first real home she's ever had.

The women start off.

LOUISE: Just a second. Franny?

FRANCES *(to the others)*:   You carry on. Yeah, Lou? You don't have to bother with it. More willing hands than makes common sense.

LOUISE: Are you really all right?

FRANCES: Me? I'm fine. You know how I love Christmas. Maire's having fun, isn't she. And Emma. Seems she's settling in. We were right, I think, to give her the job.

LOUISE: Emma's an absolute idiot. I should have thought Katha'd have had more sense.

FRANCES: It was nothing, Lou. You shouldn't blame Katha. There's no one to blame, really. *(Breaking down.)* Oh, Wheezie.

LOUISE *(moving toward her)*:   What, love?

FRANCES *(in tears)*:   I'm so unhappy.

Fade.

Act Three

Bognor Regis.
Single spot illuminates KATHA, near naked.

KATHA: For Franny, there's never been any difference between love and sex. That's been the main difference between us, I think. She's not just my sister . . . or she *is*. That's the trouble. For me anyway. Always has been . . . and she never even had a ghostly idea I felt like that.

She stretches her arm across as the spot switches to FRANCES.

FRANCES: I once told Katha, "Don't worry. You can take me for granted." At Bognor, at six in the morning. We were eating bacon butties.

Spot out. Then lights up slowly on FRANCES, asleep at her desk. PIGEON stands over her, shaking her gently.

PIGEON: Fran . . . ? Franny?

FRANCES *(drowsy)*:   Ugh? Oh . . . hallo, Piglet, what're you doing here?

PIGEON: You're at work.

FRANCES *(realizing it)*:   Oh. *(Chuckle.)* Oh, yeah. Thought you were there, in me dream.

PIGEON: You've never been here all night?

FRANCES: Have I? Just give me a minute or two.

PIGEON *(passing her tea)*:   Here.

FRANCES *(taking it)*:   Bless you . . . Ugh, mouth feels like the bottom of a budgie cage. *(Yawns.)* What time is it?

PIGEON: Half past eight.

FRANCES: . . . *day* is it? *(Chuckles.)* It is Tuesday? I think I've a hand class at nine.

PIGEON: Are you all right, though?

FRANCES *(through a yawn)*:   Not really. *(Rubbing spine.)* I think I must have slept in me chair.

PIGEON: But how long have you been here?

FRANCES: Dunno. Not awake enough yet to remember. Kids aren't here yet?

PIGEON: It's getting to be that time.

FRANCES *(rising)*:   Put me skates on then. *(She crosses down stage to clean her teeth.)*

EMMA *comes on.*

EMMA: Fran, I'd like to change the timetable for today, if it's all right. *(Looking around.)* Franny? Where are you?

FRANCES: Morning, Em.

EMMA: Oh, there you are. What's the matter? You look awful.

PIGEON: She's been here all night.

EMMA: What? She couldn't have been. That's ridic—

FRANCES: 'Course I haven't. Pigeon's exaggerating.

PIGEON: You've been here a good while. *(To EMMA.)* . . . asleep in that chair. *(To FRANCES.)* I think you should go home to bed.

FRANCES: I can't. There's too much on.

PIGEON: You're probably running a fever.

FRANCES: I've a full day and then a school meeting at five.

EMMA: You let us worry about that. You do what Pigeon says.

FRANCES: . . . and I've no home to go to.

PIGEON: What? *(To EMMA.)* She must be sickening for something.

EMMA: I think you'd better leave us.

PIGEON: She's got a hand class at nine.

EMMA: Jenny Fisher's lot, I know. I'll see to it.

PIGEON: It's only that I'm concerned about you, Fran. *(To EMMA.)* She was here when the cleaner arrived.

EMMA: We'll have her sorted between us, don't worry. Thanks, Pij. *(After PIGEON goes.)* Well, Franny. What're we going to do, eh?

FRANCES: Do you want tea?

EMMA: . . . about the situation. *(A beat.)* You'd better go home to bed.

FRANCES: I've got a hand class.

EMMA: Let me take it. You just look after yourself. Have you been eating?

FRANCES: Yes.

EMMA: Where are you stopping now . . . Louise and Brian's?

FRANCES: They offered, but . . . I've got a bedsit in town.

EMMA: I'll drive you there, come on.

FRANCES: But the hand class . . .

EMMA: That can wait. This can't.

FRANCES: The kids come first.

EMMA: Were you thinking of them when you stayed out all night?

FRANCES: It wasn't—

EMMA: I'm not bothered how long it was. You've got to take care of yourself first. Do you *want* this all round school?

FRANCES: 'Spect they already know.

EMMA: Is that what you want, though? Sympathy?

FRANCES: I don't mean I *told* anyone.

EMMA: Isn't this telling them?

FRANCES: I'm a fool.

EMMA: No, you're not. But you've got to get hold of yourself. We've got to get through this together. All three of us.

FRANCES: Is Kathie all right, Em?

EMMA: No, she's wretched, like you are, a lot of the time. This won't make her feel any better.

FRANCES: Don't tell her, please, Emmy.

EMMA: I wasn't planning to. But if you fall apart at the seams, that won't matter. She'll find out anyway. Do you see what I mean?

FRANCES: No, she mustn't find out.

EMMA: I agree. But you've got to help me. Do you see?

FRANCES: Are the dogs all right?

EMMA: No, that's not helping.

FRANCES: I just want to know how they are.

EMMA: I'll bring them in Thursday or Friday. I think they're missing you, to be honest.

FRANCES: Are they pining? Don't bring them in if they're—

EMMA: I think Kath would want you to see them. *(A beat.)* Poor Franny.

FRANCES: No, don't feel sorry for me, Em. Whatever else—

EMMA: It's my fault, in a way.

FRANCES: No, it isn't. I know you think it's natural, but this would have happened anyway, without you. As long as Katha has what she wants . . . and you're happy.

EMMA: I'd be happier if I could help you.

FRANCES: It can't be helped . . . What?

Emma moves toward her until they embrace.

EMMA: I wish I could tell you how sorry I am.

FRANCES: We both made it difficult for you . . . with something it turns out was inevitable. I just never saw it coming. I was so smug. I saw it with other couples, and I thought, "This will never happen to me." And so it did.

EMMA: You can't think about that right now.

FRANCES: I can't avoid it either.

EMMA: I know, but you've got to try.

LOUISE *(calling)*:   Franny?

EMMA: Oh, bloody hell.

FRANCES: I'll get rid of her, don't worry.

LOUISE *(coming on)*:   Are you all right?

EMMA: What're you doing here, Lou?

FRANCES: *I* didn't ring her.

LOUISE: No, Pigeon did. *(To FRANCES.)* She thought at first you might have done yourself a mischief.

EMMA: We're working, that's all. Do you work here, Louise?

LOUISE: We're concerned about her, that's all.

EMMA: Why?

LOUISE: "Why?" She stays out all night . . .

FRANCES: It *wasn't*—

EMMA: . . . and I used to live in Monks Road—murder center of the city. Am I going to come here tomorrow to find you've accused me of—

LOUISE *(To FRANCES.)*:   You don't look at all well.

FRANCES: No, look. I woke up early, and couldn't get back. So I thought I'd come in and do some work. I've got masses to do.

EMMA: So have I . . . *(To LOUISE.)* . . . and this is holding her up.

LOUISE: I want to take her home.

EMMA: It's a school day!

LOUISE: You can see for yourself she's not well.

EMMA: Let her speak for herself. She's old enough. As she said, she didn't ring you. You're in the way.

FRANCES: Emma.

EMMA: Well, all right. It's a false alarm. You've come on a fool's errand. You've got the wrong end of the stick. Which isn't the first time, is it?

LOUISE: Don't think I don't know what's going on.

EMMA: But does it concern you?

FRANCES: No, look—

EMMA: She *didn't* ring you. It doesn't concern you.

FRANCES: . . . you're both in my office . . . and I have a lot of work. *(Verging on tears.)* So would you both please . . .

EMMA: Get a hold of yourself, Franny. You've got a hand class to go to. You don't want the kids upset, do you.

FRANCES: No . . . it isn't *their* fault, bless them.

EMMA: No, now don't cry. Go on and wash your face, or they'll notice something's wrong. That's right, isn't it, Lou?

LOUISE: No, you don't want the kiddies involved. *(Turns to go.)* I guess I'll get on then.

FRANCES: Thanks, Wheezie.

LOUISE: For sticking me nose in?

FRANCES: I'll ring you tonight.

> *Lighting shift.*
> *The lights dim for the moment in FRANCES'S "office" and come up outside.*
> *PIGEON approaches LOUISE.*

PIGEON: What's wrong?

LOUISE: Not a thing, apparently.

PIGEON: But she's ill.

LOUISE: She says she's not. So what can you do? *(A beat.)* They don't want anyone else involved.

PIGEON: Involved in what?

LOUISE: Don't you know? They've split up, Pigeon.

PIGEON: Oh. Franny and Katha . . . ?

LOUISE: And they're all going round pretending they haven't, so it won't affect the school.

PIGEON: But it has to. Franny and Katha . . . they're the backbone of the place.

LOUISE: Sid hasn't cottoned on, has he?

PIGEON: Not if *I* didn't know it. But there has been . . . I don't know . . . an *atmosphere*. *(A beat.)* When did it . . . how long . . . ?

LOUISE: Since Christmas, as near as I can tell. But I knew there was something up during the last swimming course.

PIGEON: I couldn't attend.

LOUISE: And I wish I hadn't. It's probably gone on a lot longer, in fact, ever since Emma started.

PIGEON: What's it got to do with Emma?

LOUISE: Can't you guess? *(A beat.)* I'd better not say any more. They're right about that. I should know better. Brian tells me never discuss his cases, and I never do.

PIGEON: Suppose it's different with a friend. You naturally want to help.

LOUISE: And I should have done something before now. I saw it coming early enough. The way they were getting all pally . . . I told myself, "This will end in tears."

PIGEON: But she's not all right.

LOUISE: Franny? Of course, she's not . . .

PIGEON: Staying out all night.

LOUISE: She's miserable, that's why. Doesn't know where she is half the time. She's taken an awful bedsit here in town . . . forgets to eat . . .

PIGEON: She's not at all looking after herself.

LOUISE: So how can she look after kids? I've tried to get her to look for another job. Deirdre Fallon would help her and they're going on that conference together.

PIGEON: Oh, she'd find a job just like that. But . . . what would *we* do without Franny? The place would fall apart.

LOUISE: That's what makes me want to throttle Emma. She hasn't a clue the problems she's caused.

PIGEON: Suppose they were both just trying to help Emma . . . like we all were, in a way. I know how important her being here is.

LOUISE: Yeah, it's completely wrecked the place.

PIGEON: No, I mean working here.

LOUISE: As I said—

PIGEON: No, I don't think that's true. She works well, Emma. *I* get on with her fine now. I even admire her. *I* couldn't do it, I'm sure.

LOUISE: *I* don't admire her, not one bit. She's got the world by the tail, has our Emma.

PIGEON: It's all seems so . . .

LOUISE: So ridiculous, that's what.

PIGEON: No . . . unfair.

> *Lighting shift.*
> *FRANCES'S office lights up as KATHA comes on.*

KATHA *(low but hard)*:   What the hell's going on here?

FRANCES: Nothing, Kathie.

EMMA: Just some nonsense of Louise's.

KATHA: What's Louise doing here? It's 8:30 in the morning.

FRANCES: I didn't—

KATHA: You brought her here. She's not here for Pigeon, is she. Or me. She's worried about *you*.

FRANCES: I'm sorry, Kathie.

KATHA: That's not good enough, Franny.

FRANCES: Are you all right?

KATHA: No, I'm not.

FRANCES: What's the matter?

KATHA: This isn't what we agreed on, is it. You promised you'd give me some time . . . space.

FRANCES: I haven't seen you.

KATHA: I don't care. This isn't space, Fran. It's pressure.

EMMA: She didn't want you to know.

KATHA: That's bullshit. I'm right across the hall! What am I supposed to do when Pigeon comes out to the car park just now, "What's the matter with Franny?" and I haven't a clue? I thought you'd topped yourself! As it is, I dunno how we're going to keep this from Sid.

EMMA: He won't find out.

KATHA: When she doesn't bloody do her work—how can he help but know?

FRANCES: I'm here, aren't I.

KATHA: Where were you last night? The first Parents Evening in years that you haven't attended . . .

FRANCES: . . . I completely forgot.

KATHA: . . . and the *cleaner* finds you at half six, sobbing. I can't say, "She's off her food"—they think you're having a breakdown. Are you?

FRANCES: I'm fine.

KATHA: Then, for God's sake, start showing it. Get a grip on your life. Don't always look to me to sort out everything. That's why I had to leave. You're suffocating me, Franny.

FRANCES: I never meant to!

KATHA: Meaning and doing aren't the same thing. Until they are, how can you even
hope I'll come back. You've got to change, Fran. And change doesn't mean you
saying you've changed. You've got to let *me* decide.

FRANCES: I can wait forever for you.

KATHA: No, you can't. *This* isn't telling me you can. Putting pressure on Emma isn't
saying it either. It's telling me, clearly, you can't wait at all. You're as dependent
on me as ever . . . and I don't want that. I can't live with it anymore.

FRANCES: I'll always love you, Kathie.

KATHA: What I'm hearing is, "I'll always need you." That's not love at all.

This makes FRANCES weep.

EMMA: I think we'd better get back to work.

KATHA: I dunno how we're meant to when she throws a wobbily *at* work. Nobody
will ever believe she's thinking about "the job." *(Starting off.)* This isn't about
Emma, either. *(To EMMA.)* Don't let her convince you it is.

KATHA kisses EMMA on the mouth for FRANCES'S benefit. Then goes off.

FRANCES: She's right—this isn't about you. We dragged you into our troubles. Or I
did. She's right about *that.*

EMMA: I wish I could help you.

FRANCES: You have.

EMMA: . . . maybe by going away.

FRANCES: That wouldn't help at all. You heard Katha just now. She wouldn't come
back if you left. No, she needs you. I think I need you, too.

EMMA: It's all right. *(Moving into an embrace.)* I'm here.

Fade.
Lights up on the "pool." EMMA is discovered trying to remove the protec-
tive plastic from the water. She's dressed but barefoot. LOUISE comes on
fully clothed.

LOUISE: Oh, Franny not here yet?

EMMA: Franny's not coming.

LOUISE: No swimming tonight then.

EMMA: Yes, there is—I'm in charge.

LOUISE: I'm off then.

EMMA: Fine.

LOUISE: Oil and water, the two of us doing it.

EMMA: Did you hear me? I said fine.

A pause.

Pigeon's going to help me. We'll manage all right.

LOUISE: I'd just like to know how you operate.

EMMA: I'm trying to do my job, if you don't mind. Since you obviously do. I wish you'd just let me get on with it.

LOUISE: You're not fooling anybody except maybe yourself.

EMMA: We're not going to have this discussion, Louise. You're not going to wind me up.

LOUISE: Huh. You're not going to be able to stop me. You're wound up so much already, you can't help yourself. I'm going to speak me mind till they get here, and there's nothing you can do about it. Is there. You can't call anyone—I'm part of the team. Attack me, I'm stronger than you. And I shan't lay a finger on you, so you'll look silly, calling for help.

EMMA: I've got to get . . . this cover off.

LOUISE: Fine. I'll keep right on talking. We'll see which of us bottles out, shall we? *(A beat.)* You don't want any help with that, do you?

EMMA: No, thank you.

LOUISE: Of course not. Emma Swannows up Against the World.

EMMA: You wouldn't help if I asked.

LOUISE: No, you're wrong. I'd help you just like I'd help anybody. I help Franny, for instance, all the time. She asks, and I help her.

EMMA: All right, help me, for God's sake.

LOUISE *(doing so)*:   You see? That's not weakness, it's—

EMMA: . . . not a question of weakness or strength.

LOUISE: No, it's plain common sense, isn't it.

EMMA: I don't normally want help from people who aren't my friends.

LOUISE: That's plain nonsense. *I'll* take it from any quarter.

EMMA: That's where we're different.

LOUISE: Hm. Suppose you'd say that's because *you're* different. *(A beat.)* I don't see you as "disabled," you know.

EMMA: What do you want now, a "thank you"?

LOUISE: I'm just saying. I just see you as "Emma."

EMMA: And you don't like what you see.

LOUISE: What? I hope I'm not that rude. Am I? Have I ever said or done anything to you I haven't apologized for later? You have to tell me if I have.

EMMA: You know we've never got on.

LOUISE: I'm not aware of it.

EMMA: You're lying.

LOUISE: Now you're almost being rude . . . or am I being too sensitive?

EMMA: I dunno what you are . . . *I'm* being honest.

LOUISE: Is that what it is?

EMMA: Oh, come on. The swimming course . . . Maire?

LOUISE: Oh. I forgot all about that.

EMMA: *I* haven't. *(A beat.)* Then there's my permanent appointment.

LOUISE: What about it?

EMMA: You're against it. If you'd been on my panel, I'd never have got the job.

LOUISE: I'm not qualified, am I.

EMMA: No, you're not.

LOUISE: So I'd never say. If I had any opinion at all, I suppose, it would be in your favor. Franny likes you, and you know what I think of Franny.

EMMA: You could be jealous.

LOUISE: That's silly . . . schoolgirl stuff. So you think I'm jealous of Pigeon, do you? You ask Pigeon. She's also part of the team.

EMMA: She's worked here longer than you have.

LOUISE: She hasn't. But what does that mean? I left to bring up my kids. Now they're older, so I'm back at work. I chose not to work here again, but not because of Pigeon. She'd be one of the reasons for coming. No, it's the change in attitude I don't like. You ask Pigeon. She stays for Franny's sake . . . and she likes the kids. We all like the kids. We wouldn't be in "special ed" otherwise. Believe me, it's only attitude.

EMMA: And what's that?

LOUISE: Ah, well, you wouldn't know that.

EMMA: You mean Mr. Showleigh and Sid.

LOUISE: You know *about* it . . . It really was different in them days. I know you're fed up of hearing it, but your appointment wouldn't have been any problem in Showleigh's time. *(A beat.)* I expect we wouldn't have had this other nonsense either.

EMMA: You think it's "nonsense," don't you.

LOUISE: It isn't "good." You don't think it's good, do you? Can you say you're "happy"?

EMMA: I can't say I am, no.

LOUISE: Exactly. It's a mess.

EMMA *(overlapping)*:   I'm not exactly "unhappy."

LOUISE: Eh? Then you're a fool, and I'm telling you outright, to your face.

EMMA: You blame me for—

LOUISE: . . . don't *blame* you, didn't you hear me just now? I blame Sid, in large measure, for the atmosphere that made something like this possible. If it had happened before, they'd have kept it really quiet, between themselves, like a death in the family. But they brought it into the school, and that's serious . . .

EMMA: . . . and I'm part of it.

LOUISE: . . . piggy in the middle, yeah. That may not make it your *fault,* but you haven't helped matters much, have you.

EMMA: What do you want me to do?

LOUISE: Leave us, look for another job? That's too much to hope for, I guess.

EMMA: It's not common sense.

LOUISE: Makes sense from where I'm standing, but life doesn't work out that way. Brian is always telling me, "Never expect much of people."

EMMA: So that's how you see me, a criminal?

LOUISE: I say you shouldn't have done it, but who am I to say? It's never stopped anyone else, why should you be any less human than they are?

EMMA: And where am I going to find another job, without a reference?

LOUISE: Franny wouldn't give you a reference? Come off it.

EMMA: And what reason would I give? Did the training but couldn't stick the actual job. That'd impress precisely nobody.

LOUISE: You would have impressed Deirdre Fallon, no less.

EMMA: Who?

LOUISE: Head Physio, South West Region. That would have got you in any-where. Franny's been singing your praises . . . and she came to the Christmas party.

EMMA: Did you talk to her?

LOUISE: Oh, yes.

EMMA: ". . . would have impressed her."

LOUISE: Before that night, yes.

EMMA: You bitch, Louise.

LOUISE: Now you're being abusive.

EMMA: You put the mockers on me, didn't you. Now you're out to get me sacked.

LOUISE: I didn't say anything, on purpose. And she hasn't the power to sack you, over Franny's head. You dunno what a friend you've got.

EMMA: I don't believe you.

LOUISE: That makes me want to paddle your hide.

EMMA: Yeah, you wish.

LOUISE: Oh, put a sock in it, you silly girl. I don't honestly know why I bother now.

EMMA: You're pathetic.

LOUISE: Do you know why Dee was turned against you?

EMMA: I don't know or care what she was.

LOUISE: You did it yourself by that ludicrous display you and Katha put on. That may go down all right at a teenage rave wherever you come from up country . . .

EMMA: . . . but down here I'm diff'rent.

LOUISE: . . . in front of the kids, that's what done it.

EMMA: Ooh, ar. 'Tis proper shocking, that.

LOUISE: You laugh, but you go ask Katha. She and Franny always kept that side of their life away from the school . . . where it ought to be. Between anyone, I'm not being bigoted. Husbands and wives wouldn't do what you did.

EMMA: Katha was there, too.

LOUISE: She has years of good form that you haven't. You were the one people saw. Asked what they remember, people will say, "Ay, that new girl . . ."

EMMA: . . . the cripple.

LOUISE: . . . snogging away X-certificate, like . . . "Ay, you can't do that there 'ere." Get the photograph. Like I said, you took it yourself.

EMMA: Let me pass.

LOUISE: I dunno what they're gonna say about any of the rest of it . . .

EMMA: Are you going to let me get by?

LOUISE *(a hand on her shoulder or arm)*:   . . . but you'd better watch yourselves from now on. Sid's not always asleep at the switch, and he fancies himself as a local grandee.

EMMA: Take your hand off my arm, please.

LOUISE *(tightening her grip)*:   He wants the school to be a monument to his own Noble Works. Any hint of a scandal—the kind of thing *you've* been doing—Chinese whispers at work—Sidney Aldermost "is guilty of child abuse." I wouldn't want that on *my* conscience. He might try to kill you.

EMMA: Before you do it? I've asked you to let me get by you.

LOUISE: Not before you know what's involved.

EMMA: Let me go.

LOUISE: What are you *doing*? Care-ful. I'm stronger than you . . .

EMMA: That's right—*I'm a cripple.*

LOUISE: Emma! This is all wrong.

This has all happened at poolside. In her anger, EMMA tries to shove LOUISE, who merely has to stand her ground for EMMA to lose her balance and plunge into the water.

Oh, bloody hell.

Instinctively, LOUISE dives in after her. More than resisting, EMMA tries to hold LOUISE under.

You lunatic . . .

Each one spluttering, LOUISE manages to get EMMA in an armlock until all her resistance is gone.

Are you all right? Emma? *(EMMA mutters something.)* Hang on a minute. *(As she pulls her over to the side.)* Bloody hell . . . I didn't want *this*.

Quick fade.
Dogs barking again in the distance.
Lights up gradually on KATHA, on her feet, awaiting FRANCES.

KATHA: See? They haven't forgotten you. *(As FRANCES comes on.)* Cedar's sight's going, and Moonie's tripod. But they know who looks after them, all right.

FRANCES: Moonie limping along anxious to see me . . . breaks my heart.

KATHA: They're yours, Fran. You take them.
FRANCES: Landlady wouldn't allow it.
KATHA: Rubbish, it's a ground-floor flat. You've got the use of the garden.
FRANCES: It's not like here. No, this is their home.

They proceed to sit down during this opening.

KATHA: Not for much longer.
FRANCES: Are you moving?
KATHA: . . . and then you *can* have them . . . another place of your own. They may not live that long, who knows? But you'll get half when this goes on the market.
FRANCES: I don't want to think about that.
KATHA: No, you've got to. *(A beat.)* House prices have gone right through the proverbial roof. You know what one estate agent quoted for a cottage this age and size? You wouldn't believe it, *I* didn't. Half a million.
FRANCES: You know I don't care about money.
KATHA: At that price? You can't afford not to. Half a million, and we paid, what, six, eight thousand?
FRANCES: Twelve years ago.
KATHA: Well, I know, but . . .
FRANCES: I told you I don't want to think about that! *(A beat.)* When the time comes . . .
KATHA: Yeah, all right.
FRANCES: You're not planning on leaving the area, leaving work?
KATHA: Not at the moment, but that doesn't mean . . .
FRANCES: . . . I know it doesn't.
KATHA: . . . I still haven't made up my mind.
FRANCES: . . . I know.
KATHA: You mustn't wait, even "forever."
FRANCES: I'm not. I haven't pressured you lately.
KATHA: I know. You've been very good.
FRANCES: You asked to see me, and I came without hopes.
KATHA: You don't have to get all defensive. I'm not criticizing. I'm glad to see you.
FRANCES: I am, too. That's all right, isn't it?
KATHA: No, don't worry. That's fine.

They smile at each other.

I half-thought Louise might be with you . . . with a van.
FRANCES: Believe me, it's not what you think. I do dread the thought of "moving out" . . .
KATHA: It'll have to be some time.

FRANCES: Yes, I know, but that's not why I came on my own. You see, I thought
Emma might be here . . .

KATHA: I asked her not to be, on purpose.

FRANCES: . . . and if Louise came as well.

KATHA: Oh, yeah. *(A beat.)* There's something between those two.

FRANCES: I know.

KATHA: Not like us. I mean . . . they're at each other's throats. *(A beat.)* Do you
know what's behind it? Wheezer said anything?

FRANCES: Wheezer won't talk about Emma . . . and yet it's not like she's *angry* at
Emma.

KATHA: No, I know.

FRANCES: . . . more she's almost *embarrassed.*

KATHA: Yeah, that's it.

FRANCES: . . . ashamed.

KATHA: I know exactly what you're saying.

FRANCES: Emma feels like that?

KATHA: Weird, ennit.

FRANCES: Strange that they should both feel the same way.

KATHA *(laughs)*:   Perhaps they're more like us than I thought.

FRANCES: Wheezie hasn't wanted to go to swimming club, I think, because Emma
goes . . .

KATHA: . . . and Emma hasn't been going.

FRANCES: . . . because you haven't.

KATHA: I haven't been going for a long time now . . . a lot longer than the last swimming course.

FRANCES: It has something to do with me, do you think?

KATHA: Ignoring your harmless and natural vanity, I think it does have to do with
Louise. You work with Emma, don't you, well enough.

FRANCES: Perfectly.

KATHA: See? It can't be *you.* You've even been out together once or twice.

FRANCES: What?

KATHA *(smiles)*:   Don't look so worried, I mean for a *drink.* I don't mind if that's as
far as it goes.

FRANCES: I expect she feels guilty.

KATHA *(laughs)*:   Ah, Franny, you're delicious. Believe me, Emma does not feel
guilty, all right? I don't trust her, but I don't really blame her at all.

FRANCES: What do you mean, you don't trust her?

KATHA: That's private.

FRANCES: I'm sorry.

KATHA: But I'd do the same thing were I in her shoes. In fact, I'd be more like her
than she is. *(A beat.)* You don't get that, do you.

FRANCES: We both know I'm thick.

KATHA: No, you're good, you're not thick. While our Emma . . .

FRANCES: . . . *she's* good.

KATHA: . . . she "collects" people. Not like you do, out of goodness, because you genuinely like them . . . but as *trophies.*

FRANCES: You can't hold that against her.

KATHA: I already told you, I don't. But I don't trust her.

FRANCES: She's never had enough friends.

KATHA: She hasn't had many, I grant you. But then neither have I.

FRANCES: You've been loved, Kathie.

KATHA: I've been loved, that's the difference. And I've always gone out to get. Which Emma's just learning to do. And good luck to her. She deserves it.

FRANCES: We all do.

KATHA: Do we deserve to go after it, though? That's what puzzles me. I wonder if I deserved it, for instance.

FRANCES: Of course you deserved it.

KATHA: You're biased. And, much as I say she deserves it, from myself, I know pretty much what she'll do to get it. See? I don't really trust her an inch.

FRANCES: But what does that mean?

KATHA: Well, beyond that, it must mean I've been thinking a lot about Emma.

FRANCES: I have, too.

KATHA: Have you, Fran?

FRANCES: I don't mean I'm jealous. I've tried hard not to be.

KATHA: Who could blame you if you were?

FRANCES: We've always said what happened to us has nothing to do with Emma.

KATHA: I think I made you believe it.

FRANCES: No, I believe it, too, on me own.

KATHA: I don't really think we agree about that . . .

FRANCES: . . . oh, we do . . .

KATHA: . . . because now I think it does have to do with Emma, you see? She's at the center of it, in fact.

FRANCES: I don't understand.

KATHA: I know you don't. It's been hard for me to grasp.

FRANCES: I thought you said I was . . . that I couldn't be independent of you . . . I didn't give you . . . enough . . . *space* . . .

This makes FRANCES break down in tears. KATHA rushes to comfort her.

KATHA: Shh, shh, shh. It's all right now. It's all right.

FRANCES: I'm sorry, Kathie.

KATHA: It's all right. *(A beat.)* I know this is hard for you.

FRANCES *(through sobs):*   I . . . I . . . if only I could have seen you *alone.* You said you needed to be *alone.* That's what hurt. She's in my bed.

KATHA: I know. I lied to you. It was my one mistake.

FRANCES: You hurt me, Katha!

> *FRANCES strikes KATHA, then immediately breaks down for real. There are years in this outburst—an adult lifetime till now. There are years in KATHA'S comforting of FRANCES—covering not just their relationship but who they are respectively. It should correspond in stage time.*

KATHA *(softly)*:   You see? Emma's part of this.

FRANCES *(more composed)*:   I don't blame Emma.

KATHA: No, don't blame Emma, *I'm* the one you should blame. And you do. That's right.

FRANCES: Not really.

KATHA: In part, you do. That's good. It's getting you through this, Franny. You don't want to think about it, but you do, just the same. That's how you'll survive this. *(My sense is she removes physical contact here.)* As I say, I've been thinking a lot about Emma lately. I think it's important you should know.

FRANCES: Please don't . . . it's none of my business . . . and it . . .

KATHA: I think, in a way, we invented Emma. She doesn't exist, in a way.

FRANCES: Of course she—

KATHA: Not if you follow my thinking, she doesn't.

FRANCES: I don't understand.

KATHA: No, *I* didn't at first . . . it's difficult.

FRANCES *(a beat)*:   We *used* Emma . . . to cover what was wrong between us.

KATHA: . . . I think it's more than that. Who is she really?

FRANCES: I don't know what you mean. She's Emma.

KATHA: I know, but . . . isn't she merely an extension of who *we* are?

FRANCES: She was our excuse.

KATHA: I'd say she's our self-expression.

FRANCES *(a beat)*:   That's incredibly selfish, Katha.

KATHA: I *am* selfish, I've always told you. *(A beat.)* All right. How did she enter our lives, happenstance?

FRANCES: Nothing ever just . . . happens.

KATHA: No, and I don't think it did here. We only ever see those parts of a person we're able to see through ourselves anyway . . . and that's how we invented who Emma is for us. Look, she's disabled, and she works at a school for the disabled. Is that accidental? No less than you working here.

FRANCES: There's a connection.

KATHA: A very visible connection. Which you exploited in making her permanent, right?

FRANCES: . . . with the board.

KATHA: Why did you do it, Franny? Because she's so good? She came in and said straight away, "This job has my name on it"? She never said that. She couldn't.

FRANCES: Well, she *did*.

KATHA: But she couldn't *convince* you of it. Emma's *disability* is what convinced you to take her in. It convinces us all—don't feel bad about it. It's the one reason we're here, even Sidney. It's our relationship with disability.

FRANCES: We're all disabled.

KATHA: . . . another issue. Our chosen relationship with disability. We all chose, we *want* to work here. All right, why?

FRANCES: What?

KATHA: *Why* do we want to work here?

FRANCES: I can't speak for anyone else.

KATHA: Fine. Just speak for yourself.

FRANCES: I love the job. I love the kids.

KATHA: And I don't. I never have.

FRANCES: Yes, you do.

KATHA: I love you . . . and I love the kids. But I don't love the job, the way you do. I've never thrown up in my life . . . not from drinking . . . and never possibly over anything to do with work. I hate work . . . I hate working.

FRANCES: You're always too hard on yourself.

KATHA: . . . realistic.

FRANCES: All right, I skyve, too, in that sense. I "have fun."

KATHA: But it isn't your word. "Love's" your own word for what you do. It's your description of life. You love life.

FRANCES: I haven't loved very much of it at the moment!

KATHA: That's your expression of loss . . . of love lost. But you're counting on love to get it back again, aren't you?

FRANCES: . . . by pressure?

KATHA: I'm not talking about me . . . I mean the kids. You still have the kids.

FRANCES: It's true. I dunno where I'd have been without them. They pulled me through this, you know.

KATHA: . . . and that's stronger than "work," isn't it.

FRANCES: . . . isn't work. It's survival.

KATHA: . . . and I could never feel that. If this had happened to me, I could never stay here, the way you have. It would drive me mad. There'd be nothing here for me.

FRANCES: I've thought of leaving.

KATHA: But you haven't done it . . . and I wouldn't have to think. I'd be gone before a thought even entered me head . . . and that includes "pressure" as well. I'd hope to pressure you by leaving.

FRANCES: I couldn't do that.

KATHA: . . . because of the kids.

FRANCES: . . . partly, yes, you're right. *(A beat.)* I've been *using* the kids.

KATHA: . . . you've been *loving* them. "Using" is your adult word. They only know love . . . love from Franny. That's all they've ever known from you.

FRANCES: What's this got to do with Emma?

KATHA: My God, don't you *see*? Emma, to us, is part of the *kids*.

FRANCES: I don't "love" Emma . . .

KATHA: . . . because you can't. She's not a kid. At least the part of her that is a part you never see, that is, *after* they leave.

FRANCES: I see them after they leave . . . all the time.

KATHA: Do you love them then?

FRANCES: They're not here long enough.

KATHA: That's because they're no longer part of you . . . no longer here, except for Emma.

FRANCES: . . . except for Emma?

KATHA: She's the kid who came back . . . to stay. And we were curious how she turned out. *I* was. That was her attraction for me. Weren't you curious?

FRANCES: I was curious how she'd work out with the kids . . .

KATHA: . . . for the same reason. She's worked out fine.

FRANCES *(a beat)*:   I know, I can see, she has a thing with them that I *don't* have.

KATHA: And how do you feel about that? Are you jealous?

FRANCES: No! It just seems . . . right, somehow. I don't want to interfere.

KATHA: Ah huh.

FRANCES: I'll interfere, all right, if I think she's doing wrong. But . . . she never does. I can't explain it.

KATHA: It's what I'm telling you.

FRANCES: Well, like with Cassie Williams's parents. I felt obliged to stand up for Emma. She was textbook right. But then I also wanted to tell them (the dad), "What's the matter with you, man? Can't you see she's right. *Look* at her, for pity's sake. She *knows*." And yet, I have to say, Emma doesn't love the kids the same way I do.

KATHA: She's not you.

FRANCES: Sometimes I think she doesn't love them at all. She's hard in a way I wouldn't know how to be . . . never seen in a parent. Parents might well be indifferent to a child . . . might, God forbid, abuse a child . . . I suppose.

KATHA: Thank God we've never had any of *them* . . .

FRANCES: . . . but never that kind of hard. I don't understand it . . . and I think, deep down, "This is none of your business. Let 'em get on with it. You can't even learn." Which is good for me . . . means I have limitations. It makes me humble, as God wants us. *(A beat.) He* sent Emma to us . . . as a lesson.

A pause.

KATHA *(softly)*:   Fran . . . ? You know how I said I was attracted to Emma.

FRANCES: Yah. *(Quickly.) I'm* attracted to her . . .

KATHA: . . . no, not the same way.

FRANCES: I could be, very easily. You warned me yourself, "I don't mind as far as it goes." It could go further, Kathie.

KATHA: . . . sure, with Emma wanting it.

FRANCES: No, I, sometimes, I want it, too.

KATHA: All right, I believe you want to want it, but you can't. That's as far as it goes. You're still a kid, Franny. You don't know what I know, or feel the same things I feel.

FRANCES: But we loved each other . . . for years.

KATHA: We fit together for years. We never loved in the same way.

FRANCES *(hands over her ears)*:   I don't want to hear it.

KATHA: You got to.

FRANCES: Don't torment me . . . take away what I have.

KATHA: I'm not . . . I'm trying to give you something.

FRANCES: I don't want it.

KATHA: I'm not saying we didn't love each other, equally, that it was wrong. It was right . . . as right as love can be.

FRANCES: For me it was perfect.

KATHA: It was for me, too . . . and I still say it wasn't the same kind of love. Your mum and dad love in different ways, don't they? That's all I'm saying we did. That really is all.

FRANCES *(sniffing back her tears)*:   It's something I never thought about.

KATHA: There was never any need for it.

FRANCES: So what you're saying now . . . we still love each other . . . ?

KATHA: . . . differently, yeah.

FRANCES: . . . but you still love me?

KATHA: I've never stopped. How can I stop loving you, Franny? You're a vital part of me. In a way Emma could never be.

FRANCES: Is that true?

KATHA: How could I ever lie about that? Look at me . . . *(FRANCES looks.)* You know it's true.

FRANCES: Oh, Kathie.

KATHA: But just as you see the kids and the school different from me, Emma's different, too.

FRANCES: Don't you love Emma, Kath?

KATHA: Emma doesn't exist!

FRANCES: I don't understand that.

KATHA: Just follow your nose!

FRANCES: You won't ever tell her that, will you?

KATHA: . . . that I don't love her?

FRANCES: . . . because it would hurt her terribly . . .

KATHA: . . . if she was a kid. You're thinking of Emma as one of your kids. That's how you've been talking about her.

FRANCES: And you don't?

KATHA: How can I? I don't have the same relationship you do. I don't work with Emma like you do. I got to know her on that damn swimming course . . . the only thing about it I liked. You know I don't usually go. I only went then because you were stuck.

FRANCES: I always meant to thank you for that.

KATHA: Don't *thank* me, for God's sake. *(A beat.)* This is difficult to get across.

FRANCES: Don't bother.

KATHA: I've got to.

FRANCES: I know—you've told me—you were drawn to her . . . I was, too. That's when she started to work on us.

KATHA: No, but she didn't do it.

FRANCES: Yes, she did. She spent the night here. Now you're saying she's not involved.

KATHA: Think back to what I was saying about the kids . . . you got it?

FRANCES: Yeah?

KATHA: You love the kids for who they are here, right? That's how you really know them. *I* don't know them like *that*. They're slow, and they can't learn enough.

FRANCES: You're patient with them.

KATHA: I'm a teacher—I'm paid to be patient. It stops at the end of the day. With you, it never stops. Swimming club, courses, it's all to help them. You got me the job here to make your life perfect. And I love them because I love you. I don't love them for themselves. Part of me's saying, "Why can't you be better?"

FRANCES: *I* want them better.

KATHA: Not in the same way. When I clapped eyes on Emma, at first, I thought, "Wow."

FRANCES: She's attractive.

KATHA: She's *better*. I looked at her, and I couldn't help myself thinking, "That's real improvement." That turned me on.

FRANCES: You mean *she* turned you on.

KATHA: . . . yeah, by what she was . . . what she stood for—movement, progress, development, for Christ's sake. *That*, alone, made me throw a wobbily. I don't think I've stopped yet. That's what really did it for us, Franny, that taste of the future. But it's nought to do with Emma, is it. She doesn't know! I'm only telling *you—now.* It's through me own eyes that I saw it. And *I* tasted it, didn't I? No one else. And that's, finally, why we're different. I crossed over, into adulthood.

FRANCES: Are you saying I'm still a child?

KATHA: What's the matter with it if that's where you live? What was that old advert, "Nappies make nations?" You create the Emmas of this world. No one else we've known does it any better, and, without you, they might as well be strangled at birth.

FRANCES: You're just saying that.

KATHA: All right. Quit your job . . . what'll you do? If you think it's me that makes you miserable, stay off work, and see how you feel. We can end, you and me, and there's still a tomorrow. Their need will never end, will it.

FRANCES *(a beat)*:   What you're trying to tell me is . . .

KATHA: . . . it's over. For us. Yes, I am. You can see it is, can't you, the way I've explained it?

FRANCES: That gives it an ending, yes.

KATHA: I dunno. You do a thing, in a rush, and you're never clear why.

FRANCES *(quickly)*:   Are you ill, Kathie? Is that what it is? I've never heard you like this—"She turned me on."

KATHA: She did, Fran. I've been doing me best to say how . . . and why. It's clear in me own mind, at least.

FRANCES: . . . and I may never understand it, in your sense.

KATHA: . . . in that sense, no, I hope you don't. *(A beat.)* You won't make the world any worse by not knowing, will you.

FRANCES: Will I? Won't I?

KATHA: And there'll always be room for return visits.

Lights begin to fade. A children's round begins quietly, off.

FRANCES: I'll try . . . to take a closer look.

VOICES: I love to sail in my big blue boat

Big blue boat/my big blue boat

I love to sail in my big blue boat

Out on the deep blue sea.

Final (gradual) fade.

Contributors

Nancy Bezant, an accomplished and well-known actress, has been performing in North Carolina for many years. She is also a writer.

Tess Chakkalakal is a visiting lecturer in American and African-American literature at Williams College. Her dissertation traces the figure of Uncle Tom in African-American fiction.

Ruby Cohn is professor emerita of Comparative Drama at the University of California at Davis. She is author of over a dozen scholarly books, including *Anglo-American Interplay in Recent Drama, From Desire to Godot: Pocket Theater of Post-war Paris,* and *Just Play: Beckett's Theater.*

Pamela Cooper, an associate professor of British and American literature at the University of North Carolina at Chapel Hill, is author of *The Fictions of John Fowles: Power, Creativity, and Femininity.* Her recent research interests include a book on postcolonial fiction which applies aspects of poststructuralist theory to representations of the body in literary texts.

Thomas Fahy received his Ph.D. in American literature from the University of North Carolina at Chapel Hill. He was recently an assistant editor and contributor to *A Modern Mosaic: Art and Modernism in the United States* (2000). His work has also appeared in several journals, including *Prospects, Shofar, Style, Mosaic,* and *Women's Studies.*

Kimball King is professor of English at the University of North Carolina at Chapel Hill. He is general editor of Routledge's *Studies in Modern Drama* series. His book-length publications in drama include *Twenty Modern British Playwrights* (1977), *Ten Modern Irish Playwrights* (1979), and *Ten Modern American Playwrights* (1981), as well as *Sam Shepard: A Casebook* (1989).

Kanta Kochhar-Lindgren, director, choreographer, and scholar, is currently co-editor for an anthology on the aesthetics of disability. Other research interests include dance and disability and South Asian diasporic performance. She teaches at Central Michigan University.

James MacDonald is currently a writer-in-residence at Exeter University. His most recently published plays include *Left-Handed Enterprise* and *Kleptocrats.*

Lilah F. Morris received a B.A. in English from the University of California at Berkeley. For the past several years she has been involved in the economic and clinical aspects of medical research, publishing in peer-reviewed medical journals including *Thyroid* and *Journal of Clinical Endocrinology and Metabolism.* Ms. Morris is currently a second-year medical student at Tulane University School of Medicine.

Sarah Reuning graduated from Davidson College and received an M.A. in English from the University of North Carolina. She currently works as an assistant editor for both the University of North Carolina Press and *The Technology Source.*

Johanna Shapiro is a professor in the Department of Family Medicine at the University of California Irvine College of Medicine, where she has taught and conducted research for the past twenty-three years. Dr. Shapiro was recently appointed Director of Medical Humanities for the UC Irvine College of Medicine, and she has authored or coauthored over 75 refereed publications. Dr. Shapiro is also feature editor of the *Family Medicine* column, "Literature and the Arts in Medical Education," and faculty coadvisor to *Plexus: UCI-COM Journal of Arts & Humanities.*

Robert C. Spirko is a doctoral candidate in the English Department at the University of North Carolina at Chapel Hill. His research interests focus on twentieth-century American poetry, cultural studies, and affect.

Index